Prisoners of Colonialism

The Struggle for Justice in Puerto Rico

Ronald Fernandez

Common Courage Press   Monroe, Maine

Library of Congress Cataloging-in-Publication
Data
Fernandez, Ronald.
Prisoners of colonialism : the struggle for justice in
Puerto Rico / Ronald Fernandez.
p. cm.
Includes index.
ISBN 1-56751-028-0. — ISBN 1-56751-029-9 (pbk.)
1. Puerto Rico—Politics and government—1952-
2. Self-determination, National—Puerto Rico—
History—20th century. 4. Nationalists—United
States—History—20th century.
I. Title.
F1976.F392   1994
320.97295—dc20   94-7629
CIP

Common Courage Press
P.O. Box 702
Monroe, ME 04951
207-525-0900 fax: 207-525-0934

First Printing

Contents

Dedication

To Zulena Segarra Berríos,
born in captivity
because her parents loved their patria,
Puerto Rico

Acknowledgments

My greatest debt is to the prisoners, or more accurately, to those prisoners who shared their experiences and beliefs with a man who was a virtual stranger. To Luz Berríos, Antonio Camacho Negron, Luis Colón Osorio, Eddie Cortés, Elizam Escobar, Ricardo Jiménez, Oscar López Rivera, Roberto Maldonado, Filiberto Ojeda Ríos, Alicia Rodríguez, Juan Segarra Palmer and Carlos Alberto Torres I want to say thank you. It has been a privilege to write this book.

In many instances prisoners willingly agreed to speak with me but correctional officials refused to allow me to enter the prison in which they were held. This is the primary explanation for what may appear to some readers as a lack of focus on particular political prisoners. While the book was not harmed by the roadblocks erected by correctional authorities—e.g. the same "universal rules" were applied in some federal prisons but not in others—a more complete analysis can be written only when the political prisoners are once again free women and free men.

For their hospitality in Chicago I wish to thank Jose López, Fifo Rodríguez, Rafael Marrero, Evelyn Rodríguez, Jan Susler and Mary Taylor. In Puerto Rico I owe thanks to Manuel Caballer, Blanca Canales, Rafael Cancel Miranda, the incredibly gracious Diaz family of Arecibo, Laura Albizu Meneses, and Rosa Meneses.

This book was written as a result of a request by Luis Nieves Falcon. All of the prisoners—and all

Puerto Ricans—owe him a tremendous debt of gratitude.

Linda Backiel was of enormous assistance through this project. She provided everything from the book's title to friendship, from assistance with interviews to especially helpful criticisms of my ideas and approach to the prisoners—and Puerto Rico's—political situation.

Greg Bates and Flic Shooter are publishers with a purpose. I want to thank them for a wonderful experience.

Without Brenda Harrison this book would not exist.

I am responsible for any errors and for all interpretations of the revolutionary groups and their activities.

Introduction

I Can't Promise Anything

The judge was Irish. So much so that instead of the stars and stripes, Judge James Bailey flew Ireland's green, white, and orange. Court watchers claimed he was a sympathizer of the Irish Republican Army, a revolutionary organization that produced support, contempt and controversy whenever anyone discussed the bloody streets of Belfast, Northern Ireland.

Luis Rosa saw the flag. He didn't know what to expect but he knew it wasn't empathy when two sheriffs began to punch and kick him right in front of the judge and his flag. The sheriffs used force because Luis Rosa and Alicia Rodríguez shouted "Viva Puerto Rico libre" (Long live a free Puerto Rico) when they entered Chicago's Cook County Courtroom on April 25, 1980. Their passion produced similar shouts from the many spectators who, even before the defendants appeared, had received orders to stand at attention until the judge gave them permission to sit.

Disobedience had no place in James Bailey's courtroom. As two sheriffs grabbed Ms. Rodríguez by the chin and neck, pushed her head backwards and dragged her from the room, another three sheriffs continued to punch and kick the now bloody Luis Rosa. Meanwhile, Judge Bailey, "screaming and waving his hands" ordered that spectators be removed from the courtroom and the courthouse.

7

They could return to their neighborhoods or take a flight to Puerto Rico, but they were not staying in a Cook County judicial facility.

One of the lawyers got arrested when he pleaded with sheriffs to stop beating Mr. Rosa. They continued to kick Luis, and then, under the judge 's orders, they grabbed Attorney Brian Glick. The presumed charge was contempt of court, later disregarded when Judge Bailey released the attorney without pressing formal charges.

Mr. Rosa and Ms. Rodríguez faced life in prison. Along with nine others, they were apprehended on April 4, 1980. Police spotted a stolen truck near the campus of Northeastern University and arrested Luis and Alicia when they tried to enter the vehicle. It looked like a simple car theft until anxious residents told police they spotted a number of other people walking in and out of a van parked in the vicinity. Officers rushed to the scene and immediately arrested nine people dressed in jogging suits. At the time police had no idea what was planned; later they said it was "an as yet unknown terrorist action." But, whatever the group's goal, the six men and five women were arrested with a stolen truck, several stolen vans and cars, 13 weapons, and a number of disguises and false identifications.

The specific charges filed against Luis Rosa and Alicia Rodríguez included armed robbery of the two vans, unlawful possession of weapons, transportation of a stolen vehicle across state lines and seditious conspiracy because they were allegedly members of the FALN, the Spanish acronym for the Armed Forces of National Liberation.

Sedition is a federal offense. Since the 1920s,

no one except Puerto Rican revolutionaries went to trial for "conspiring to overthrow, put down, or destroy by force the govern ment of the United States." In this case, all the arrested Puerto Ricans were charged with seditious conspiracy, but, in what attorneys believed was an effort to create informers, only Alicia and Luis received the special treatment offered by Judge Bailey and his assistants. For example, "while Luis and I always experienced physical and psychological abuse," Alicia recalls "that the other companeros(as) were escorted into a deliberation room for the entire trial. While the only thing in our bullpen was a cold cement floor, the others sat in chairs around a large table and with a bathroom in the adjoining room. Even though the only one of us who had a toilet was Luis, his was in clear view of every passerby. What separated us was only a thin metal sheet."

Marrying everyday abuse and humiliation to serious federal *and* serious state charges, the government hoped to get what it wanted: reliable information about a group that had, among other things, bombed military establishments and taken over the Chicago campaign offices of President Jimmy Carter.

One initial problem with the government's approach was the attitude of the defendants: Claiming the status of prisoners of war, they refused to participate in the judicial proceedings. Indeed, one reason for the actions in Judge Bailey's courtroom was his contempt for a political position that had a long and respected history in the Caribbean. For more than eighty years, many Puerto Ricans had challenged a claim made by Senator Albert

9

Perkins on April 2, 1900. He told his colleagues in the Senate that Puerto Rico came under the U.S. flag as "a prize of war."[1] Perkins said this was legal; the islanders who were a battlefield reward said this was nonsense. They argued that U.S. authority was always illegitimate because, among other reasons, no Puerto Ricans had been asked if they wanted their homeland to be a piece of real estate for the Spanish or war booty for the Americans.

Luis and Alicia wanted to explain why they were prisoners of war. Puerto Rico was a U.S. colony, illegally invaded and maintained by force of conquest since July 25, 1898. Under international law, "anticolonial combatants" had the right to use all legitimate forms of struggle, including armed struggle, to secure the independence of their country. The FALN took the war to the United States to help create a revolutionary conscience among the Puerto Rican people and to serve notice on Washington that colonialism was an intolerable political condition. Finally, they argued that it was absurd to believe that the colonizer could fairly judge his own crimes. To the defendants, only an international tribunal had legitimate authority to judge their revolutionary stance and their admittedly revolutionary activities.[2]

Judge Bailey refused to let the accused speak. He removed their chosen legal advisor and imposed a public defender despite Luis Rosa's "knowing waiver and strenuous objection."[3] When Attorney Michael Deutsch tried to explain the defendant's rights under international law, he was immediately threatened with contempt, and Judge Bailey ordered sheriffs to restrain Deutsch when the attorney tried to approach the bench. Meanwhile, Luis

Rosa was sentenced to six months in jail for contempt of court. (He also later received a sentence of
30 years on the state charges to be followed by a 75
year federal prison term for seditious conspiracy
and membership in the FALN.)

Alicia Rodríguez received special treatment.
Perhaps it was the passion in her voice and eyes. Or
her gender. Or some other factor which moved the
judge to hold her over until the next day. Whatever
the case, a jail employee warned Alicia she would be
sentenced for contempt the following morning. That
leak enabled Alicia to tell her family and legal advisors, and they produced such a show of support
that there was another confrontation before Alicia
ever appeared in court.

When roughly forty friends tried to enter the
courtroom, bailiffs not only barred their entrance,
they forcibly removed them from the building.
Alicia's supporters waited outside while attorneys
Deutsch and Siegal tried to speak to the judge. He
refused to see the attorneys; he barred Deutsch
from entering the courtroom; and he failed to tell
either attorney what he had already done with
Alicia.

"They took me from my cell, walked me to a
hallway, handcuffed me to a wooden chair outside
the judge's chambers, and when he appeared he
was foaming at the mouth; he looked like he wanted
to eat me for lunch."

Judge Bailey had a question: "Are you going to
keep quiet today?"

Alicia had a response: "I can't make any
promises."

The judge then ordered that Alicia be gagged.

11

"They stuffed two handkerchiefs in my mouth and then wrapped wide tape over my lips and surrounding areas. I felt violated when they muzzled me. I felt as if they were attempting to bury alive, not me—Alicia the person—but the revolutionary I had become. It goes without saying that rage and indignation accompany every *puertorriqueño* who views colonialism as unnatural and intolerable."

With tape and cloth, the judge thought he had silenced a strong-willed woman. What he didn't know (or, perhaps, care about) was that the Puerto Rican anti-colonial struggle was almost as old as the Irish; and, in both, one generation of revolutionaries learned from their predecessors.

Early in her incarceration, Alicia Rodríguez received a very significant visit from Lolita Lebrón. In 1954, Ms. Lebrón and three other Puerto Rican revolutionaries attacked the United States House of Representatives. As a result of an unconditional pardon, Ms. Lebrón was released from prison in September of 1979. In public, President Carter suggested that humanitarian considerations motivated his actions, but in a memo stamped "secret" he had received this advice from National Security Advisor Zbigniew Brzezinski: "Lolita Lebrón and three other Puerto Rican nationalists have been in federal prison for 24 years. *No other woman in the Hemisphere has been in prison on such charges for so long a period; a fact which Communist critics of your human rights policy are fond of pointing out.*"[4] (emphasis added)

Ms. Lebrón visited Alicia Rodríguez because the younger Puerto Rican had worked for years to "free the political prisoners." Chicago was the national headquarters of the effort that helped move President Carter to pardon the Puerto Ricans, and the neighborhood center where Alicia worked was proudly named after Rafael Cancel Miranda, another of the four revolutionaries who shot at U.S. congressmen in 1954.

During their visit in Chicago, Ms. Lebrón offered Alicia this advice: Make use of all the educational opportunities available in prison and, in the meantime, "lotion yourself up."

Alicia did as she was told. She entered the "no spectators allowed" courtroom gagged, taped, handcuffed from behind, and accompanied by three "big" deputies. Attorney Mara Siegal explained the defendant's position: "This court does not have jurisdiction to try her. She is a prisoner of war. It is her demand and the demand of all her friends that they be transferred to an international tribunal where their case can be heard and they be adjudged as prisoners of war. This is an outrageous display of the United States' cruel and inhumane treatment...."[5]

The judge interrupted. He ordered the attorney arrested for contempt, fined a thousand dollars, and held in the Cook Country jail until the fine was paid. The bailiffs removed the attorney. No one knew about the lotion on Alicia's face.

"I was pressed up against a table in the courtroom. I was spread-eagled, handcuffed from behind, and on either side of me a deputy was stepping on my feet. They were trying to muzzle me like a dog but, thanks to the lotion, the tape loosened. I could speak. I told the judge he was an imperialist and, before I could say another word, three guards punched my nose, jabbed my eyeballs, and punched me in the back." Meanwhile, Sheriff Rita Geoghegon made this remark: "Ms. Rodríguez is nothing but a Communist terrorist and should be shot."[6]

The judge, once again outraged, ordered that Alicia be "retaped." She was removed from the courtroom, the tape (which held tight in some places) was ripped off and "this time they put three handkerchiefs in my mouth before they fastened the tape over my lips and around my head. I was taken back to court, forced to once again assume the position in front of the wooden table, and I immediately tried to talk. I couldn't do it. So I tried again. Still no words. But, there was no way they were going to keep me quiet. I had to do something." Alicia began to hum. And she continued humming until the infuriated Judge Bailey gave up. He ordered Alicia removed from the court, and she was immediately placed in a holding cell near Attorney Mara Siegal. The two women waited while Michael Deutsch once again tried to speak to the judge.

Deutsch's first job was to get his law partner out of jail. But he had no written arrest order from which to appeal. When he went to ask Judge Bailey to put his contempt order in writing, he was met by a burly judge who, leaving his desk, told Deutsch, "I'm going to throw you out of the fucking window, motherfucker." Deutsch made a strategic retreat, and, still without an appealable order, filed a complaint with the Judicial Inquiry Board and the Appellate Court of Illinois which subsequently reversed Mara Siegel's contempt citation and denounced the treatment of Alicia Rodríguez as "an affront to the dignity and decorum of judicial proceedings."[7]

There was an affront, alright. And a crime. But it was not merely to the dignity of the court. Luis and Alicia argued that the proceedings themselves were no less an affront to the dignity of the Puerto Rican people than the hated presence of the "Black and Tans" in Belfast or the Tories quartering their troops in Boston. The crime at the core of their case was neither robbery nor sedition; it was colonialism. It had existed in Puerto Rico for over five hundred years—first under the Spanish, and, since 1898, under the United States of America—and it added (and adds) a unique dimension to the charges against the Puerto Rican political prisoners who are at the center of this book.

Gags could never silence a revolutionary like Alicia Rodríguez. Nor could tape seal up the arguments she wishes to present to any international forum that will listen. Puerto Rico is the oldest colony on earth. She and the other prisoners are incarcerated on foreign soil, and subjected to cruel and unusual punishment. Most important of all, presidents from McKinley to Clinton have refused to honestly address an undeniable fact. Imperial politics is the key to any understanding of the actions, arrests, convictions and treatment of the Puerto Rican revolutionaries.

The women and men who appear in these pages are the *fourth* generation of Puerto Rican political prisoners. Like Luis Rosa and Alicia Rodríguez, many of them—e.g., Carmen Valentín, Ricardo Jímenez, Lucy Rodríguez—first became involved in political activities while trying to free the third generation revolutionaries who, in 1954, opened fire on

15

the House of Representatives. And, of those who fired in 1954, at least one—Rafael Cancel Miranda— places his political roots in a 1937 attack on his parents, then struggling as members of the second generation of Puerto Rican revolutionaries.

This is a story which spans one hundred years. To fairly understand the prisoners, *Prisoners of Colonialism* begins in the year that, as Senator Millard Tydings acknowledged, "we acquired Puerto Rico by conquest."[8]

Political Prisoner # 0001

"The glorious Nationalist Party, headed by Pedro Albizu Campos, sowed the revolutionary seed, and extended its roots in an irreversible manner."

—Filiberto Ojeda Ríos,
Administrative Segregation
Metropolitan Correctional Center,
September 23, 1988

"It would be outrageous for me to claim that Albizu didn't influence our Prisoner of War position and our politics...Personally I'm not embarrassed to admit and make no apologies that I'm closer to Albizu than to Marx."

—Oscar López, Marion
Penitentiary, September 10, 1992

His name is Manuel Caballer and he is a revolutionary, a lawyer, a homeopath, a Catholic, a Nationalist, a devoted son, and a Ponceño.

This last word means nothing to a Northamerican, but for a Puerto Rican it's often impossible to disentangle a sense of self from a reverence for birthplace and family. Watch a person's eyes when he or she tells you about towns like Aibonito or Arecibo, Caguas or Vega Baja and you often perceive a mischievous combination of love and pity: They love their "hometown," and it's a pity God let *you* be born elsewhere.

Since Don Manuel is from Ponce—the "cultural soul" of the Puerto Rican people—he is unquestionably entitled to a special sense of pride. Through four hundred years of Spanish colonialism Ponce

17

was lucky; it lay so far from the military bastion called San Juan that its residents had a chance to create a world of their own. The narrow streets are filled with wood and stucco homes decorated by painters using a uniquely Caribbean palette. On the street that houses Don Manuel's law office I counted three shades of aquamarine but even more distinctive was an exquisite combination of white, brown and orange. The house asked to be noticed because that is the essence of Ponce's claim to fame: Using color, cement, wood, wrought iron and tile, islanders created homes that, for all their beauty, are also a form of personal and political resistance. You—the Spanish and now the Northamericans— may control the island, but you can't control our spirit. Just look at Ponce.

Don Manuel has lived in Ponce for seventy-four years. He left only to enter prison in San Juan— after the revolution of 1950—and returned to celebrate a city whose pride is so generous it even extends to unwanted imports. This became apparent when, after almost four hours of interviewing, I, at least, was hungry. Where could we go for lunch? "How about the local Bonanza?," said Don Manuel. This surprised me but once we entered the restaurant the choice made sense. Ponce and its people had somehow transformed the mass culture of the metropolis into a Puerto Rican eatery. The splashy signs and costumes were of course "made in the U.S.A." but the music was Latin, *mofongo* was the special of the day, the staff treated Manuel like family, and the salad bar was a forty foot source of particular Ponce pride. Don Manuel pointed to the many types of local fruit, the (I think) four varieties

18

of beans, and he even waxed eloquent about a potato. It looks like small onion, but it's quite tasty and
an obvious favorite of many Ponceños.

Manuel was never a "booster." He was not selling Puerto Rico or Ponce to a visitor about to invest.
Part of his warmth sprang from the everyday hospitality which is mandatory for any Puerto Rican but
even more basic was an undeniable fact: Manuel
Caballer loves his country, its fruits, its people and,
even more obviously, his father.

The Caballer family is a part of Ponce's—and
Puerto Rico's—political history. In 1887 Don
Manuel's father—Luis Caballer Lotero de Mendoza—
spent time in San Juan's El Morro, a prison fortress
that is a frigid mountain of cement and stone. "*Mi
papa* helped organize resistance to Spanish colonialism; and he lost four fingers when Spanish soldiers brutally tortured him and other Puerto Rican
political and social leaders." Ultimately scores of
islanders spent time in jail but, since Don Manuel's
father owned and edited one of Ponce's principal
newspapers, he was a special target of *los com-
pontes*, the Spanish phrase which stimulates memories of Spanish soldiers pulling out the nails from a
prisoner's fingers.

"Mi papa" expected better from the Americans.
In fact, using a tone of voice filled with both love
and admiration, Don Manuel explained that "my
father sincerely believed the Americans would never
continue a policy of colonialism. How could a people
responsible for the Declaration of Independence
impose on Puerto Ricans the very colonial system
which was the cause of their own revolution?"

On July 25, 1898 General Nelson Miles invaded

Puerto Rico. He and the first contingent of a 16,000 man army landed at Guánica, proceeded to Ponce, and, once there, Miles acted like a dictator: He declared martial law, silenced the press and only released Luis Caballer from a Spanish imposed house arrest so that U.S. soldiers could use his newspaper to print—in English and Spanish—the first public announcement of the United States' motives and intentions. The elder Caballer had so much faith in the United States and its representatives that he printed General Miles' message to the Puerto Rican people. On July 28, 1898 islanders read that "we have not come to make war upon the people of a country that for centuries has been oppressed but on the contrary to bring you protection...to promote your prosperity, and to bestow upon you the immunities and blessing of the liberal institutions of our government."

Nobody disagreed with this ideal. It was reality that posed a problem. The "Charter of Autonomy" signed with the Spanish in 1897 gave Puerto Ricans a considerable amount of self rule; they enjoyed meaningful voting representation in the mainland Spanish government, they received the power to negotiate trade and shipping agreements, and, certainly the most important provision in the 1897 law, Puerto Ricans also had the legal right to initiate or veto any proposed changes in their political status.[1]

When islanders complained about U.S. treatment, General Miles fixed bayonets. Or, as Senator Millard Tydings said in 1943, and Senator Henry Jackson (of Washington) repeated in 1974, "Puerto Rico became part of the United States by an act of conquest."[2] General Miles even Americanized the

20

spelling of the island's name; Puerto Rico instantly became Porto Rico, so that until Congress finally changed the law in 1932, a man like Manuel Caballer had to knowingly misspell the name of his beloved *patria*.

To change the situation, Puerto Ricans generally played by the rules established in Washington, D.C. For example, disillusioned and exasperated by almost two years of military rule, island politicians cited Article 1 of the U.S. Constitution when they asked Congress (in February of 1900) for an immediate "redress of grievances." Puerto Rican officials reminded the United States Senate that the "sacred pledges" made by men like General Miles were a principal cause of the "spontaneous support" received by the army of occupation. But, patience was not only wearing thin, in one loud voice the people of Puerto Rico wanted answers to these questions: "Who are we; what are we? Have we been invited to come under the sheltering roof, only to starve at the doorstep? Are we citizens, or are we subjects? Are we brothers and our property, territory, or are we the bondmen of a war and our island a crown colony?"[3]

Congress responded with the Foraker Act of 1900. Puerto Rico was not only a colony—in 1902 President to be Howard Taft helped write a book titled *Opportunities in the Colonies and Cuba*—it was the first unincorporated territory in U.S. history. Louisiana, Arizona, Alaska, and even Hawaii (in 1895) entered the Union with the explicit promise of statehood. It might take a while but they and their citizens never would be permanently excluded from the constitutional rights, privileges, and obligations of all U.S. citizens.

Puerto Rico was different. While it "belonged to" the United States, Congress had no specific status plan in mind. The islands inhabitants were "citizens of Porto Rico" but the island was not, according to U.S. law, a nation. Thus, Puerto Ricans were not U.S. citizens because they were officially a race of stateless people. As Senator Joseph Foraker told his colleagues on March 2, 1900, "We have gotten out into the sea and we have come here to legislate for another race, who speak a different language...."[4]

The emphasis varied with the speaker but "they" were children, oppressed, ignorant, black, "mongrels," Spanish and lucky. Senator Perkins, for example, agreed that Puerto Ricans had never asked, perhaps had never desired to become a part of the United States, but they would nevertheless thank Congress for its "unprecedented generosity." As all civilized men knew, "the peoples of a country cannot, like Aaron's rod, blossom and bear fruit in twenty-four hours." Somebody first had to sow seeds and nourish the soil; that was America's destiny and, despite their obvious "ingratitude," Puerto Ricans would eventually applaud Congress because "no Territory of the United States has ever been treated in so liberal a manner as this government now proposes to treat Porto Rico."[5]

In Ponce, Luis Caballer tried to comprehend the meanings of lucky and liberal. The new Puerto Rican government was deliberately and proudly modeled after British imperial practice in the Caribbean. The governor was appointed by the president of the United States; the 11 members of the Executive Council were also presidential appointees

22

(for over a decade only five were Puerto Ricans); and the elected House of Delegates had so little power that the Americans cynically let the Puerto Ricans think they controlled the budget. To do otherwise was to face the harsh realities of colonial status. As W. F. Willoughby, president of the Executive Council, boasted in the United States, "the actual administration of island affairs was exercised out of the hands of the people of the island itself;" Puerto Rico had good government because, "from the administrative standpoint," Puerto Rico's was "an autocratic government...similar in all essential respects to that of old Germany."[6]

The old Germany Willoughby had in mind was headed by a Kaiser and ruled by politicians like Otto von Bismark. Did Senators like Joseph Foraker sincerely believe that Puerto Ricans would thank them for an autocracy imposed by bayonets and bullets?

Yes, they did. Reading the congressional hearings and debates of the first thirty years of the twentieth century a reader is struck by the literal invisibility of the Puerto Rican people. "They" were a constant topic of discussion, but, even in the presence of their non-voting representative, congressmen consistently made statements like these: "Marriage among the natives is still a luxury indulged in by very few but race suicide is not seriously threatened. On the contrary, the production of children, especially of the dark color, is largely on the increase. It costs nothing to raise them...the country ones are naked until they reach the age of 10 or 12 years...and their food consists mainly of the windfalls of fruit and refuse, if they beat the dog or the hog to it. (Laughter)"[7]

23

Racism was still a joke in 1909. In Washington, it often was considered funny and never contradictory to label as inferior, men and women who were part of a culture which had been developing on Puerto Rican soil for at least three centuries before the Declaration of Independence was signed in Philadelphia. Meanwhile, in Ponce, Manuel Caballer tried to understand a civilization that sanctioned discrimination every bit as Jim Crow as that in Georgia or Mississippi.

For example, at Guanica—the site of General Miles' 1898 invasion—a Delaware company called South Porto Rico Sugar built the then-largest sugar center in the world. Spewing out contamination, the smoke stack stood at the center of this gigantic cane plantation. Scattered round the stack were the shacks of the "peons" who cut cane; around them were the few Puerto Ricans who had positions of power; and, at the edges of the racial circle were the homes of the Americans. As a reporter from *The New Republic* wrote in 1916, their homes were not only "spacious and modern," a few were "quite pretentious;" tropical flowers blossomed beside the paths to these homes. There was also a YMCA and, for those so inclined, tennis and squash courts.

The only thing missing was a Puerto Rican. None, "however high his position, or however proud his family or, for that matter, however white his color, may venture here for any social life."[8]

Like Africans in Johannesburg, Puerto Ricans were aliens in their own land. Proud men like Luis Caballer despised the realties of colonial life, but they compromised because the alternatives seemed worse. In 1905 the United States took over the cus-

24

toms houses in the Dominican Republic; in 1906 it once again staged a military occupation of Cuba; in 1916 it gave the Danes the choice of selling the Virgin Islands or having American soldiers conquer them; and, in 1916, the United States began an eight-year military occupation of the Dominican Republic and a sixteen-year military occupation of Haiti. In 1917 U.S. Marines used bayonets to force Haitians to build roads; and, in what would later be called "search and destroy missions," American soldiers systematically killed thousands of Haitian and Dominican resisters. In Congress, Senator Pomerene admitted there "were cruelties of such a character as to make an American hang his head in shame."9 In Puerto Rico, many islanders argued that, for all its indignities and exploitation, their nation, at least, had avoided the horrors in Haiti and the Dominican Republic.

The situation changed when sons began to follow in their fathers' footsteps. Manuel said, "It was one thing for my father to accept American control as the inevitable fate of Puerto Rico—in 1924 Governor Horace Towner accurately claimed that 'The United States still has absolute control because in its legislation Congress can do anything it wants to.'10—but when I volunteered to defend statehood in a class debate, my father gave me the strongest reproach imaginable. My father actually told me, 'I do not recognize you as my son.'

As Don Manuel told this story I glanced at a wooden machete on the wall of his law office. Stamped on the tool was the title of a popular song: *Coño Despierta. Coño* does not translate well, but it is serious slang in Puerto Rico. In a tone that moves from rage to exasperation it might be translated as "Go! Dammit" but, coupled with *despertar* (the verb "to wake up") the words are a call to action. "Wake up God Dammit! It's time for action."

Change was what Don Manuel's father had in mind. He rebuked a son who loved and respected him because, at an age when Manuel might be expected to defend his nation with the passion and purity of youth, the unforeseen consequences of accepting colonialism became evident: A son imitated his father's terrible compromise.

In the school debate Manuel involuntarily made the case for independence. He was the class' best speaker, so the teacher, a closet *independentista*, used Manuel's skills to convince her students of the need for a free Puerto Rico. Like Luis Caballer, the teacher was a Puerto Rican of the "second level." She kept her real beliefs hidden because she feared the employment implications of openly advocating independence.

"Second level " Puerto Ricans are a colonial norm. For nearly a century, U.S. analysts have discussed the political aspirations of the Puerto Rican people without recognizing that public statements— especially to Northamericans—often have little to do with private beliefs. From 1921 to 1923, for example, E. Montgomery Reilly was the Governor of Puerto Rico. He wanted to "rule" Puerto Rico, so he bluntly told his inaugural audience that their present political desires were irrelevant to Washington: "There is no sympathy or possible hope in the United States for independence for Porto Rico, from any individual, or from any political party...and there never shall be. As long as Old Glory waves

26

over the United States, it will wave over Porto Rico, and will never be hauled down."[11]

Reilly's systematic exclusion of all independence advocates from positions of political and economic power represents a system of patronage and political discrimination that survives to this day. Like many others, Don Manuel's father had given in to "King Monty" by eliminating independence (in 1924) from the political plank of the then-dominant Unionist Party. Luis Caballer had reluctantly accepted colonialism, but the thought that his 10-year-old son was already doing the same thing came as a shock. He took his young son to the family's library, and together they researched the past. Ultimately they made a resolution that has lasted a lifetime: Viva Puerto Rico libre!

For Don Manuel there is no way to separate political ideals from fatherly love. Indeed, the profound importance of "family values" in the lives of so many Puerto Rican political prisoners contradicts stereotypes about revolutionaries. Strong, loving families are definitely one key to understanding these Puerto Ricans' political activities; another is the speeches and actions of a Ponceño every bit as important to Don Manuel Caballer as his own father.

Pedro Albizu Campos

Don Manuel's office is filled with roughly a dozen paintings of the same man. Some are examples of realism, some are abstract; one especially arresting portrait is derived from a photograph taken in 1944. Pedro Albizu Campos was in New York's Columbia hospital recovering from a heart problem exacerbated by seven hard years in Atlanta's Federal Penitentiary. The FBI had even bugged his hospital bed, but, despite so much unsolicited attention, the portrait nevertheless reflects the love, strength and commitment which defined the man. He was pure principle. Or, as they say in Puerto Rico, he remained so "vertical" that even though he could have left prison in 1941, he remained for two additional years, because, as the FBI noted, Albizu "refused to execute the necessary conditional release papers on the grounds that by doing so he would be recognizing the United States Government...."[12]

Pedro Albizu Campos made himself a revolutionary. Like Don Manuel's father, he was born (in 1891) in a Ponce dominated by Spain, soon to be conquered by the United States. He first entered school as Presidents McKinley and Roosevelt forcibly changed Puerto Rico's educational policy; English became the mandated medium of classroom instruction during Albizu's childhood and it is amazing that his, or any of his classmates', intelligence shone through in a system which demanded that Puerto Ricans teach in a foreign language to students who did not understand the English their teachers could not speak.

In the cultural capital of Puerto Rico, students like Albizu began the day with the Pledge of Allegiance to a foreign flag; they also sang the *Star Spangled Banner*. This was sometimes followed by *God Bless America*, and, in schools named after Washington, Lincoln, and Jefferson, Albizu learned arithmetic by adding and subtracting fruits he had never seen—apples and pears instead of bananas and pineapples.

Albizu graduated with honors. He was president of his class and so much the pride of Ponce that he received a scholarship from the often-revolutionary Loyal Order of Masons. The Masons sent Albizu to the University of Vermont (in 1912) because, like Samuel Adams, Benjamin Franklin, and George Washington, they believed in a new hierarchical order. Theirs rested on "real worth and personal merit;" it was linked to brotherly affection and sincerity. Empathy was the hallmark of any genuine Mason because the elites of England or Germany had "scarcely ever thought about the existence of their inferiors." Thus, the willingness of the Masons to believe that "the other" had a reality equal to one's own was a powerful force in producing a call to begin the world all over again...[13]

By 1912, the ideals of George Washington had been transformed into the British-inspired colonialism that mandated English-only schools in a Spanish-speaking country. Albizu, nevertheless, got the chance for a higher education because many Masons still recognized intelligence, merit and ambition when they saw it. Albizu, for example, spent only one year at the University of Vermont. Harvard came calling, and Albizu did so well at Cambridge that he became president of the University's Cosmopolitan Club. In a portrait taken in 1916, Albizu and his classmates look stodgy; they are all dressed in black suits, wearing the starched collars that apparently choked the smiles out of virtually every club member. However, as in a class picture taken in Ponce in 1910, "Pete" sits at the center of the photo and appears content because, by all accounts, he had every reason to congratulate himself and his Mason supporters. His classmates said he was both high-minded and idealistic; and they jealously reminded him years later "of the charming members of the opposite sex whom you used to seduce with your wiles."[14]

Albizu was patriotic as well as popular. In an article published in the Harvard *Crimson* eight days after the U.S. declaration of war, the 26-year-old Albizu sounded like Don Manuel's father. He explained that Puerto Ricans had welcomed General Miles because "they looked to this country as their liberator...we welcomed the American flag in 1898 because we believed it, and still believe it, to be a symbol of democracy and justice. It was conceived in that spirit."[15]

In 1917 Albizu was committed to a peaceful resolution of Puerto Rico's problems and assured his Northamerican readers that he and his compatriots would not only volunteer to swat the Hun, "we will give good account of ourselves in actual voluntary military cooperation with the United States."

What happened? How did the patriot from Harvard become such a revolutionary that, by 1934, he refused to concede the right of an American president to set foot on Puerto Rican soil;[16] and by 1950 he ordered members of his party to attack Blair House, the residence of President Harry Truman.

At the White House, at the FBI, and at the Offices of Naval Intelligence, officials had no problem assessing Albizu's motives and behavior. The man was a deranged fanatic, his behavior the result of racial prejudice experienced during World War I. As President Roosevelt put it in 1936, "I am informed that Albizu Campos, at that time (1917) a firm admirer of our democratic institutions, subsequently became imbued with a deep hatred of the United States, due, chiefly, to his being assigned during the World War to a colored officer's training camp."[17]

There is only one problem with this explanation: It's not true. Pedro Albizu Campos was what Northamericans would call black, but a man born minutes from the smoke-stack segregation at Guanica never needed to enter the U.S. Army to experience hatred rooted in racial or ethnic slurs. For the second decade of Albizu's life, U.S. political and economic representatives excluded Puerto Ricans from positions of power to social clubs, and openly boasted that, except as servants, Puerto Ricans never entered their homes. As the governor of Puerto Rico (1929-31), Teddy Roosevelt, Jr., later wrote in a book entitled *Colonial Policies of the United States*, "we have one besetting sin in common with many other peoples, including the British. We think we are better than other people. Anyone who does things different from us is either comic or stupid. We regard being a foreigner in the nature of a defective moral attribute."[18]

Thus, Albizu's most noteworthy trait was not his supposed hatred of Northamericans but rather, his high level of personal and political idealism, despite daily encounters with racism and paternalism, which endeared him to his classmates at Harvard.

Long interviews with everybody from his closest associates to his youngest daughter (Laura Albizu) indicate that Albizu never spoke disparagingly of his military service. He never regretted volunteering to go "over there;" and, just as important, he never hated Northamericans. His complaint was colonialism and what he argued were the demonstrable contradictions of U.S. policy. For example, in congressional hearings, the federal officials who (in 1936) charged Albizu with seditious conspiracy, simultaneously admitted that U.S. policy in Puerto Rico represented "the establishment of Old World colonialism, under the Stars and Stripes, something which should be repugnant and repulsive to our ideas of democracy."[19] However, in explaining Albizu and his movement, those same officials resorted to individual psychological explanations for a revolution that had some of its deepest roots in pamphlets like *Common Sense* and political principles like freedom, liberty and self-determination.

Tom Paine, for instance, clearly despised the British system of colonial government, but would anyone ever argue that his violent, revolutionary resistance was caused by psychological pain? Or, what about Samuel Adams and the Mohawks who destroyed the tea in Boston Harbor? Was it bitter, personal humiliation that fueled the mobs which often destroyed significant amounts of public and personal property before and during the American revolution?[20]

The colonizer's stress on an individual's personality is a form of self-defense. It reduces complex social and historical issues to psychological phenomena and thus avoids the need to accept either personal or collective responsibility for the economic and political exploitation which are an essential component of any colonial situation.

After the war, Albizu returned to Harvard. He completed all but two of the courses required for his law degree, and he then returned (in June of 1921) to a *patria* at war with itself and with the United States. As Governor Reilly—now "King Monty" to the Puerto Rican people—wrote to President Harding, it was true that his anti-independence inaugural address had produced an intense response; "I received a number of letters threatening my life, others telling me that if I did not leave the island in 48 hours I would be killed, and if I drove through the streets I would be murdered." However, "I could not show the white flag so I drove through the streets and around the plaza that afternoon."[21]

What a governor. And what a burden for the Puerto Rican people. They had voted for change, but Congress refused to concede, not only independence, but even the possibility of an elected Governor. Albizu, analyzing the situation from Ponce, initially was hopeful. When Reilly expelled independence advocates from their bread and butter positions in the island's government, Albizu joined the Unionist Party (in October of 1922) supported by Luis Caballer. This surprised some political activists because Albizu was already associated with a nationalist position. However, he joined the Unionist party because he believed that the political indignation expressed against Reilly could produce a rebellion capable of ending colonialism. The new governor was potentially a godsend because his flagrant and humiliating disregard for the expressed will of the Puerto Rican people might finally recreate the moral atmosphere that, in 1868, produced a revolution against the Spanish. Called *Grito de Lares* (the shout of Lares) in Puerto Rican history, it was the moral ideal against which Albizu measured success and failure.

Albizu struggled. Through 1922, 1923 and into 1924 he wrote a series of conciliatory articles, all creatively suggesting various methods of ending colonialism without a revolution: an alliance with the Statehood Socialists, a constitutional convention, yet another resolution to the United States Congress. Albizu knew that, in 1924, besides Puerto Rico, the U.S. also was occupying Haiti and the Dominican Republic, used only soldiers to rule the Virgin Islands, and rewrote the Cuban constitution. Facing that level of U. S. arrogance and intransigence, Albizu offered every imaginable proposal, but he also advanced the idea that if the Yankees closed their ears to the words of Puerto Ricans, those ears would be opened with gunblasts.

By 1924 none of the major parties listed independence as a status option; equally important, island politicians actually raised the white flag before the very officials responsible for men like E. Montgomery Reilly. As Antonio Barceló, president of the Puerto Rican Senate told the House Committee on Insular Affairs (in February of 1924) "among ourselves, the members of the delegation, there is a complete unanimity of judgment in this petition for a larger degree of self government. We only differ in regard to our future political status which is as uncertain to us as it is to you."[22]

At the same time, Albizu wrote of death—the death of the Unionist Party. From hundreds of formal and informal conversations with men such as Luis Caballer, Albizu thought he knew the truth:

34

"The great majority" of the people in Puerto Rico's dominant political party were proindependence "to their very bones." They loved their culture; they relished their language; and they abhorred the "kaiserism" imported from Washington. Yet, instead of challenging the United States, "we offer an exceptional spectacle; the people are action, their leaders reaction; the people, the vanguard, their leaders, the impediment."[23]

Albizu resigned from the Unionist Party in May of 1924. He immediately joined the recently founded (in 1922) Nationalist Party, where he hoped to create the sense of moral outrage that would forever avoid the submissiveness of the Union Party. Even when Congress answered the age-old questions—who are we? what are we?—with "who knows, talk to me in a decade or two," Albizu's former colleagues acquiesced. They were perfectly willing to walk into a future "as uncertain to us as it is to you."

Albizu was on fire. The famous photo suggests his intensity, but it misses the *moral* dimension—always rooted in the inalienable rights guaranteed by natural law—which was the perpetual touchstone of Albizu's revolutionary politics. Fully fifty years before the United Nations called colonialism a crime against humanity, Pedro Albizu Campos believed that U.S. policy was morally repugnant. Forget the economic exploitation. Ignore the use of Puerto Rico as a military bastion. Overlook the discrimination. Disregard the assault on culture. And focus on the moral compass that drove this man: Colonialism was something the world had not yet named—genocide.

Albizu was right—in 1925 and in 1994. What

Pedro Albizu Campos

happened, however, was that instead of focusing on his accurate analysis of history or the behavior of U.S. colonial officials, people too often focused on Albizu himself. Before a famous speech in 1925, he quietly mounted the platform, slowly walked around the stage, and, only after he removed each and every American flag from the podium, did Pedro Albizu Campos speak to *his* people, in front of *their* flag, on *their* sacred soil.

People said Albizu was bold. Audacious. Rude. Crazy. Fanatical. The comments varied with the critic, but the focus of this Ponceño never varied through thirty years of confrontational politics. Asked, "Do you have a political platform?" Albizu responded "Yes, sir. Our program, its general thesis, is to restore to the Puerto Rican people the moral intensity which they expressed in 1868...then they preached the revolutionary creed. We seek to translate that moral indignation into all the forms of resistance that will enable us to dispose of American colonialism."[24]

Because he was an open revolutionary, because he and his followers never hid their revolutionary intentions, Albizu Campos shocked his contemporaries and astonished one American president after another. How could a man who graduated from Harvard threaten to overthrow the United States of America? Where was his gratitude? And why did he insist on any confrontation that would somehow question the legitimacy of U.S. cultural, political, and economic authority?

The questions should be reversed. Revolution was a right, colonialism the crime. Thus, what needed to be changed was the acquiescence of the Puerto Ricans; and what needed to be challenged was the hypocrisy of the Northamericans. As then-Governor of Puerto Rico Rexford Tugwell told a San Juan audience on the Fourth of July, "The Declaration of Independence did not end colonialism but it removed that system to a moral category which made it indefensible."[25]

Albizu agreed. His aim was to arouse the moral indignation of his people and offer its youth answers to 450-year-old questions: Who are we? We are Puerto Ricans. Who could ask for more? What are we? We are free. But only if we are willing to dedicate our lives to the *valores* that give historical significance to the anticolonial struggle of any Puerto Rican patriot.

In Ponce, Albizu Campos bought a house next door to the Caballer's and, as if by fate, Don Manuel found an answer to his father's request to free Puerto Rico. *Albizu gave direction to people's lives.* Like the U.S. Congress, in 1927 or 1937 nobody in Puerto Rico offered a vision for the future. Where are we going? Traditional politicians offered only this answer: We don't know. Or, more accurately, we must wait until the Yankees make up their minds.

For those with Albizu's sense of moral indignation, the wait was over. Albizu spoke of *valores* (e.g., sacrifice, family, patriotism), and in my interviews with this first generation of political prisoners the word is said with a deep sense of pride and significance. There was a self-sacrificing quality about the Nationalists' commitment—Nathan Hale's "I regret that I have but one life to give for my country" comes immediately to mind—and, like the sense of self linked to the sense of place, it is impossible to disentangle *valores* from religious and cultural affirmations.

Never confuse *valores* with fanaticism. As Nathan Hale suggests, assessments of motivation

are grossly colored by political—and more specifically—colonial prejudices. Hale's willingness to give up
his life for his country makes him an unforgettable
U.S. patriot, but when a Nationalist like 83-year-old
Blanca Canales makes the same commitment, she
turns into a fanatic who hates the United States.

anything anti-US is wrong

That is not only nonsense, it is poor history.
The sense of commitment expressed by many
Nationalists has a sacred quality because its roots
are partly religious in origin.

In 1930 Puerto Rico was still an overwhelmingly
Catholic country, full of people who wanted to
defend their faith against the missionary zeal of
hundreds of American-Protestant ministers. So, as I
listened to <u>Blanca Canales</u>' assure me that she recognized the legitimacy of all religions, the door to
her apartment nevertheless contained a beautiful
picture of Jesus and Mary. Like so many of her
Nationalist comrades, this woman had a deep love
for Catholicism; she believed in its teachings and
she also believed it was an elemental part of Puerto
Rican life. For example, in 1930 and in 1993, Puerto
Rico closes down on Good Friday. Believers do *nothing* on the day God died.

Blanca Canales is tiny—4'9" on a good day. But
in October of 1950, she was an important member
of the revolutionary forces in the mountain town of
Jayuya. Her comrades first assaulted the local
armory and, when she spied the smoke produced by
their successful attack, she unfurled Puerto Rico's
one star flag and proclaimed the Republic. National
Guard planes (accompanied by U.S. pilots) eventually defeated the revolutionary forces, but Blanca's
most painful memories are from an assault on the

nearby town of Utuado. She went to help comrades who, even after they surrendered, were slaughtered by native and Yankee soldiers.

Blanca Canales explained her revolutionary commitment by using a healthy dose of self-depreciation. While it was very hard to believe, she smilingly insisted that her role model in 1930 was the governor's wife, Mrs. Theodore Roosevelt, Jr. "We watched what she did, and we even wore little pairs of white gloves." I had a really hard time believing the glove story—Blanca Canales had to be one of the century's first feminists—but she swore it was true.

The problem was that by following the lead of Mrs. Roosevelt this Latin American woman felt like half a person—half American, half Puerto Rican. She was "disoriented" and what Albizu did was remind her of her mother. *Mi mama* was always an independentista; she rarely made a political mistake, and she always argued with *mi papa*, pushing him to take more aggressive political positions ."

As with Manuel Caballer, these memories of childhood are recounted with affection and respect. Freud was never needed in the Canales home. However, what Blanca needed as a young adult was a sense of direction; half this, half that, she felt like a puzzle in search of a solution. Thus, when Albizu preached pride and social change, Blanca Canales discovered a movement that simultaneously affirmed a sleeping political commitment and a deep respect for all aspects of Puerto Rican culture. Religion, language, affection, hospitality, dignity, respect: Albizu always celebrated the best aspects of the Puerto Rican character, and in a woman like Blanca Canales he found individuals who were perfectly willing to dedicate their lives to a revolution that, as it struggled against colonialism, affirmed what was best in Puerto Rican society.

The Impossible Charge: Seditious Conspiracy

By 1935 the struggle had definitely come to a head. In numbers, the Nationalists were still a small party, but any focus on size misses the enormous spiritual significance of Albizu and The Nationalist Party. What the Nationalists did—by organizing a military group called the Cadets of the Republic, by issuing bonds in the name of the Republic, by, in essence, declaring war against the United States— was arouse the proindependence sentiments "in the bones" of the Puerto Rican people. Then (and today) few Puerto Ricans were willing to make the commitments of a Blanca Canales or a Manuel Caballer. But they were quite willing to live vicariously through the actions of Albizu and his comrades. Indeed, they were even willing to support Albizu when he publicly suggested that someone execute the island's American Chief of Police, E. Francis Riggs.

In an October 1935 speech at the University of Puerto Rico, Albizu had criticized students for their lack of political and cultural commitment. They wore Blanca Canales white gloves instead of raising clenched fists. Days later some students organized a demonstration against Albizu, and, when four Nationalists left the University after being denied access, they were killed by police under the authority of E. Francis Riggs.

By late 1935 Riggs and Albizu were bitter ene-

41

mies. In fact, while most histories of their antago-
nisms focus on the murder of the four Nationalists,
Manuel Caballer says that Albizu had long before
come to the conclusion that Riggs meant to kill him.
Albizu believed that, while representing the United
States in Nicaragua in 1934, Riggs had both ordered
and paid for the assassination of Augusto Sandino. I
have been unable to verify this charge, but whatever
happened in Nicaragua, in Puerto Rico Albizu did,
in fact, face an assassination attempt by one of his
Nationalist associates. The fellow's name has been
forgotten—Caballer said that Albizu ordered him to
forget the man's name, and he unfortunately followed orders—but the attempt did occur and the
would-be assassin, confronted by Albizu, claimed he
had been paid ($11,000) by E. Francis Riggs.

Albizu decided to act. In a speech to 8,000 people at the burial of the young Nationalists, Albizu
told his listeners that Riggs had sent the police to
the university "with the deliberate intent of assassi-
nating the Nationalists representation of Puerto
Rico." The only alternative was an eye for an eye, or,
as Albizu declared, "we swear that assassination
will not go unpunished in Puerto Rico."[26]

E. Francis Riggs was killed by two members of
the Nationalist Party—Hiram Beauchamp and Elias
Rosado—on February 23, 1936. Legend teaches that
it was this assassination which moved the federal
government to charge Albizu with seditious conspiracy, but, as Cecil Synder (the U.S. Attorney in
Puerto Rico) explained the situation to President
Roosevelt, special agents first arrived on the island
weeks before Riggs' death. Their job was to accumu-
late evidence of revolutionary intent, and, given

42

Albizu's open defiance of the colonial government, they not only had an easy task, "they had already completed their investigation and left Puerto Rico before Colonel Riggs was murdered."[27]

While Albizu welcomed the confrontation, an indictment for seditious conspiracy—the same charge leveled 44 years later against 11 of the contemporary Puerto Rican political prisoners—surprised and worried many Northamericans. From Washington, Ernest Gruening (director of the Interior Department's Division of Territories and Island Possessions) told Puerto Rico's governor "that I think the charge of treason is not a desirable one to bring...simply because it glorifies Albizu Campos and raises an issue which can be disguised in terms of patriotism." To Gruening—in a classified letter to another official—"the people of Puerto Rico must know perfectly well that they are free and always have been free..."[28]

While freedom was, of course, the issue, Gruening managed to forget his own words. In 1931, for example, he had written to Governor Teddy Roosevelt, Jr. that "Puerto Rico, unlike the Philippines, was unequivocally and permanently U.S. territory."[29] In a letter to Blanton Winship in 1936, he said that "independence agitation is, in my judgement, very largely the natural reaction from longstanding unemployment and want; he then cited a series of "grossly unfair" U.S. economic policies.[30] Finally, it was Gruening who, in 1937, noted that thirty-five year old U.S. sugar policies "are essentially going back to the factors which caused us to seek our independence from Great Britain, and which caused the rebelling of the Colonies against the tyranny and oppression of mother countries in the Old World."[31]

If men like Gruening lied to themselves, they had a much harder time lying about the reaction of Puerto Rico's political elite. For example, on July 16, 1936 Colonel John Wright included these items in his "weekly list of subversive activities": The Woman's Federation had sent a "radiogram" to the Pope asking that he intercede to stay the proceedings against Albizu and the other Nationalists. Only two days after the trial began, eighteen Municipal Assemblies (e.g., Arecibo, Ponce, Jayuya, San German, and Quebradillas) had already passed resolutions requesting that the trial be stopped; and, most important of all, the heads of the Republican (Statehood) and Liberal (one day independence, the next day something else) Parties had actually sent a cable to President Roosevelt asking that the trial be stopped.[32]

In social visits that also made the weekly subversive list, Albizu thanked his colleagues for a level of support that suggested a 180 degree turn in Puerto Rican politics. In 1923 the elite refused any direct challenge to a governor who bluntly ridiculed its desire for independence. By 1936 that *same* elite asked that charges of admitted execution be overlooked. In Washington Ernest Gruening was aghast; he pressured a future governor of Puerto Rico (Luis Muñoz Marín) to condemn Albizu, but despite economic threats, the administration's best friends deserted it when the issue was support for the Nationalists' struggle. Even a year later, Muñoz sent a long letter to President Roosevelt, closing with this statement: The members of my political organization

44

"unanimously approved to request the freedom of persons imprisoned on political indictments."[33]

Albizu trusted the people. Even those who were theoretically the most Americanized. Remember that in the federal courts of Puerto Rico all trials are in English; that excludes most Puerto Ricans from any potential jury pool (even in 1991 only 20% of the Puerto Rican people were bilingual), but Albizu never worried about judgment by less than a jury of his peers. He thought he knew what was in people's bones, and he was right. The first trial for seditious conspiracy ended in a hung jury; the seven Puerto Ricans refused to convict, the five Northamericans said Albizu should go to jail. For a long time.

Cecil Snyder was angry. As he later put it to President Roosevelt, "this was the most important criminal case ever tried in Puerto Rico...it was the major preoccupation of this office for six months...."[34] And it was a case Cecil Snyder meant to win. So, Snyder called for a new trial in less than a week and, in a country with 5,000 Northamerican and one million Puerto Rican residents, he created a jury of 10 Yankees and two Puerto Ricans. As American artist Rockwell Kent later revealed in a sworn statement, Snyder boasted at a San Juan party that "this time" he would get Albizu. The means was Snyder's flaunted list of preselected jurors, all committed to declaring Albizu guilty as charged.[35] In fact, this jury did condemn Albizu and his colleagues but, two years later, one juror told President Roosevelt what really happened.

Elmer Ellsworth explained that the two Puerto Ricans "were closely associated with American business interests." They were the kind of men any

45

colony contains—recall, for example, that Benjamin Franklin's son was imprisoned by George Washington for aiding the British[36]—and, along with the 10 Americans, they were "a jury that all seemed to be motivated by strong if not violent prejudice against the Nationalists *and were prepared to convict the Nationalists regardless of the evidence.*"[37] (emphasis added)

The president read Ellsworth's letter and filed it. Meanwhile, the results of the administration's other efforts to deal with the Nationalists and the independence movement were "bearing fruit." In a May 18, 1936 cabinet meeting, the president and his advisors decided to draft a bill offering independence to the Puerto Rican people. Ernest Gruening would write the bill in his office at the Interior Department's Division of Territories and Insular Possessions but, under no circumstances, would the bill be associated with the Roosevelt administration.

Hiding the president's involvement was a Senator who argued that Puerto Rico required radical social change. Millard Tydings told Puerto Ricans that "ever since 1898 your destiny has been what Congress said it should be;" and now was the time for change because Puerto Ricans were far too dependent on the United States. "When you have difficulties down there," Congress "appropriates some money for relief. That carries you over to the next year. Then the next year we appropriate more money for relief. That carries you over to the following year. There is no solution and if I were a Puerto Rican I would want to know what my destiny was. I wouldn't want to go on under that kind of a hand-

46

out government year after year after year. It is disgraceful. It is a blot on the American system."[38]

Tydings echoed Pedro Albizu Campos. The two men were at one until Tydings explained his conception of self-determination. The bill was written in Washington and no Puerto Ricans were ever consulted before it was introduced. Asked if this was a slight to the people of Puerto Rico, the Maryland Senator· offered this response: "The Puerto Ricans weren't consulted when Puerto Rico was annexed to the United States. It was not necessary to consult them about independence. It was a matter for us primarily to decide, although no discourtesy was intended."[39]

Tydings reconciled his various statements in this fashion: He and his Senate colleagues had decided to keep the U.S. "permanent possession" but to do it in what appeared to be a democratic manner. Thus, Congress proudly promised a vote while Puerto Rico's leading newspaper asked this question: Was the Tydings bill a plebiscite or an ambush? The paper decided it was an ambush because of changes made by Ernest Gruening and supported by everybody from the president to Millard Tydings.

The model for the bill was the independence legislation offered to the Philippines. But, instead of the twenty-year economic transition provided its Pacific colony, Gruening only offered the Puerto Ricans four years. And, in an additional twist of the knife, the bill stipulated that as soon as independence arrived, all federal funds would disappear.

In his autobiography Gruening admitted that it was "partly right" to characterize the Tydings Bill as

47

a "brutal act."[40] This was so because the bill neglected the results of forty years of economic change.

In 1897 fifteen percent of Puerto Rico's exports went to the United States and twenty-one percent of Puerto Rico's imports came from the United States. By 1905 the figures were eighty-four and eighty-five percent; by 1920, eighty-eight and ninety-four percent; and by 1930 ninety-five and eighty-seven percent.[41]

In 1936 Puerto Rico's economy was married to that of the United States. It was an unhappy relationship—official unemployment in 1935 was twenty-four percent for the men sixty-six percent for the women—but primary responsibility for the consequences of 38 years of political and economic change must rest with the United States and its colonial representatives. As William Willoughby first boasted in 1905, both political and economic power had been taken out of the hands of the Puerto Rican people. This accurate claim had been reasserted time and again (e.g., Governor Towner's 1924 declaration that Congress had absolute power) so, *with autocratic power comes primary responsibility*. One cannot reasonably claim the one without the other.

The Tydings Bill did just that. It was meant to frighten the people of Puerto Rico, and it succeeded. The Nationalists willingly accepted any sacrifice to achieve independence, but the other parties cried starvation, and the independence bill died in committee. Meanwhile, with Albizu and seven of his colleagues serving ten year prison terms in Atlanta's penitentiary, nobody boldly challenged U.S. authority, thus, U.S. authority boldly challenged Puerto

Rico.

In a letter written by Ernest Gruening but signed (on April 8, 1937) by Franklin Roosevelt, the president set the tone for another generation of colonialism. He indicated his chagrin at an unacceptable fact: "Today hundreds of thousands of Puerto Ricans have little and often virtually no knowledge of the English language." Indeed, "even among those who have had the opportunity to study English in the public schools, mastery of the language is far from satisfactory."[42] Roosevelt wanted change, but in assessing the failure of the English-first movement he ignored not only his own ethno-centrism but a major reason for the dismal results achieved by the Americanization effort—the English-first movement.

Consider, for example, a comment made by Filiberto Ojeda Ríos, one of the contemporary political prisoners. Ojeda started school in the late thirties, and he accurately described the situation: "The English language was forced upon all the Puerto Rican students as the main vehicle of learning. Many teachers in those days expressed resentment of this fact, and their resentment carried an *independentista* message directly to their students. The preservation of our national language became an important tool against colonialism in the absence of sufficient strength to oppose the fierce repression through other means."[43]

Ojeda was right. And so, too, the mother of Haydée Beltrán, one of the contemporary political prisoners now held in California. Ms. Beltrán says that after 35 years in the United States, "my mother does not speak one word of English. To her that

49

means a lot. To her that means 'I've never given into staying here'... she's very proud...we never spoke any English in the house...she would not listen to us. If we spoke to her in English she would turn and say, 'I do not understand.' That is how we kept our language."[44]

In Puerto Rico and in the United States, presidents like Franklin Roosevelt created the *cultural resistance* that helped create revolutionaries. In childhood, Filiberto Ojeda Ríos sat, as if in clandestinity, learning English, but, like Ms. Beltrán's mother, he spoke Spanish whenever he wanted to be at peace with himself and his people. Ojeda resisted, not only a horrible educational system—in 1941 *Fortune* magazine prophecized that the educational system was likely to produce "illiteracy in two languages and a general negativism"[45]—but a reassertion of U.S. colonialism. As the president put it in his public letter, "it is an indispensable part of American policy that the *coming generation* of American citizens in Puerto Rico grow up with complete facility in the English tongue. It is the language of our nation."[46] (emphasis added)

Nonsense. And proven nonsense if an observer analyzed the 1940 electoral campaign of a new Puerto Rican political entity: The Popular Democratic Party of Luis Muñoz Marín. On the issue of political status Muñoz wanted to postpone any discussion until the war ended; he always suggested, hinted, alluded, promised that his real goal was independence, but he nevertheless preached patience and accommodation because of the island's dismal economy. Let's get that in order, and then we can discuss political status.

To talk to the people Muñoz never used his perfect English. Instead he followed the lead of his schoolteacher wife. She had battled the use of English throughout the 1930's and, among other influences, hers shows up in the campaign tactics of the Populares. In essence, to win the 1940 election, the United States' man in San Juan cleverly used the Spanish language to celebrate the most elemental symbols of Latin American and Puerto Rican culture.

The Party's political emblem was Pan, Tierra, y Libertad (Bread, Land and Liberty), a slogan which deliberately echoed the antiamerican cries of Emiliano Zapata during the Mexican Revolution. The Party's newspaper was *El Batey*. This is an Indian word taken from the Taínos, the first inhabitants of Puerto Rico; the batey was a ballfield used by the Indians for religious purposes and used by Muñoz as an instant way to gain the attention and respect of the Puerto Rican electorate.

The Party's emblem was the profile of a "jíbaro" (literally a hillbilly but often said in Puerto Rico with a great deal of respect) in a pava (a straw hat) and one of Muñoz best political assets was his ability to talk to the people in their language, using all the idioms that only a "jíbaro" would easily comprehend.[47]

Inextricably rooted in Puerto Rican culture, Muñoz won a smashing political victory in 1940. In Washington, officials breathed a sigh of relief; they expected to control Muñoz but they had no way to control what was still in the bones of the Puerto Rican and Latin American people.

An Absurd Position

Trouble came in many shapes and forms. At the White House officials worried about mid-1942 letters from a "very important" Argentinean politician. Dr. don Alfredo Palaciós thanked President Roosevelt for "correcting the imperialistic policy of the governments of the United States which divided the continent in antagonistic forces." America had changed; "therefore the free men of America cannot conceive why Pedro Albizu Campos...is in prison since 1936, in the Penitentiary of Atlanta, for the crime of directing the liberation movement of his countrymen."[48]

Palaciós reminded the president that "Puerto Rico, Sir, is in the power of the United States against its will. In that colony which cannot resign itself to being so...." a man of Albizu's stature reminded the Argentinean of a great American: Abraham Lincoln. So, "invoking Lincoln's memory, which is sacred for all the oppressed throughout the world, I ask of you the freedom of Albizu Campos, the imprisoned liberator...the first Hispano-American."[49]

Colony. Oppressed. Lincoln. Liberator. The first Hispano-American. Palaciós stressed a theme which runs through this book: South of the border, independence revolutionaries are heroes, not criminals. Liberators, not terrorists.

In response to the Argentinean letter, the White House lied. It sent data drawn from the files of Governor Blanton Winship and (here is the lie) it assured Palaciós "that the action against Señor Albizu Campos was taken entirely because of his adjudged complicity in the murder of certain police

52

authorities in Puerto Rico." Since Roosevelt had received and read the 1938 judicial summary of prosecutor Cecil Snyder, the president knew that the case against Albizu was decided before the murder of Francis Riggs. However, since there was apparently no defense against the liberation analysis of Palaciós, the White House simply told the Argentinean Senator that he had been "misinformed." Albizu was an assassin.

In May of 1942 Palaciós responded "with the frankness proper to a man who was born in a free country." The president of the United States had adopted an "absurd" position: "To call the Puerto Rican patriot who is fighting for his country's freedom an 'assassin' as does the 'official report' appears absurd to us who venerate in our America the memory of the heroes who through their abnegation and sacrifice gave us independence."[50]

Once again the president read the correspondence. And once again Palaciós received a response that not only refused to see Albizu through a Latin American lens, it refused to accept the arguments of the State Department official who actually wrote the president's replies to Palaciós. Planning for the postwar world in August of 1942, Assistant Secretary of State Sumner Welles asked this question in then secret discussions with the British:

> There is a great moral question here and *it is a question that will shape and color the history of the world after this war is over.* To get right down to the question, what inherent right has France to territory (i.e., Indochina) which she has seized, sometimes by war, as recently as the 1880's, any more than has Japan to seize by

force certain territories of China which she has now occupied? The only difference is in point of time.[51] (emphasis added)

Welles was right. He had raised a "great moral question" with great moral implications for the United States. Indeed, since even Senator Millard Tydings agreed that "we acquired Puerto Rico by conquest"[52] , what right did the United States have to a nation "seized by force," not in the 1880's, but in 1898?

In Washington, Welles refused to answer the question he himself raised. The British, angered by what they called self-righteousness, pushed him on Puerto Rico. Did the same principles used to condemn the French and the British apply to the United States? Not on your life![53] Welles refused to concede the legitimacy of his own questions when they applied to the Western Hemisphere, so, once he threw morality overboard, Albizu Campos tried to rescue it.

In Atlanta, officials told the president they had received many letters asking that Albizu be pardoned. The problem was the prisoner. To put an application on the president's desk, Albizu had to ask for executive clemency. "This he persistently refused to do for the reason that the United States has no jurisdiction in Puerto Rico, and if he acknowledged any kind of supervision by the United States government it would be acknowledgement of the United States over him."[54]

Albizu agreed with Sumner Welles. The United States had no "inherent right" to a nation seized in war. Thus, like so many of the contemporary Puerto Rican political prisoners, he refused to ask for a pardon or for parole. On principle Albizu stayed in jail two years longer than was necessary and, even after his release, he still gave U.S. officials years of anxious moments because he refused to report (again on principle) to his probation officer. Judge Robert A. Cooper, the official who sentenced Albizu in 1937, wanted to immediately return him to jail since he flaunted his contempt for American authority; and, even more important, "the State Department was now in possession of evidence tending to show that Albizu and the codefendant Juan Antonio Corretjer are at present engaged in activities in the City of New York in furtherance of their objective of overthrowing the government of the United States in Puerto Rico."[55]

The judge wanted action. The State Department said not now. And Albizu did his best to foment revolution from his exile in New York. For a year all sides remained "satisfied" with the stalemate but, in August of 1944, Governor Rexford Tugwell urged "an immediate pardon or commutation" of Albizu's sentence. In San Juan, rumor had it that corrections officers meant to arrest Albizu for parole violations, and Tugwell told his superiors in Washington "that a resentence would have a deleterious effect on our relations with Latin America and would strengthen the independence group within the Popular Party."[56]

From Washington, the Interior Department tried to allay Governor Tugwell's and the State Department's fears. Albizu was not going to be arrested. What happened was that a probation officer from the island's had left new forms at Albizu's house. As usual he refused to sign them but the arrest rumors began because of the appearance of this zealous official. However, to assure no future problems, Tugwell should pressure the judge to close his eyes to Albizu's admittedly open defiance of the federal government. Granted there was no legal way Washington could stop the judge, but, unless he was blind to Caribbean realities, officials "assumed that he [Judge Cooper] is familiar with the consequences that would occur in Puerto Rico if he ordered Albizu returned to Puerto Rico for revocation of his parole."[57]

What were those consequences? Nobody knew for sure but, except for Albizu, all concerned wanted to avoid any confrontations because, if the Puerto Rican people were with the prisoners in 1936, by 1944 *independentistas* had actually taken over Puerto Rico's dominant political party. As Tugwell told his superiors, at the Popular Party's August convention, "the independentistas were very wild and wooly and ran away with the whole show, putting Muñoz on the defensive and, although they appear not to have known it, putting him into a state of near panic for some time."[58]

Muñoz feared the worst: He would be displaced as party leader after the November elections. Thus, since "he says that independence is inevitable," Muñoz decided to swim with the tide rather than against it. He would weakly advocate independence but definitely promise a plebiscite in which the people could decide among three alternatives: statehood, independence, or some form of dependent independence.[59]

Since Governor Tugwell believed that "about 90% of these [Popular] politicos" were proindependence, he worried about the results of the coming election. Muñoz had once again argued that status was not an issue, but Tugwell correctly believed that "it has gone such a distance that it is conceivable they may throw him (Muñoz) out after winning an election in which independence is *deceptively absent* as an issue. They will claim a mandate afterward and put pressure on Muñoz."[60] (emphasis added)

In November of 1944 the Populares won one of the most decisive victories in Puerto Rican political history. They amassed sixty-six percent of all votes cast and, confirming Tugwell's biggest fear, they sent independentista representatives to assume 17 of the senate's 19 seats, and 37 of the 39 seats in the colony's lower house.[61]

Meanwhile, in Washington Senator Millard Tydings once again introduced an independence bill in the U.S. Senate. Whether he was serious was a matter for speculation, but, once the bill was set for hearings, all interested parties reserved their seats for a decisive test of the democratic fiber of the Roosevelt administration. Recall that in negotiations for the creation of the United Nations, Washington officials had consistently pressured their French and British allies to respect the self-determination of colonial nations. So, would President Roosevelt follow his own advice? That was a question on many minds, when, with the sudden death of the president, it was now up to a man from—of all places— Independence (Missouri) to shape America's response to a "great moral question" of the postwar world.

The End
of The Beginning

"The arrangement between the United States and Puerto Rico is one of the most unsatisfactory relationships between two governments that I have ever encountered, on the face of the earth."

—Senator Millard Tydings,
Congress, May 1943[1]

..".the system can fairly be called colonial."

—Luis Muñoz Marín,
Congress, June, 1943

Radiation Treatment

This chapter begins with a statement from Laura Albizu. It is an account of one aspect of her father's imprisonment in 1953.

"While jailed at La Princesa Albizu was subject to what he diagnosed, and we later realized, was radiation. He was bombarded from some part of the building by a strange light whose origin he could never determine.Sometimes it appeared to him as a very beautiful light that would dance around the room. He had a very scientific character, and was very skeptical of these visions, but he could not deny the burns that appeared all over his body, and the burning sensation he felt. He kept himself wrapped in wet towels as the only way to calm this burning and, he hoped, may protect himself somewhat from the dangerous rays.

"He would never let me stay very long, although I wanted to visit with him as long as I could. He told me it was dangerous for me to stay. One day I prevailed, for whatever reason and stayed the whole day. When I left I was accompanied by a journalist who had come from Peru. Although the government denied it, and said this was proof that Albizu was crazy, the world knew that Albizu was suffering and seriously ill from the torture he was receiving. The press was waiting as we left. As I stood there in front of the microphones with scores of journalists asking about my father's condition, I suddenly felt this tremendous hemorrhage. The journalist who was next to me saw that something was wrong and immediately put me in a cab. I was bleeding and bleeding. Nothing like this had ever happened to me before and no doctor I talked to could explain it.

"Years later when I was in Peru I went with some friends to the beach. I never spend long in the sun but we went for the entire day. I spent hours stretched out in the sand, absorbing the suns' rays. That night, I began to hemorrhage. The doctor asked if this had ever happened before. Not that I could recall. Then I did recall. But I couldn't explain. The doctor asked me what I had done that day to provoke this. "Nothing. I went to the beach, that's all." How long did you stay, she asked. "All day." Well, that explains it. "Explains what?" Your hemorrhaging. The rays. The radiation. From the sun. That was the effect of radiation. At that angle, you lying there all day, you absorbed a lot of radiation from the sun. "Radiation?" I asked, remembering the other time, and my father's torture.

Radiation she affirmed."

After his arrest in 1950, Pedro Albizu Campos remained (with one short interruption) a prisoner until his death in 1965. Like so many of his Nationalist comrades, he endured a substantial amount of pain and abuse. But he also left such a powerful legacy of struggle that the political prisoners today in prison used Albizu's efforts as a foundation for their own.

As early as 1922 those efforts were rooted in Albizu's absolute refusal to accept colonial authority; but, during and after 1945, the United States government provided a number of new reasons for any Puerto Rican's legitimate resort to revolution.

The Meaning of Self-Determination

To many people self-determination is easy to define. Alone, on their own, without unwanted help and interference from outsiders, a group of people decide what *they* wish to do with their political, economic, and cultural future. This seems clear cut, but, as the 1945 congressional hearings progressed, Senators offered a different definition of self- determination.

Start with statehood. Puerto Rican advocates came to Washington to plead their case, but two powerful Senators immediately ruled it out and Senator Ellender "went so far as to say that so long as a single word or syllable of Spanish is spoken in Puerto Rico, there can be no serious talk of statehood or annexation."

The choice, said Dr. Luis Perea, "is between independence or the status quo. Statehood has been altogether outlawed, I might say, by Senator Tydings and the rest of the Senators. There is only one Senator who believes in the possibility of statehood." And, in the House of Representatives not one congressman was willing to support statehood. So, "Mr. Chairman what is the use of talking about the supposed alternatives?"[2]

One answer was public relations. For international consumption it was essential that Puerto Ricans openly discuss their status options. The hearings would produce stories; the stories would correctly note that petitioners had expressed their desires; and, all other things being equal, the actual tone and substance of congressional dialogue would never become a part of everyday discourse.

Senator Tydings agreed with the need for public relations. But he also suggested that you could carry it to unacceptable limits. As he told Dr. Perea, "we cannot offer you the right to vote on statehood and then have you vote on it, and subsequently refuse to give it to you, without putting ourselves in the position of offering you something, and then, after you have said, 'All right we want it," saying to you, 'You cannot have it.'[3]

Okay. But why talk about self-determination? How was anyone free to decide their destiny if Congress arbitrarily foreclosed options before the Puerto Rican people had a chance to vote?

In 1945 Puerto Ricans were asking these same questions. They knew Congress needed to be strongly prodded; so before they appeared in Washington, the independence majority tried to *peacefully* foreclose Congress' options before Congress foreclosed Puerto Rico's. What happened was that, despite strong pressures from Luis Muñoz Marín, island politicians sent two cables to Senator Millard Tydings. The first contained the signatures of 11 (of 19) Senators and the second the signatures of 22 (of 39) representatives. They all wanted independence, and they were backed up by the public support of 42 of the Popular Party's 73 Puerto Rican mayors.[4]

Through their representatives, the people had spoken. They wanted to be free and that posed immediate problems for Senator Tydings and his colleagues. Even before the hearings began, Tydings had indicated that "military establishments and rights must be *permanently enjoined* by the United States in Puerto Rico. The United States Government will, of course, counsel and determine what these military establishments and rights should be."[5]

Since, in 1945, the United States military controlled over thirteen percent of Puerto Rico's most arable land (see Chapter Three), Tydings was once again foreclosing economic development options before they even existed. Puerto Rico is 35 miles by 100 miles. To permanently enjoin roughly thirteen percent of a small island's land was a congressional limitation on Puerto Rico's self-determination.

While the military proposal was controversial in its own right, Senator Ellender brought things to a head in a dialogue with Luis Muñoz Marín.

Senator Ellender: ."... my guess is at this moment that Congress would not give the Puerto Ricans full independence nor statehood. It would be in between as far as I can see." And, later, in a discussion of economic assistance, Ellender blasted

Muñoz for seeking congressional aid: ..".you cannot hope to obtain your full independence. You would have to depend on something or may I say, some preference accorded to you by us. In other words certain relationships must be maintained between you and us that would exclude complete independence, as we know it."

Muñoz Marín: "We are always glad to do things that you ask us to do anyway."[6]

Not Albizu. Not the Nationalists. And not, as it turned out, many members of Muñoz's own party. Their leader might be willing to happily follow congressional orders but his colleagues did everything possible to expose what they believed to be congressional contradictions. They planned to hold a plebiscite. Let Puerto Ricans vote and, once they did so, let congress deal with the expressed will of the people.

The very idea of a plebiscite confounded Senator Tydings. As an aide explained to President Truman (on October 3, 1945), "Senator Tydings spent 20 excited minutes telling me how terrible it would be, that Congress would never consent to statehood for example, and that it would be improper to submit statehood as a possible alternative to Puerto Rico knowing full well we would not give it to them."[7]

A president who prided himself on never passing the buck now had a chance to decide a great moral issue. Thus, President Truman told Congress the time had come to ask islanders what status they preferred, and he also said that, in the interest of good faith and comity between the people of Puerto Rico and those of us who live on the mainland,

Congress should not submit any proposals to the Puerto Ricans which the Congress is not prepared to finally enact into law."[8]

In New York, Pedro Albizu Campos tried to grasp how it was in the interests of good faith and comity to deny the self-determination Truman simultaneously affirmed. Albizu was angry and so, too, the majority of representatives who had peacefully and democratically asked for independence. In February of 1946, the Puerto Rican legislature passed a plebiscite bill which was immediately sent to Governor Rexford Tugwell. On the radio, Tugwell said that "we believe in liberty, in home rule, in self-determination. But we are holding onto Puerto Rico without the expressed consent of its two million people." Nevertheless, Tugwell vetoed the plebiscite bill, and when the Puerto Rican legislature overroad his veto, the buck once again stopped at President Truman's desk.

The 1917 legislation which governed Puerto Rico gave the president of the United States ultimate authority over Puerto Rico. So, even when the Puerto Rican legislature overruled the appointed governor, the president could overrule the two bodies that represented the only appearance of democracy in the colony.

In explaining his veto, Truman said that approval of the plebiscite "might erroneously be construed by the people of Puerto Rico as a commitment that the United States would accept any plan that might be selected at the proposed plebiscite...." As Congress had clearly indicated, statehood and independence were out of the question, so the president refused to publicly humiliate himself and his country. He would continue to talk of self-determination but never allow the Puerto Ricans to democratically express their status preferences.[9]

With this second veto the president unintentionally raised another great moral issue: When, in the course of human events, is revolution a legitimate political alternative? When do people have the right to use violence to change unacceptable political and social conditions?

These are excruciatingly difficult questions. The U.S. Declaration of Independence offers this guide: To secure life, liberty and the pursuit of happiness "Governments are instituted among Men, deriving their just powers from the consent of the governed—That whenever any form of government becomes destructive of these ends, it is the right of the people to alter or abolish it...." And, "when a long train of abuses and usurpations, pursuing invariably the same Object evinces a design to reduce them under absolute Despotism, it is their right, *it is their duty*, to throw off such government...."[10] (emphasis added)

In the case of President Truman's plebiscite veto, Washington not only refused to permit a government based on the consent of the governed, it also refused to allow the governed to even express their particular preferences. This alone was a substantial reason for men like Albizu to do their revolutionary duty, but, in the colony of Puerto Rico, there was also "a long train of abuses and usurpations."

In 1899 the Puerto Rican people asked for a democracy. They got the colonial autocracy designed by, among others, Senator Joseph Foraker and William Willoughby.

> "He has refused his Assent to Laws, the most wholesome and necessary for the public good."

In 1917 (see Chapter Five) Puerto Ricans were made U.S. citizens against their will. Despite the unanimous vote of the Puerto Rican legislature to remain only citizens of Puerto Rico, Congress gave them this choice: Accept U.S. citizenship or be aliens in your own nation. In adopting this legislation, Congress had two principal aims: to eliminate the independence movement and symbolically prove to islanders that they were "a permanent possession of the United States."[11]

> "He has combined with others to subject us to a jurisdiction foreign to our constitution, and unacknowledged by our laws;"

In 1921 E. Montgomery Rilley (with the approval of President Harding) repressed the independence movement which then held sway in the island. He also increased pressures to make English the first language in the Puerto Rican school system.

> "He has erected a multitude of New Offices and sent hither swarms of Officers to harass our people and eat out their substance."

Until 1934 Puerto Rico was controlled by the Department of War. The attitude of that organization is best expressed by Major General Frank McIntyre, the man who, for twenty years, headed the War Department's Bureau of Insular Affairs: "An island or a small group of islands acquired for naval purposes does not differ greatly from a war vessel or fleet at anchor. It would be as improper to transfer the administration of such an island or island group from the Navy to another department as to turn over war vessels to any other than the Navy Department."[12]

"He has affected to render the Military indepen-dent of and superior to the Civil Power."

Commenting (in 1926) on proposed naval bases in the Virgin Islands, McIntyre cautioned Congress because, "we had an Army and Navy board there (in Puerto Rico) and they took everything, and as a con-sequence, San Juan has been crowded ever since because the Army and Navy took so much."[13]

"For quartering large bodies of armed troops among us."

In 1941 Congressman Fred Crawford, a sup-porter of colonialism, nevertheless told his col-leagues that, "getting down to some things that we have done, I think our legislative approach from an industrial standpoint in Puerto Rico, has been noth-ing short of diabolic."[14]

In every stage of these Oppressions We have Petitioned for Redress in the most humble terms. Our repeated Petitions have been answered only be repeated injury."

Albizu could easily extend this list. The problem was the inability of U.S. officials to face their own contradictions and, linked to this, the virtual invisi-bility in the United States of Puerto Rico and its people. Explain to an "average" American what really happened and (at least in my experience) he or she immediately grasps the likelihood and/or the legitimacy of revolutionary resistance. The Declaration of Independence is a revered document to so many contemporary U.S. citizens that they instantly empathize with a nation subjected to a long train of abuses and usurpations.

However, in 1946 Puerto Rico was rarely a topic for detailed and *honest* public debate. Between normal indifference and the onset of the Cold War, Puerto Rico was a very low priority for the United States. Thus, when a man like Albizu Campos resorted to violence Americans judged his actions in a social and historical vacuum. Few took time to study the issues, and even fewer did so in a manner that took account of fifty years of colonialism, culminating in a refusal to even allow the Puerto Rican people to express their status preferences.

In 1946 the stage was set for a violent outburst of revolutionary resistance. And then President Truman did something that both flabbergasted and appalled Pedro Albizu Campos.

The Blood Tax

Puerto Ricans who live in their homeland do not pay federal taxes. This policy began in 1900, and it had nothing to do with congressional goodwill. On the one hand, to tax Puerto Rico was to admit it was part of the United States; this was unthinkable since it opened the door to possible statehood. On the other hand, taxation was unconscionable because, in 1900, taxation without representation still equalled tyranny. Since Puerto Rico's Resident Commissioner had no right to vote in

Congress, some powerful officials agreed they had no right to impose federal taxes on the Puerto Rican people.[15]

Disguised taxes were another matter. In 1940 Puerto Ricans became eligible for the first peacetime draft in United States history; most accepted what they regarded as an unjust imposition of federal authority but the Nationalist Party counseled resistance. Refuse to accept the "Blood Tax" and serve *your* country by saying no to Washington's outrageous expansion of its colonial powers.

As J. Edgar Hoover later told President Truman, "by October of 1943, 45 members of the Nationalist Party had been convicted and sentenced to various federal penitentiaries in the United States for wilfully violating the Selective Service Act." This accurate count missed a vital historical fact: In resisting the draft, the Nationalists were peacefully following a tradition with deep and violent roots in U.S. history. When President Lincoln instituted the draft during the American Civil War, he met stiff and determined resistance because many citizens believed that the federal government had no legitimate authority to impose itself over the separate states. In the first four months of conscription, 98 of the registrars who came to Northern cities were killed or wounded. Meanwhile it became hard to complete the draft because potential registrars were threatened with the firing of their homes or the loss of their lives.[16]

J. Edgar Hoover was oblivious to this argument: The injustice claimed by the Northern states paled before the colonial claims of presidents like Franklin Roosevelt. How was it legitimate to ask people to risk their lives in war yet refuse to allow them to

The End of the Beginning

vote for the president who would determine when to go to war, and against whom? How was it moral to compel people to fight for the United States yet continue to emphasize that they were definitely *not* a part of the United States?

Albizu was genuinely appalled at this extension of colonial authority. He always argued that the Selective Service law was, with respect to its application in Puerto Rico, totally unconstitutional within the legal framework of the United States Constitution. Thus, once the Truman administration reinstituted the peacetime draft in 1948, Albizu's speeches reflect a level of increased indignation: Puerto Ricans asked for independence and you said no; Puerto Ricans asked for a plebiscite and you said no; but, when you ask for our bodies, we must say yes. Or, as Albizu told an audience at the site of General Miles' 1898 invasion: "Who is the devil that can comprehend the U.S. Congress...here we have tyranny."[17]

To Albizu the greatest irony of all was the Cold War. In the battle between the free world and the one enslaved behind an Iron Curtain, Puerto Ricans were ordered to soldier for the independence of others. Germany, Italy, Korea: Puerto Ricans had to do their part or wind up in a federal penitentiary. Meanwhile, the Truman administration sponsored a law that contained, not Communism, but the independence of the Puerto Rican people.

La Mordaza. The gag law. It became a part of Puerto Rican life in June of 1948—Albizu had returned on December 15, 1947—and its explicit intention was to muzzle, not only the Nationalists, but the "deep in their bones" independence senti-

71

ments of a substantial portion of the Puerto Rican people. As an early 1948 survey of voter sentiment showed, even in the most loyal bastions of Popular Party support fully a third of the people had no idea which way they were going to turn. And, with Congress even more opposed to statehood than to independence, Luis Muñoz Marín sensed the possibility of a "back door" victory for the likes of Pedro Albizu Campos.[18]

Muñoz found a loyal ally in J. Edgar Hoover. The FBI director boasted that he had "thoroughly and continuously" investigated the Nationalist Party since 1936.[19] Albizu was a subversive, and the best way to eliminate him was to follow the lead of Congress: Make speech a crime. Imitate the precedent set by the 1940 Smith Act and argue that it was a felony "to foment, advocate, advise or preach, voluntarily or knowingly, the necessity, desirability or suitability of overthrowing, destroying, or paralyzing the Insular government...."[20]

The gag law literally copied its Smith Act model. This surprised few of Muñoz's critics since, as he assured Senator Ellender in 1945, "we are always glad to do things you ask us to do." But, in this case, Muñoz led as much as he followed. The sentiment for independence threatened his plans for what is today called Commonwealth. Thus, if only because of his ego—Muñoz once told Ernest Gruening that "the destiny of Muñoz Marín and the destiny of Puerto Rico are inseparable"[21]—Muñoz championed democracy as he made free speech a felony.

One effect of surveillance on Albizu was to bring out a much neglected facet of his personality: his keen sense of humor. He *loved carcajadas*, the Spanish word for belly laughs. Thus, as he walked around the narrow, one way streets of Old San Juan, Albizu sometimes lost the many agents following him in their automobiles. They were blocked by the one-way streets so, to avoid confusion, Albizu often told them his destination. To my knowledge there is no record of the agents' reaction to Albizu's "kindness."

In the Puerto Rico of the late forties, the roads were often rudimentary. It took time to travel from one city to another, so, when nature called, or people tired of so much time in the car, Albizu and his associates often stopped for a rest. Occasionally, Albizu would walk to the FBI or Insular Police cars stationed behind his and tell the agents to also get out and relax. I do not know if Albizu told them how long "we" would be staying at this particular stop.

Albizu loved cats. His youngest daughter Laura says that he would even allow the cats to eat from his plate. Thus, when a beloved cat was lost in 1949, he and a friend searched the area in front of his Old San Juan residence. They looked behind walls and even under cars. No cat. So, they returned to Albizu's apartment and, looking through the window, roared as "undercover" agents checked every spot searched by Albizu Campos. The one agent laying under a car apparently thought that Albizu had planted a bomb.[22]

It was funny. Yet very serious. In the files at the Truman Library the folders contain a number of now declassified reports on Albizu and the Nationalists. One is an April 1948 report from the District Intelligence Office, Headquarters, Tenth

Naval District, San Juan. Along with the local police and the FBI, sailors were also tailing Albizu, and they assured all readers of the "restricted" document that "Albizu has not been apprehended by the FBI for fear of creating a martyr situation." However, "he and his followers are being watched closely and in the event of probable violence, a special law enforcement squad is organized to arrest him immediately."[23]

A 1950 report from J. Edgar Hoover looks like an advertising pitch; it's in a shiny black plastic folder, the white lettering catches your attention and inside is a "personal and confidential, delivered by special messenger" file on Albizu. The man had a "burning hatred" of the United States and "public statements by leaders of the organization clearly reveal that the organization stands for the violent and forceful overthrow of the United States Government in Puerto Rico as the only means of gaining independence for Puerto Rico."[24]

This was never a secret. Nationalists never hid their anti-colonial intentions, so in 1948, '49, and '50 Albizu gave revolutionary speeches from one end of the island to the other. In many instances he openly took notice of the "undercover agents" recording his words; and, as in 1925 or 1936, Albizu's speeches always had the same aim: to create the *moral* intensity which moved Puerto Ricans to try and overthrow the Spanish in 1868.

Albizu must have succeeded. How, after all, could J. Edgar Hoover create a martyr unless a substantial number of people believed Albizu was being crucified? Whatever the case, the speeches reveal a concern with everything from the draft to Santa

Claus, from colonialism to Catholicism, from economic exploitation to the National Forest Service (which had just declared most of Puerto Rico a U.S. national forest).

Albizu focused on a figure like Santa Claus because his ascendancy symbolized an assault on Puerto Rican culture. The *gordo* (the fat man) should be returned to the mainland because of his weight, a lack of snow, and three very popular Kings. In a speech given on December 19, 1949, Albizu spoke of the birth of Jesus and the lovely tradition practiced by Puerto Ricans, not on December 25, but on January 6. The night before the three Kings (in the U.S. the three Wise Men) arrive children place grass in shoeboxes and leave it as food for the Kings' camels. In return, the Kings leave presents. It is the highlight of Navidad and so beloved a tradition that, in 1942, nine-year-old Filiberto Ojeda Ríos won a prize in New York for an essay that celebrated Puerto Rico's version of Three Kings Day. Forty-five years later Ojeda told this story sitting in New York City's Metropolitan Correctional Center. We were surrounded by glass, guards and guns but he displayed a joy that would have gratified Pedro Albizu Campos.

In the Santa Claus speech, Albizu used ridicule to underline the American attack on one of Puerto Rico's most revered traditions. "We are all waiting for the snowstorm from San Juan...the Nationalist Party convention was going to be celebrated in the middle of a great snowstorm. And Santa Claus was going to appear in Arecibo under a giant pine tree."[25]

With so many magnificently flowering flamboyans, who needed pine trees? Where was the snow? Why adopt a custom the Yankees borrowed from the Germans? And, in a very poor country, with indigenous and African roots, why have an obese, pink-cheeked man as a symbol of giving? To the Catholic Albizu it was obscene for Santa Claus not to lose a few pounds and, like Jesus, share the food he never needed with those who were starving. Santa Claus looked like a pumpkin; he was a bloated symbol of a colonialism that, like a balloon, could be punctured by a people eager to defend their culture and its customs.

In response to Albizu, U.S. authorities noted that he was "a psychopathic case, perhaps actually insane."[26] However, in their eagerness to write off Albizu as deranged, U.S. officials missed two essential points: It was always impossible to disentangle the political revolution from the defense of Puerto Rican culture, and to find *definitive* proof for the charges that moved the Nationalists to revolution, it was only necessary to read a very public document—the Congressional Record.

Fred Crawford was a congressman from Michigan. He had a long standing interest in Puerto Rican affairs and he was also an architect of the "Commonwealth" legislation then being considered by the House and Senate. On May 5, 1949, Crawford told his colleagues that "I do not know of any better time than today, this week, and next week, for us to learn something about our colonial possessions (i.e., Puerto Rico and the Virgin Islands) and our subjects."[27]

Our subjects. Congressman Crawford used the word even more passionately in a second comment—"Mr. Chairman, we are working with the emotions, the lives, the desires, and the souls of subjects of the Congress of the United States"—and yet, again, none of his colleagues objected. In fact, when the Commonwealth legislation finally came before Congress on June 30, 1950, Crawford openly explained its meaning: "At no time have I ever come to a conclusion where I thought Puerto Rico could ever support statehood. Certainly Puerto Rico cannot support any type of independence. She would have to be a puppet of some other country. *But Puerto Rico can be a colonial possession and have a great deal to say about her own government, under which the Puerto Ricans live.*"[28]

Albizu was never the problem. The problem was the truth. Too many Northamericans refused to face it; therefore, instead of being appalled when a congressman spoke of subjects and colonial possessions, other prominent members of Congress echoed the sentiments of Fred Crawford. The Senate committee which approved the bill to allow Puerto Ricans to write their own constitution emphasized that "the measure would not change Puerto Rico's fundamental political, social, and economic relationship to the United States." And in the House of Representatives, Jacob Javits of New York stated that "this is a very serious issue for us in the United States, especially today, because this is a possession of the United States." Thus Javits wanted to clarify a particular point: "this bill does restrict, *and let us have that very clear*, the people of Puerto Rico to a constitution which is within the limits of the (1917) Organic Act for Puerto Rico. Their fundamental status is unchanged."[29]

Like Pedro Albizu Campos, Fred Crawford called Puerto Rico a colony in 1949. If Puerto Rico was a colony in 1949, and the Commonwealth legislation made no fundamental changes in its political status, then—*let us have this very clear*—Puerto Rico was still a colony after the creation of the Commonwealth.

Congress' open and proud reaffirmation of colonialism was both obvious and undeniable. However, at home Luis Muñoz Marín not only tried to hide the truth, he forgot the pledges made in his thoroughly successful 1948 gubernatorial campaign. Then, the people were promised the plebiscite denied by Truman in 1946; now, given Congress' refusal to offer either statehood or independence, Muñoz told Congress (but not his own people) that "we would hope that Puerto Rico, having shown its capacity for self-government, would mean that the attitude of the bill generally should not be paternalistic."[30] Muñoz nevertheless settled for a bill whose opening paragraph said that Puerto Rico "belonged" to the United States; and his Resident Commissioner told Congress that "the federal provisions of the present Organic Act (of 1917) would be reaffirmed" in the new legislation. Puerto Ricans only "wished to adopt a local constitution and reaffirm their station within this union...we are asking to live under the Constitution of the United States *as heretofore*."[31] (emphasis added)

For Albizu this was nothing less than a humiliating reaffirmation of colonialism. Thus, he decided to stage a revolution. He knew that, unlike the conclusion drawn by Tom Paine in 1776—"*the time hath found us*"—1950 was an awful time for a revolution.

Agents posing as nationalists had already informed the island's government of his plans, and, instead of confronting a military power separated by thousands of miles of ocean, the United States had more than 20 active bases right on Puerto Rican soil. Albizu understood that any chance of success was, at best, negligible, but his hope was to create the sense of moral outrage which might move the Puerto Rican people, and the rest of the world, to condemn and prohibit continued U.S. colonialism.

In pursuing revolution Albizu represented a minority. Independence still had a very substantial first and second level following—no less a figure than Muñoz's Speaker of the House said that eighty percent of the dominant Popular party wanted independence[32]—but, no matter how much they applauded revolution after three drinks, people expressed fear when they were sober.

Puerto Rico suffered from a case of patriotism limited, a situation consistently faced by men like George Washington and Alexander Hamilton. Revolution, no matter how gross the injustice that propels it, is never a popular alternative. Contemporary Americans forget that, in 1776, it was a violent minority who forced their beliefs on a reluctant and/or passive majority. One modern estimate is that at least twenty percent of the American colonists were Benedict Arnolds; John Adams estimated that one-third of the people favored independence, another third supported the King, and the remainder had no political preference. They were the "grazing multitude" who turned a deaf ear to the calls for social change.[33]

Fighting for a New York Artillery Company,

Alexander Hamilton said that "our countrymen have all the folly of the ass and all the passiveness of the sheep...they are determined not to be free." Meanwhile, Washington raised recruits by offering them everything from land to cash on the barrel-head; as early as October 30, 1775, he complained "that a very great Proportion of the Officers of the Rank of Captains and under, will retire, from present appearances I may say half, but at least one third;" and, throughout the revolution, Washington used one half of the Army to keep track of the other, because "without including drafts who never joined the Army it can safely be stated that at least half of the militia enrolled during the (Revolutionary) war deserted."[34]

Minorities start revolutions, so on the day—October 30, 1950—Harry Truman signed the new Puerto Rican Federal Relations Act into law, Nationalists staged a revolutionary resistance that, among other things, declared a Republic, attacked La Fortaleza, the residence of Governor Muñoz Marín, and assaulted everything from the armory in Arecibo to the temporary home of the president of the United States in Washington, D.C.

While Albizu sanctioned the November 1 attack on Blair House, the men who carried out the assault never regarded the president's death as their primary aim. Oscar Collazo said that he and Griselio Torresola took an oath to defend *la patria*; they agreed to give up their lives for their country, so they assaulted Blair House, not to kill Harry Truman, but "to focus the attention of the world on the colonial status of Puerto Rico and its people."[35]

The world noticed. Virtually every serious periodical on earth headlined news about the Nationalist assault on the president of the United States. But, as in 1936 and 1942, Albizu and his supporters were fanatics instead of revolutionaries, assassins instead of liberators.

Especially in the United States, the attack on the president was judged from a perspective containing equal measures of arrogance, ethnocentrism and ignorance. For fifty-two years Puerto Rico had been, not only an unincorporated territory, but an insignificant part of even congressional debate. Thus, in the June 1950 debate about Puerto Rico, Congressman Engle of California matter-of-factly said, "The newly elected president of Puerto Rico is for this bill is he not?"[36] No one corrected Engle, a man whose obvious ignorance of Puerto Rico and its government was shared by most of his colleagues.

On a mental map made in the U.S.A. Puerto Rico was a pint-sized possession, located in an American Lake. Thus, when the Nationalists attacked the president they were arrogantly dismissed as fanatics, and the man who did the official labeling was none other Fred Crawford. The congressman who called Puerto Ricans "subjects" saw nothing contradictory in commissioning a study that never mentioned either colonialism, the Blood Tax, the gag law, or the pending plans of the Interior Department: As an assistant secretary told Congress in 1948, "I am working on a program to settle a number of them on the Alaska Railroad in Alaska...and find jobs away from the sugar fields. If we don't find jobs for them they will continue to be the peons they were in the 1920's...."[37]

Responsibility. Congress refused to accept any

when King Monty ruled in the 1920s, and it also refused to accept any responsibility when Fred Crawford dominated in the late '40s and early '50s. The congressman's report again explained the "acid tongued" Albizu in terms of personal pathology;[38] it made a tortured attempt to link him to the Communists; and it never tried to empathize with either Albizu or with the revolutionary Oscar Collazo.

Collazo was simply a fanatic, "whipped into a frenzy" by the insane Albizu. But, as his daughter explained to the police who questioned then fifteen-year-old Zoraida Collazo for fifteen hours, her father was a loving parent. When he first came to the United States, he wrote her every week, and when she finally arrived in New York, he made her so much the center of his life that, over forty years later, father and daughter are still inseparable. The beautiful love that binds these two adults is very real but to recognize its existence is to make the simple, complex; it is to accept the humanity of a man with a gun and to pose a monumentally difficult question: What would you do if, after fifty-two years of colonialism, your masters said you must continue being subjects?

The one person who answered this question was Senator Millard Tydings. He said that "as far as I am concerned, if I were a Puerto Rican, I would be for independence and I will tell you why...there are more precious things than being helped out of economic difficulties, and that is the right to be master of your own destiny...if I were a Puerto Rican that (help without power) would not satisfy me, just like it did not satisfy George Washington, Thomas

Jefferson and Simòn Bolívar. That is something you cannot have a substitute for...."[39]

Senator Tydings made that remark in 1943. It had little impact. In 1950 Oscar Collazo was condemned to the electric chair. When Zoraida Collazo returned to high school after the attack on Blair House, the teacher said "you do not have a seat in my classroom." Eventually, Zoraida was permitted to sit at the back of the room, but, forty-two years later, the experience remains a very painful memory for Ms. Collazo. It was, of course, personally humiliating but, on a deeper level, it was a rejection of her father and his beliefs. As she suggested, one way to look at the revolution was that neither Oscar Collazo nor Pedro Albizu Campos wanted a seat in that or any other American classroom. They only wanted to be free, but, instead, Zoraida got a seat in the back of the classroom and "colored" men like Albizu got a seat in the back of the bus.

Nothing changed after the 1950 attack, so in San Juan and New York, Nationalists made plans for another assault on world opinion. This time they would attack Congress because it was senators and representatives who imposed not only Commonwealth, but the "Blood Tax" that symbolized one of Washington's gravest contradictions: the tyranny of taxation without representation.

Pardon Everyone or Pardon No One

Albizu Campos was arrested on November 2, 1950, after a more than two-day siege of his Old San Juan residence. Comrades kept the police at bay by blocking doors with books and firing warning shots whenever police approached the house. But when the frustrated authorities filled the house with gas, Albizu reluctantly agreed to surrender. Almost overcome by gas, he waited for Alvaro Rivera Walker, who, just before they left the building, attached a white flag to a broom handle. It was the middle of the night, with no audience in sight, so Alvaro feared that the police might use this "golden opportunity" to assassinate Albizu. The white flag would hopefully offer a shield against the bullets that had so far missed Albizu.[40]

Albizu was never charged with ordering the death of either Harry Truman or Luis Muñoz Marín. He was indicted for violating *La Mordaza*—the gag law. His crime was what he thought and said; and his sentence was a minimum of nine years (and a maximum of 50) for the speeches that criticized everything from the Blood Tax to Santa Claus.

With Albizu and virtually every other Nationalist leader in prison, Governor Muñoz Marín successfully prepared the people for Commonwealth status. In a 1951 referendum that gave Puerto Ricans the choice of remaining a colony or adopting the new status, Muñoz's position won seventy-six percent of the vote but the referendum was nevertheless marred by a low voter turnout. Elections normally brought out eighty percent of Puerto Rico's registered voters, yet the figure for the 1951 referendum was fifty-eight percent. And for the 1952 referendum that approved the Constitution rewritten by the U. S. Congress, only fifty-two percent of the Puerto Rican people voted. Meanwhile, in the 1952 elections, independence advocates actually won nineteen percent of the island's vote and, even more ominously, Washington officials publicly and privately ridiculed the governor and his claims of political authority.[41]

Commenting on the Commonwealth's new constitution, the House committee that monitored Puerto Rico said, "It is important that the nature and scope of S.3336 [the bill which allowed islanders to write a constitution] *be made absolutely clear*. The bill under consideration would not change Puerto Rico's fundamental political, social and economic relationship to the United States."[42](emphasis added)

And, finally, forgetting the promises of no paternalism, Fred Crawford lectured Puerto Rico's Resident Commissioner in this fashion on May 28, 1952: "Suppose Puerto Rico misbehaved, let us say, and you decided to call them to task, to spank them a little bit...." Well, it could be done because Congress retained all the "necessary power" to change any and all facets of Puerto Rican life.[44]

Muñoz was lucky. Even after fifty years of Americanization only a small minority of Puerto Ricans read or spoke English; and, of that small minority only a handful of book worms read documents like the Congressional Record or House and Senate committee reports. The truth was rarely a part of Puerto Rico's public discourse, but in Washington, J. Edgar Hoover had no problem openly discussing the realities of Puerto Rican life.

Hoover wrote nasty reports about independence activists to one president after another. When one of Muñoz's most trusted aides publicly suggested that Puerto Rico have its own currency, postal, customs and immigration laws, Hoover warned Eisenhower in the same way he had warned Franklin Roosevelt:

Muñoz was straying from the colonial fold. He had to be kept in line because he had actually indicated "his disapproval of its [the English language] use in the offices of the Puerto Rican government...and in the last session of the Puerto Rican legislature all alternate English versions of Legislation enacted were thrown out."[45]

While Hoover made no specific suggestions, he could not resist "certain recently coined phrases which explain in a joking manner what the recent expressions of members of the Commonwealth of Puerto Rico amount to." The jokes? Muñoz "wanted to make the divorce final and increase the alimony. He wanted to bolt his cake and have it too." And, finally, "the Popular Democratic Party desires to have a banana republic with United States air conditioning."[46]

In jail, Albizu never knew that he and J. Edgar Hoover finally agreed about the political realities of Puerto Rican life. Now 61 years old, Albizu was so ill that his condition worried both Luis Muñoz Marín and American ambassador to the United Nations Henry Cabot Lodge. In New York, the United States was seeking to remove Puerto Rico from the U.N.'s list of non-self-governing territories. Among others, Hoover warned the president that Albizu's death in jail would produce violence in San Juan; thus, the man who ordered the attack on Blair House was nevertheless released from jail so that his death would not impede the U.N.'s stamp of approval for Puerto Rico's new political status.

Albizu refused to leave the jail. He demanded pardons for everyone or pardon no one. In fact, as if quoting Senator Tydings' 1943 remark, Albizu stressed that there were more important issues than economic well-being. If only his bones left jail, "so be it...because more than the life of Albizu Campos, what interested all Puerto Ricans was the political future of *la patria*"[47]

Albizu was nevertheless removed from jail. In theory, his forced freedom supposedly eliminated the threat of violence; in reality, it helped set the stage, first, for the March 1, 1954 attack on Congress, and, second, for a series of "top secret" negotiations that rank among the most controversial aspects of a century of U.S. /Puerto Rican relations.

The Attack on Congress

We met in the plaza. Virtually every Puerto Rican town has a plaza, but the park-like center of Cabo Rojo contains something special: a huge statue of Ramón Emeterio Betances. Betances was the author of "The Ten Commandments of Free Men," the principles of the 1868 Lares uprising, and, despite the recent election of a statehood governor, the huge sign that dominated the plaza in 1993 proudly broadcast this message: "Cuna [cradle] de Betances." Birthplace of the man who helped end slavery in the Antilles and home to a revolutionary who offered this observation to an American president: "To the bogus interpreters of the Monroe Doctrine we should always say this: Yes. Certainly. America for the Americans; but the Antilles for the Antillians. That is our salvation."[48]

Albizu agreed. He dedicated the memorial in 1926 and twenty-three years later he made one of his "seditious" speeches in front of the statue of a medical doctor who, right up to the American invasion in 1898, raised money in Europe to free the Puerto Rican political prisoners then held in Spain.

My appointment was with Rafael Cancel Miranda. For attacking Congress in 1954, he spent more than 25 years in U.S. prisons; like Albizu, he had refused a number of conditional releases and only left prison (among other facilities, Cancel Miranda spent years in Alcatraz and Marion) when he received an unconditional pardon from President Carter in 1979. Since his release was partially the work of the contemporary political prisoners, one of Rafael's first stops after leaving prison was Chicago, to thank people like Carmen Valentín and Alberto Rodríguez, and to see the neighborhood school which had been named in his honor in 1974.

I wanted Rafael to walk me through the day of the attack. Politely but firmly, Rafael refused to start in 1954. The attack in 1954 was rooted in the Ponce Massacre of 1937. Nationalists seeking to march peacefully through the city in commemoration of the abolition of slavery had their permit revoked at the last minute. The result was the Ponce Massacre—nineteen people died. The American Civil Liberties Union issued this contemporary assessment of the murders: "The Ponce Massacre was due to the denial by the police of the civil rights of citizens to parade and assemble. This denial was ordered by the Governor of Puerto Rico, Blanton Winship."[49]

Rafael's parents', members of the Nationalist Party, participated in the march in Ponce. His parents survived the bloodbath, but, for the seven-year old-boy, the massacre was a turning point in a life that had hardly begun. "You must understand," he said, "that they shot at my mother and father." Forever after, the American flag was a symbol of oppression; in school Rafael adamantly refused to pledge allegiance to that flag; and, later, he also expressed contempt for the advocates of Franklin Roosevelt. Rafael felt that "the American teachers wanted us to blow our noses in English." He refused, and, in 1949, he also said no to the Blood Tax. He was convicted of draft resistance and sentenced to two years in the federal penitentiary at Tallahassee. He was horrified by the racism of the corrections officers. The teenager had not seen this kind of hatred—or the racial segregation of the prisons—in Puerto Rico, and it further alienated him from the Yankees and their culture.

When Rafael returned to Puerto Rico in 1951, he was once again arrested; he again refused military service: and, finally in 1952, he was declared an "undesirable" by the United States government. He was released from prison, and, following the lead of thousands of victims of political repression, he went to New York. There he worked with the Nationalist Party members then seeking to counter President Eisenhower's efforts to remove Puerto Rico from the United Nations list of non-self-governing countries.

In Washington, officials wrote one thing and said another. In a spate of then-confidential correspondence, Governor Muñoz Marín was quickly put in his place. He might think that Puerto Rico had ceased to be a territory of the United States, but, as James Davis (director of the Interior Department's Office of Territories) told him, "If Puerto Rico has not become an independent nation or a State of the

Union, and we are all agreed that it is not, then as a matter of domestic constitutional law, it must still be a territory of the United States."[50]

There was only one problem with Muñoz' interpretation of the meaning of commonwealth: the U.S. Constitution. Muñoz wanted to tell the United Nations that laws enacted in Puerto Rico "could not be repealed or modified by external authority." However, Article 4, Section 3 of the U.S. Constitution unequivocally stipulated that "the Congress shall have power to dispose of and make all needful rules and regulations respecting the territory or other property belonging to the United States." This translated into absolute power over *all* U.S. possessions, but, since Puerto Rico was still a second class (i.e., an unincorporated) territory, its "small t" status equalled "capital C" colonialism.

The truth became an obstacle to political success for the Eisenhower administration. Washington officials anxiously asked themselves why the United Nations would remove Puerto Rico from its list of non-self-governing territories if, as the Interior Department stressed, congressmen like Fred Crawford and Jacob Javits still had absolute power over all things Puerto Rican?

Ambassador Lodge and his colleagues decided to lie. At the United Nations, they boldly claimed that Puerto Rico had a powerful measure of real sovereignty and, along with a considerable degree of arm twisting, that claim produced the resolution which, in November of 1953, removed Puerto Rico from U.N supervision.[51]

Albizu resolved to produce another commotion. He ordered Lolita Lebrón to stage an assault that would catch the world's attention and, in early 1954, she ordered Rafael Cancel Miranda to "explore" Washington. Since none of the Puerto Ricans knew the city, Rafael's job was to act as a tourist and discover the best plan of attack. He carefully surveyed the capitol and subsequently chose the House of Representatives as a target because it was the easiest chamber to enter unobtrusively.

Rafael and his comrades were not anxious to sacrifice their lives for *la patria*. Forty years later, Rafael jokingly remembered that he and his wife used to Mambo. They loved to dance, and he loved life and his wife and children. No Nationalist wanted to die. However, they had all made a solemn commitment to place love of country above all other loves and obligations. Before anyone questioned their sanity or morality, the four Nationalists asked critics to answer this question: After 56 years of pleading for an end to colonialism, was a resort to revolutionary violence either surprising or illegitimate? How else did Puerto Ricans get Northamericans to finally resolve this contradiction: owning one person was despicable but owning an island that housed two million was acceptable. As the new law stressed, Puerto Rico and its inhabitants "belonged" to the United States.

The conspirators met at Penn Station. Since they expected to die, they bought one-way tickets, and when they later entered the House gallery, they sat near but not with one another. For a short while, they even listened to the debate. Representatives were discussing "Mexican wetbacks," and shortly before the Puerto Ricans opened fire, Congressman Lane shouted that "those who encourage this modern slavery in the Southwest wrap themselves in the American flag...[T]he bootleg traffic in wetbacks is a practice that will not be tolerated by American public opinion. It is an affront to human dignity and a menace to our labor standards."[52]

Representative Halleck took the floor. He was the representative who told his colleagues that the new Puerto Rican legislation meant that the island "would be governed as before." When it came to "wetbacks," he also wanted to leave well enough alone. "There are about 40,000 of these Mexican workers now in the Western part of the country and if they leave, it will create a vacuum which will persuade more wetbacks to come in here to meet the situation.... so why not proceed toward action and get on with other business before us."[53]

Lolita Lebrón agreed. Right after Halleck finished she unfurled a Puerto Rican flag, shouted "Free Puerto Rico," and fired eight shots at the roof of the House of Representatives. As she later told reporters, "I know that the shots that I fired neither killed nor wounded anyone."[54]

That was not the case with the shots fired by two of the three men. Although Andrés Figueroa had a gun that failed to function, the other weapons worked. Both Rafael Cancel Miranda and Irving Flores emptied their pistols by firing at the crowded floor of the House; some members thought it was youngsters with firecrackers, but five congressmen were wounded by the assault. Congressman Bentley was shot through the lung, and the newspapers correctly headlined that his condition was critical.

The End of the Beginning

The first headlines said that three Nationalists had "sprayed bullets from gallery." The error in the number occurred because, after the attack, Irving Flores walked out of the House of Representatives. He calmly left the gallery, saw a squad of police on the run, and walked into a room housing statues of America's revolutionary heroes. With his overcoat over his arm, Irving admired Washington and Jefferson while the police ran into the House gallery to apprehend Rafael, Lolita, and Andrés.

Irving was apprehended at the bus station. The four Nationalists were questioned endlessly about their aims and associates. The FBI offered every enticement possible for their cooperation but finally gave up after an eye-opening meeting with the four revolutionaries. The agents were exasperated and angrily threatened to send them all to the electric chair. Nobody said a word until Andrés Figueroa raised his hand. Frustrated by the failure of his weapon, Andrés felt that he had let down his comrades and his country. So, in what Rafael laughingly described as very halting English, Andrés politely offered: "Me first, electric chair."

The agents never returned. The four revolutionaries went to prison, and neither they nor the American people were ever aware of "top secret" negotiations then taking place in the Eisenhower White House. At the same time that Secretary of State Dulles was telling reporters that the four Puerto Ricans who attacked Congress represented a "fanatical rejection of the democratic process," the Eisenhower administration was actively trying to convince Muñoz Marín to accept independence, even though he didn't want it and the Puerto Rican

93

people had just overwhelmingly endorsed the Commonwealth status so proudly celebrated by Ambassador Lodge at the United Nations.

It's an interesting story, which begins at a November 20, 1953 breakfast meeting at the White House.

President Muñoz Marín

Krishna Menon was a pain. The Indian ambassador to the United Nations kept making statements which were, as Ambassador Lodge told the president, "right straight down the Communist line." He wanted independence for the colonial people's of the world; he never stopped criticizing the United States; and he was even offering impediments to U.S. plans for Puerto Rico.

Nobody had a suggestion until, at the November 20th breakfast, the president said to offer the Puerto Ricans independence. Make a dramatic announcement which would keep people like Krishna Menon off guard and then use the offer of independence to break up the roadblocks to Commonwealth.

Secretary Dulles missed breakfast, but by dinnertime he had heard about the proposed offer, checked with congressional representatives, and placed a worried call to Ambassador Lodge. "A dramatic announcement re: Puerto Rican independence would not sit well in Congress." Lodge responded that "he had not thought of doing this until the president brought it up." However, it was a very good idea, and, in any event, the secretary should remember that the president "would not be offering them independence, anyway, only Congress can do that, he will just be saying how the president feels."[56]

Dulles was still worried. On November 24, he sent an "eyes only" telegram to Lodge and agreed that "you know better than I whether the president's authorization with reference to Puerto Rico was made after adequate consideration and weighing of relevant facts." However, Dulles urged consultation with Congress or the announcement "would be apt to have a bad reaction." Also, someone should tell the Puerto Ricans: "I assume. that consideration should be given to the effect of the statement upon the loyal elements in Puerto Rico and whether this will undermine their position and seem to build up the disloyal minority." And, finally, "would this announcement on our part be seriously embarrassing to the French and be used by the extreme nationalists and perhaps communist inspired elements in North Africa?"[57]

The problems multiplied, but Lodge still made the announcement. He told the Puerto Ricans the day before he took the floor of the United Nations, and, the day after his speech he wrote this to President Eisenhower: "Your idea about Puerto Rico turned out to be a ten-strike. As you will have seen in the papers I made the announcement in the General Assembly yesterday—one week to the day after you mentioned it at breakfast—and received unprecedented burst of applause from the delegates...the effect will be tremendous in Latin America and in all colonial areas and it will regain some of the ground which unavoidably we lost earlier because of Tunisia and Morocco."

At the end of the letter Lodge included a hand

written P.S.: "Krishna Menon has just praised the Puerto Rico statement! His first pro-U.S. statement since I have been here."[58]

Within a month, Lodge asked associates in the State Department to see what they could do "to stimulate the Puerto Rican legislature to adopt a resolve requesting the United States to give full independence to Puerto Rico."[59] This would have a tremendous effect on Krishna Menon; it would score points for the U.S. all over the globe, and give Lodge moral power in the General Assembly.

But, what about the Puerto Ricans? How could the United States get them to accept a new status when they and we had just spent eight years devising what was now called Commonwealth status? So, as Rafael Cancel Miranda and his colleagues planned their attack on the U.S. legislature, Lodge planned his assault on the Puerto Rican Senate and House.

First, as the State Department's Mason Sears told Lodge on January 8, 1954, "There are certain fixed factors in the situation." Nothing could change "without Puerto Rican approval." And that would be very difficult to get "considering that the principal reason for the existence of the Popular Party has been the belief that as an independent nation the Puerto Ricans could not enjoy the close integration with the United States economy, which is necessary if they are to stand on their own feet economically."[60]

With his eyes on Krishna Menon, Lodge had neglected to focus on the short or long term effects of independence on Puerto Rico's economy. For five years Muñoz and Washington had touted

"Operation Bootstrap." It was supposedly the economic linchpin of the island's future, and it would certainly disappear without the federal tax benefits that quickly became the primary inducement for U.S. manufacturers.

The economy posed a problem. And, while Sears also worried about "the number of people who may wish to migrate to the United States while it can be done without any restrictions," Sears nevertheless offered a plan of attack. "It should be explained to the governor" that his economic benefits would continue. Then, "some formula must be devised to permit him to make an about-face without risking a political loss of face." Sears suggested that Muñoz simply announce that "the operations of the government under the 1952 compact had proved so much more successful than anticipated that...the time had definitely come when there would be great advantage to the Puerto Rican people if they were to become fully independent and on an equal footing with all other Latin American countries."[61]

While that had been Pedro Albizu Campos' plea for thirty years, Sears never considered anything except his bosses' request for a workable scheme. Thus, he stressed that "it would do no harm to hint at the almost certain honor that attaches itself to Governor Muñoz should he become the first president of Puerto Rico." And, saving the highest priority for last, Sears suggested that "it should be explained to the governor that the establishment of independence in Puerto Rico in the near future would have an international impact in view of the colonial issue which is so red-hot in most parts of the world. It would be received with great satisfaction by the Asiatic-African nations and would enhance the influence of the two American continents in world affairs."[62]

The files at the Eisenhower Library contain no evidence of a response from Governor Muñoz. Presumably it was an about-face he could never manage, but once President Eisenhower read this "top secret" correspondence, he immediately grasped its potentially explosive nature. What would Krishna Menon say if, as the United States accused the Nationalists of disregarding the will of the people, a Puerto Rican produced the State Department correspondence of Ambassador Lodge and Assistant Secretary Sears?

On the top of the letter is this comment in the president's handwriting: "File Secret Files. DE." The DE is scrawled but, as the library archivists note, it is unmistakably Ike's.

Lodge still refused to give up. On March 27, 1956 he wrote a letter to the president's executive assistant concerning "an idea which I think has a great deal of merit. It is that Congress adopt a resolution offering independence to Puerto Rico ...."[63]

While Lodge apparently never had spoken to a Puerto Rican, he included a suggested resolution with the letter, and he also explained his aims: "If the offer were accepted many problems would be solved. If the offer were rejected, our Congress would at the very least have taken a step which would be interpreted as "anti-colonial" and do us great good throughout the world—notably in Afro-Asian countries."[64]

After 58 years as a colony, Puerto Rico had now

become a chip in the poker game popularly known as the Cold War. Independence was good public relations and a big hit with Congress. When Lodge and his associates checked with Speaker of the House Joseph Martin, the Speaker said that "the Congress would gladly *shed* Puerto Rico at any time and to give him a proposed resolution which he will talk over with some of the boys."[65] (emphasis added)

The boys agreed, but Muñoz presumably did not. In any event, the records contain no indication of the governor's response to the United States' request for Puerto Rican independence.

As Rafael Cancel Miranda and the contemporary Puerto Rican prisoners see it, these White House plans for independence offer nothing less than incontrovertible proof that, in relation to Puerto Rico and its people, the Eisenhower administration was morally bankrupt. For the prisoners, the Lodge correspondence displays a level of contempt and cynicism that would have surprised even Pedro Albizu Campos. Nevertheless, federal officials like Henry Cabot Lodge are at the center of the contemporary struggle—and at the center of the chapters which follow.

The University
of the Sea

"Only in the Roosevelt Roads complex can we
train, simultaneously in all varieties of missile
firings, air to ground ordnance, surface gunfire
support, underwater, surface, and air launched
torpedo firing, submarine calibrations, amphibious operations, and electronic warfare. All
this...makes the complex our university of the
sea for training our Atlantic Fleet and allied
navies."

—Rear Admiral Arthur
Knoizen, Congress, 1980[1]

Luis Colón Osorio was arrested on March 17,
1992. The charge was bail-jumping, and one part of
the punishment was a trip to Roosevelt Roads, the
<u>largest naval facility in the world</u>[2]. It is located in
Ceiba, Puerto Rico, and, among other functions, it
houses American soldiers who guard Puerto Ricans
such as Luis Colón Osorio.

Luis never denied the bail-jumping charge. On
the contrary, as soon as he left in 1991, Luis (along
with his immediate superior, Filiberto Ojeda Ríos)
made a roughly two-hour television "documentary."
It was widely publicized on Puerto Rican news programs, and it clearly established that Luis was a
comandante in the *Ejército Popular Boricua-
Macheteros.* Moreover, while the word *Machetero* (literally, cane cutter) had a 150-year history in Puerto
Rico's struggle to end colonialism, Luis traced his

101

efforts to a 1960 resolution of the United Nations: The *Macheteros* was "a political-military organization dedicated to the eradication of colonialism and the fulfillment of the United Nations Declaration 1514 on the Granting of Self-determination to Colonized Nations and Peoples. "

Luis was a political prisoner who asked that his captors recognize the provisions of the Geneva conventions relative to the treatment of anticolonial combatants. However, since the United States claims it has no political prisoners, Luis received treatment which pointedly confirmed, yet legally denied, the validity of his political position.

He was handcuffed and shackled at the legs. Luis protested when he was transported (after five days in the federal building in San Juan) by military helicopter "out of my own country" to the military base at Roosevelt Roads. There, Luis became a piece of war memorabilia. The chief of the base as well as a variety of other officials, used Marshall Colón's camera to ceremoniously position themselves near the still-shackled *Machetero*. As the camera clicked, they smiled with satisfaction as one photograph after another confirmed both their courage and Luis' status as a prisoner of war.

In a military cargo plane, Luis finally was flown to the Air Force base in Charleston, South Carolina, registered at a local jail under the name of "Cooper Scott," and on Sunday, March 22, 1992 deposited at the federal correctional institution at Otisville, New York. Luis had now been in custody for nearly a week, but had not yet been permitted to bathe, to receive a pencil and paper, or even to call his attorney.

The University of the Sea

Otisville is one of many prisons that has cropped up among the abandoned cow pastures and silos of up-state New York. It is about two and one-half hours from New York City, in a hamlet with little other "industry." The driveway snakes in S-curves up densely wooded steep hills. The S-curves are not designed to facilitate driving through the hills but, to hinder those fleeing from prison. The prison is ultra-modern, sprawling behind several levels of razor wire and chain link fences.

Opened in 1980, Otisville "houses an overflow of pretrial and holdover inmates" from New York's Metropolitan Correctional Center, and by 1992 the overflow was so great that an institution built to hold 667 prisoners somehow squeezed in over 1,000.[3] Nevertheless, Otisville officials not only gave Luis his own cell, they made certain that he was in the middle of an empty section of the segregation unit, with no one on either side, no one across the corridor.

Luis was in "the hole." He calls it "white torture" because it leaves no physical scars. To prison officials "administrative detention" is the "separation of inmates who pose a serious threat to life, property, self, staff, other inmates, or institution property. It is the result of a classification committee action and is not imposed as a punishment for specific acts."[4]

Luis was not being punished for a specific act but for his political affiliations with a revolutionary group. This form of punishment was so severe that federal guidelines mandate that "A psychologist should make a thirty-day evaluation to insure that the inmate is not deteriorating."[5] In essence, as long as the inmate has not yet "deteriorated", he or she may be returned to the detention cell.[6]

When Luis finally got a pencil and paper, he wrote a diary, which contains this summary of "segregation": "It means locked down in modern dungeons. In a little room, completely shut off from the rest of the world. It is 12 feet long by 6 feet wide, completely sealed, with a steel door that has a little slot with a padlock. You spend 24 hours a day, alone in there. Three times a day they unlock the little door and slide it open to shove a tray of food in...There is also a window facing the corridor so they can watch you, shining a light in your face 23 or 24 hours a day."

> Tuesday, March 24: I was not allowed to bathe; I had no toiletpaper, soap or towel; I was offered but not given recreation; I had no writing paper or stamps; I was not allowed to make a phone call. I am still in isolation.

> Tuesday, April 7: No bath, no recreation, no newspapers, they made me change cells, the FBI came to bring me a paper, no medical services.

> Tuesday, April 14: Still in isolation, they gave me one hour outside,without any jacket or warm clothing; I am not given medical services, no newspapers, no library, no bath, no telephone.

> Tuesday, April 21: Still in the hole; Recreation: 1 hour outside in a Doberman cage with nothing.

> Tuesday, May 5: Still in the hole; no papers, no library, no appropriate recreation, no phone, no

medical services, no bath.

Friday, May 14: Still in the hole; no appropriate recreation, no medical treatment, no library; I got an infestation of body lice from the jail clothing. The clothing is not mine; it is used by everybody. It is not hygienic even after washing. They gave me a shampoo. The label reads "Lindane Shampoo. Shampoo hair." No telephone. I asked and they didn't give it to me.

Thursday, May 21: I begin a fast for liberation with God. Still in the hole. No bath, no appropriate recreation, no library, no medical treatment, no papers, no telephone.

However revealing, Luis diary neglects essential aspects of life in administrative detention. The doberman cage, for example, was an actual dog run, with a wraparound grille, one prisoner to a cage. And Luis' cell, in which he spent 23 hours a day, had a metal shelf for a bed and a toilet with no lid or seat. To Luis it was "white torture" because the aim is to attack the mind and spirit instead of the body. As in the case of Albizu Campos, a prisoner's claim of torture was cited as evidence that the revolutionary movement was led by fanatics, lunatics, and distorted personalities.

To leave his cell for any reason at all—e.g., to cross the corridor to take a shower or make a phone call—Luis was required to back up to the door of his cell, stick his hands through the slot to be handcuffed, pull his cuffed hands back into the cell, turn around and wait for the guards to open the door. If he was taken out of the unit for a legal or social visit, or to see a doctor, the handcuffing procedure could not be done by the guards then on duty.

There were special orders that Luis could not be taken from the segregation unit unless a lieutenant and at least four other guards were present.

Prisoners sometimes avoid visits because of the required strip and (sometimes) cavity searches. In a cavity search a guard takes his or her fingers and sticks them up the rectum. If the prisoner is a woman (like FALN prisoners Alicia Rodríguez or Alejandrina Torres), the guard might search the vagina. In Luis' case, he was asked to lift his penis and testicles. He also had to run his fingers through his hair, bend both ears forward with his hands, and, depending on the corrections officer, either open his mouth and move his tongue, or, as if a horse, pull down his lip so that the officer could inspect this final body cavity.

Inmates in the hole have no access to the library, no newspapers, and no TV. Luis did have a radio, but books sent by friends were often confiscated as "unauthorized packages." He once received five weeks of mail on the same day. No explanation required. None offered.

Luis was allowed to make short phone calls to relatives once a week. Calls to friends or journalists were forbidden, and, as a practical matter, he was also unable to initiate phone calls to his attorney. When Attorney Linda Backiel came to discuss some documents the prosecution had just turned over as part of the evidence it seized at the time of Luis' arrest she discovered the jail had built two special booths for her and her client. She and Luis were forced to sit in different rooms, separated by a plexiglass window through which they could speak only by telephone. When Backiel pointed out the impossibility of consulting about voluminous, handwritten documents without her client being able to see them, the prison assigned two more guards: one to watch the two rooms at all times, the other to take the documents, inspect them page by page, and slide them under the door to the other room.

On October 6, 1992, a man said to be serving a life sentence—he was in the hole for fighting—was put in Luis' cell. Six other empty cells were available, but prison officials, nevertheless, confined a man who speaks only English with a man who speaks only Spanish.

Luis believes his visitor was part of an attempt to provoke him. Or perhaps set up a situation in which he was accused of some offense. Prison officials have never offered any explanation for their actions.

Despite being a devout Catholic, Luis' religious beliefs were not respected. He was forbidden to attend mass, and his attorney had to obtain a court order for him to receive Holy Communion during Holy Week. When he was belatedly offered medical services on Good Friday, the two cultures clashed. Luis explained that on Good Friday he did nothing but meditate, fast, and pray. A judge interpreted his behavior as evidence of obstinacy and lack of seriousness, failing to understand that in Puerto Rico, the streets of San Juan are abandoned because no one does anything on Good Friday. Even the radio stations deliver nothing but religious or solemn classical music.

Luis finally went to trial in December of 1992. A jury which included no Puerto Ricans quickly found him guilty of bail-jumping, and on Friday, January

29, 1993, Luis appeared for sentencing in Bridgeport's federal court. The judge was T. Gilroy Daly, a man who began the proceedings by noting that Luis' case was unique even among unusual cases. The original charge was conspiracy. Luis had served 18 months of preventive detention on that charge; he fled when released on bail, and now, just before his sentencing in Bridgeport, the prosecutors suddenly dropped the conspiracy indictments. That left bail-jumping as a charge, but it left the judge with a moral, if not necessarily a legal, quandary. Prosecutors wanted a sentence of 24 months. Since Luis had served only ten months he would have returned to the hole if the judge agreed with the prosecutors.

Ms. Backiel asked about the 17 months of preventive detention on the conspiracy charges. She knew that the federal sentencing guidelines prohibited Judge Daly from counting the time spent on the underlying charges, but she nevertheless asked that they be considered. "Enough is enough" was her blunt, almost angry, summary of the defense's position.

The judge agreed with Ms. Backiel. Indeed, he was apparently so moved by what he called ten months of "hard time" that he tallied Luis' period of incarceration so precisely that the Puerto Rican revolutionary would leave the court a free man that very morning.

The United States had other plans for Luis. A new warrant had been secretly sent up from San Juan the night before the hearing. It called for Luis Colón Osorio's arrest for alleged possession of weapons at the time of his arrest on March 17,

1992. Mere possession by an ordinary person is not a crime, but federal law makes it a crime for "fugitives" to possess them. Prosecutors asked Judge Daly to order Luis detained until they could get him sent back to San Juan for the lodging of formal charges and a full detention hearing there.

Through his lawyer, Luis offered to go back and appear at the hearing the following Monday. The prosecutors would not agree. Meanwhile, the judge was obviously disturbed. Colón Osorio had been in custody for almost a year. Why hadn't they charged him during that time? He ordered the prosecutors to tell him, within half an hour, whether they could guarantee Colón Osorio would be in San Juan that very night and have a detention hearing no later than 10 AM the following day—a Saturday.

After half an hour of frantic phone calls, the prosecutors reported that everything was set. Accompanied by FBI agents, Colón Osorio would be sent on a commercial flight leaving in less than three hours. His attorney specified that her client was not, under any circumstances, to be questioned by the agents. Judge Daly then issued an order confining Colón Osorio until 10 AM the next morning. After that, he emphasized, the government was "at its peril." He, at least, was giving prosecutors no more authority to confine the defendant.

In a whispered conversation, Chief Prosecutor Albert Dabrowsky told Ms. Backiel that Colón would be on a 3:40 Delta flight leaving from Hartford. If she hurried, Ms. Backiel might make the flight and so be in San Juan to represent her client at the Saturday hearing.To Ms. Backiel, this information-was "a courtesy." Perhaps Dabrowsky was embar-

rassed by the timing of the new charges,and, therefore, was helping her to assist her client.

Ms. Backiel rushed to Hartford. She had not
been paid for her ten months of work for an indigent
client, money was now in short supply. However,
two friends provided the funds, and, with ten minutes to spare, she made the plane. Ms. Backiel was
surprised that her client was not aboard the plane.
When she arrived in Puerto Rico (at 11 P.M.) he was
still nowhere to be found, and, despite the public
promises made to Judge Daly, Luis had not yet
arrived in Puerto Rico.

While it is rare for prosecutors and the FBI to
disregard the orders of a federal judge, there was
precedent in Puerto Rico. When President Carter
discovered that the FBI had interfered in a variety of
illegal ways in the 1967 Puerto Rican status
plebiscite and in the 1968 gubernatorial elections,
even Jimmy Carter could not obtain all the documents he desired. His aides indicated that "in all
probability documents had been withheld" by the
FBI from the president of the United States.[7]

Ms. Backiel finally found her client. He had
arrived at 2 AM, but, instead of the commercial
flight promised to the judge, Luis had flown in a
"four seat plane of the FBI." In court, Ms. Backiel
had stipulated that all contact between the FBI and
her client had to be made formally and through her;
one of the agents nevertheless "launched many
accusations and provocations during the trip. He
also offered to 'help' me if I 'helped' them. I emphasized that I do not get involved in discussions of
that sort, and did not react to his provocations."[8]

In Puerto Rico, no Saturday morning hearing

was scheduled. And no judge would even see Ms. Backiel. She wanted to file a habeas corpus petition for Colon's release now that Judge Daly's order had expired.

Meanwhile Luis was kept in San Juan's federal building. Since this facility has no cells, Luis was kept in the "bullpen," —a waiting room which contained nothing more than a toilet and plastic benches attached to two walls. A cot was Luis' bed, total nakedness his new brand of punishment. Lights stayed on 24 hours a day to facilitate "the constant passage of marshals and prisoners...there was no privacy whatsoever. Guards and prisoners, both women and men, twenty-four hours a day. There was constant noise of chains during the day. They didn't let me out for recreation...."[9]

Luis lived like this for nearly a week. He saw his mother, his two daughters and his grandson (for the first time) through a "thick metal mesh that made it hard to see." Then, on Friday, February 5, 1993, Luis was taken in chains to a helicopter which flew him to the military base at Aquadilla. From there, with sirens roaring, Luis went to a penal institution, was questioned, and then taken in chains to another helicopter. This one took him to a federal detention center on the west side of the island, almost three hours from his lawyer and his family. Here he was locked in a cell for 24 hours a day and the one visit permitted his mother and daughters immediately resurrected the pain experienced at Otisville: "Although they had made a trip of three hours to get there from San Juan, the only visit allowed was for half an hour. The visit was through a window, by telephone. They had me handcuffed on the other side of the window."[10]

On March 5, 1993, Luis was finally released on bail. The conditions stipulated that he had to stay at his mother's house 24 hours a day and that he wear an electronic monitor which allowed authorities to record his every movement. The bracelet is a 4" band of mesh attached to a 5" square of black plastic. Luis wears his on his leg, and he shows it with a sense of pride.

I saw Luis at his mother's home. She is a warm, affectionate woman who is an avid proponent of statehood. Like so many other Puerto Rican families, hers is split over the issue of status, but Luis will always be her beloved son, even if he is "too much of an idealist." Lucia obviously respects her son's commitment, but she wishes he would stop making so many sacrifices for his people.

Luis smiles. He wants to spend time with his children, and he knows that his notoriety makes a clandestine life forever impossible. But his commitment is as deep as ever. So, too, his sense of integration with the community. In the neighborhood he is the universal handyman and a religious community put up its property as collateral for Luis' bail.

To Luis, the church's commitment is one obvious proof that he is not a terrorist but a part of the Puerto Rican family. After all, why would a priest, six nuns, and an entire congregation stake their property on a *Machetero* with a recent bail-jumping conviction unless they felt a deep sense of identification with a persecuted patriot. The congregation's support is not cultural, political, religious or personal. It's all those things at once in a culture that also produces the Ponceño pride of Manuel

112

Caballer, the Three Kings delight of Filiberto Ojeda Ríos, and the new name of Chicago's Division Street: Pedro Albizu Campos Boulevard.

* * *

Imagine an altar set in the woods; worshippers walk down a tree-enclosed path and then enter a concrete shell which is open on all sides. Surrounding the shell is an amazing proliferation of flora and fauna; the trees are gigantic; the leaves are often a foot wide;and the weather changes from sun to storm so quickly that the sense of being in a rain forest is real rather than imagined. Inside the shell, five long rows of twenty-foot pews encircle an altar which contains no lavish display of gold— it is a monument to the culture as well as to God.

The music is Latin, *jíbaro* to its *campo* (country) core. There are two bongo players, one fellow with a tambourine and a fourth who knows what to do with the strings of a cuatro. Before the service begins, a nun leads the congregation in singing while the padre sometimes sings along, sometimes talks to members seated behind the altar, or casually finds humor in almost any gesture or statement.

The atmosphere is informal. Newcomers are exhorted to stand and tell where they come from; one or two are asked to give their reactions to the atypical mass at its conclusion. During the service, everyone who wants to offer the mass for a sick or dying relative, a son who has gone astray or a family that is coming apart, is urged to do so—aloud. The Sermon on the Mount is taken quite literally, reiterating the duty of the faithful to visit the sick, shelter the homeless, work with AIDS victims and dig deeper for a collection dedicated to a local family whose home has just burned. On one occasion a former political prisoner was invited to speak from the podium about his "prophetic" experience. To Padre Alvaro, this case was a classic example of persecution for ideals, with a suffering capable of transforming an entire people.

The congregation is mixed in color, social class, education, and barrio of origin. Puerto Ricans come from everywhere to hear the padre, and they contribute generously when a petitioner explains his or her predicament. The week I attended, we all gave money to help a woman with a family member in medical need. She spoke; we all gave what we could; and, when the donations were counted, the padre announced the sum ($678). Everyone clapped, and he immediately gave all the money to the woman in need.

Afterwards, the congregation sang songs like this:

The jíbaro was both good and seditious (bullanguero).

The stranger found sweet soil in his house.

Today there exists no joy,

seeing how my people live,

nervous, covetous, and demented.

The stranger had overturned the society.

Wake up! My people to this message.

It signals all that is bad. Wake up now!

The University of the Sea

If anyone doubted who the stranger was, the padre cleared up the confusion in his "sermon." In the June mass I attended, he complained about the assault on Puerto Rican culture in general and the corruption in San Juan in particular. In a tone that dripped with sarcasm the padre explained that instead of adequately funding the groups which resisted Northamerican culture, the dummies in San Juan had actually reduced support for the organizations that preserved and nourished Puerto Rico's uniqueness. And, as if that wasn't bad enough, the officials were dishonest. Reading from a newspaper article, the Padre paused for a laugh; he seemed to ask, "Can you believe these people?," and he was answered by a member of the congregation who was also a government employee. This gentleman explained what was happening and how the people could resist more destruction of their *jíbaro* past.

This church lives. It sings of a Jesus who is the *gran Libertador,* and, as I watched the children in the congregation, it was easy to imagine a number of potential revolutionaries. As if in clandestinity, they sat in their pews absorbing the spirit of resistance that was best displayed at midnight on Holy Saturday. The church is darkened. There is no light, only the moon, the stars and the sounds of the forest. The congregation enters carrying candles. At this year's Easter mass, as the candles burned in the forest, a proud patriot solemnly marched to the altar to affix the flag of Puerto Rico during the reading of the story of the Exodus of the Jews and the eventual victory in their struggle to create a homeland nation capable of assuring the survival of their identity as a people. Thus are sown the seeds of change that can spring up *anywhere* in Puerto Rico.

"Anywhere" is a big word, but, as the community's interpretation of Jesus suggests, U.S. colonialism produces so many sources of possible and probable conflict that the spirit nourished in the rain forest can also blossom near a U.S. pharmaceutical factory, a branch of Citibank, a food stamp office, or on and about Roosevelt Roads. Luis Colón Osorio, for example, grew up on a tiny island called Culebra, and, to fully comprehend his desire for revolutionary change, it is necessary to understand that the deepest roots of his religious commitment are secular as much as sacred— military as much as ecclesiastical. Luis grew up with bombs as his childhood companions and those bombs created his first role model: John Wayne.

Culebra and Vieques

Puerto Rico includes four significant islands. That is a well-known fact in the Caribbean, but on the Northamerican mainland few people know about Mona, Vieques, and Culebra. The first is virtually uninhabited but the second and third have been a source of revolutionary resistance for the last fifty years. Many of the *Macheteros'* (and the FALN's) most violent actions were directed against U.S. military activities in Puerto Rico. In the 1943 words of President Franklin Roosevelt, Puerto Rico was "the center" of a "vast natural shield for the Panama Canal...*its possession or control by any foreign power—or even the remote threat of such possession—would be repugnant to the most elementary principles of national defense.*"[11] (emphasis added)

Once the U.S. seized Puerto Rico, the four

islands assumed strategic importance in the minds of American sailors and soldiers. For forty years nobody put them to significant military use, but the Caribbean was nevertheless an American Lake, to be employed in any way that benefited the United States. As Secretary of State Robert Lansing counseled President Wilson in November of 1915, "the Monroe Doctrine should not be confused with Pan Americanism...in its advocacy of the Monroe Doctrine the United States considers its own interests. The integrity of other nations is an incident, not an end. While this may seem based on selfishness alone...."[12]

Lansing was a Washington rarity who told the truth and used no ideological gloss to hide his nation's admittedly selfish motives. Thus, Puerto Rico was a "permanent possession" of the United States of America. It wasn't needed in 1915 or even in 1935, but who knew about tomorrow or the day after? Alliances changed, weapons were invented and strategic contingencies multiplied with the ever-increasing complexity of world geopolitical thinking.

It was a difficult time for a world power. So, until 1940, Puerto Rico was a military ace in the hole; its political future forcibly married to a world-view that thought of any Caribbean nation's independence as incidental but never an end of U.S. foreign and domestic policy.[13]

God put Puerto Rico in the middle of the Caribbean. God put Puerto Rico in front of Panama. And God put Puerto Rico 550 miles from the coast of South America.Presumably God had no military strategy in mind. Franklin Roosevelt did. He accompanied the U.S. Navy on its 1938 Caribbean maneuvers. He watched Navy planes carry out a mock bombing of San Juan. He soon agreed to accept the advice of his military strategists: Puerto Rico would become the Pearl Harbor of the Caribbean.

To Roosevelt, the three Puerto Rican islands were perfect. The U.S. owned them. The U.S. governed them. And the U.S. would transform them because of the military possibilities of a new weapon: the airplane.

Suppose, said military theorists, a powerful enemy controlled Brazil or Venezuela. Suppose that enemy brought planes to South America. And suppose Germany used those planes to first occupy Puerto Rico and then bomb states like Florida or cities like New Orleans.

In 1939 no one knew if this would happen. To forever avoid such a contingency, the dormant military potential of Puerto Rico was immediately and explosively actualized. On the main island, the Navy expropriated 340 acres in the center of San Juan; that became the San Juan Naval Air Station at Isla Grande, a top priority project because it was "a major air base, equipped to serve two squadrons of seaplanes, one carrier group" and also contained all the industrial equipment required for major repairs of planes or boats.[14]

Culebra received a facelift. The island is four by seven miles wide and sits midway between Puerto Rico and another American colony, the Virgin Island of St. Thomas.[15] In 1903 President Theodore Roosevelt set aside a considerable portion of Culebra's land for unspecified military uses. Meanwhile, roughly a thousand people were permitted to live on the island because, despite the appeal of its finely sheltered harbor, Culebra received only infrequent prewar use. It had a sod-surfaced airstrip, a camp site and the debris left over by the generations of Marines who, every winter, used Culebra to stage amphibious assaults. In 1939 the Navy took over another 276 acres of Culebra for substantially expanded air facilities; it modernized the runway and it also revamped everything from the sewer systems to the cold storage facilities. The hope was to have a much needed emergency landing field, but, when Luis Colón Osorio was born in 1950, Culebra still had no hospital. Thus, his pregnant mother faced this terrible choice: risk crossing the ocean to travel to the "Mother Island" or remain at home and risk a medically unattended birth on the "Daughter Island."

Vieques is four by twenty miles long and lies seven miles off the east coast of the main island. In 1939, it was the only place in Puerto Rico capable of accommodating a base designed to be a second Pearl Harbor. The Navy expropriated almost 7000 acres on the main island (this was the Ceiba base where Marshall Colón took the trophy photos of Colón Osorio) and another 29,000 acres on Vieques. Together these "real estate" holdings added up to the largest naval complex in the world. Sailors called it Roosevelt Roads, a facility designed to house the entire British fleet, if England fell to the then-mighty armies of Adolf Hitler.

In 1940 Vieques had a population of roughly 10,000 men, women and children who survived on jobs derived from sugar; the island contained vast tracts of cane which had long been the principal, yet always fragile, source of the island's economic base.

Nevertheless, the Navy paid an average of $47 an acre for the "best sugar land" on Vieques and, as Supreme Court Justice Abe Fortas told Congress in 1944, "by acquiring so large a portion of the island and taking it out of civilian use and occupancy, the Navy effectively destroyed the economy of the community....the situation has now deteriorated to the point where almost the entire population of Vieques is dependent upon the insular government for subsistence."[16]

The Navy moved about 3,000 islanders to the Virgin Island of St. Croix. Another 4,000 were resettled in the center of Vieques, but, since the Navy paid no taxes, the municipality found itself in the same situation as the population: It was broke, with no way to pay for everything from schools to sanitation. Luckily, some islanders found work on "Rosey Roads" and, however terrible in the short run, the prospect of a world war obviously demanded sacrifices from everyone. Viequenses did their part, satisfied that the Navy would keep its word and, with victory, return Vieques to Puerto Rico and its people.[17]

The military's plan was to build a fourteen mile breakwater between Vieques and the mainland. The rock would be mined in the new quarry built on Vieques; the fleet would dock behind the breakwater; and, in the event of a need for repairs, ships would use the gargantuan drydock constructed on the Puerto Rican mainland. Workers also built a hospital, a fuel depot and another major air station for both land and seaplanes.

With no voting representation in Congress, Puerto Rico nevertheless had been drafted; in fact, within three years it had been transformed into the centerpiece of an island armada that stretched from Trinidad to Bermuda. In the lend-lease deal of 1941, for a bunch of antiquated destroyers President Roosevelt had received 99-year military leases on a variety of British possessions. Puerto Rico was essential because it would be a second Pearl Harbor and because it was the American center of a thousand mile shield of well-armed U.S. and British colonies. As Admiral William Greenslade counseled the president in 1940, "complete control of the Caribbean is fundamental to our national defense. Not only is this control a vital factor in our communications with South America under our responsibilities in Hemisphere Defense, but such control is of even more importance in assuring the defense of the Panama Canal and our own continental United States in the vital Gulf area."[18]

After more than forty years, Puerto Rico's potential had suddenly turned into such an important military command that the president of the United States suggested it was "repugnant" to think of Puerto Rico under anything other than American control. And, Senator Robert Taft echoed the president when he told his congressional colleagues in May of 1943, "I can understand a certain amount of autonomy, but I cannot understand how you can reconcile complete independence of the Island with the effective and necessary use of Puerto Rico for a military control of the Caribbean."[19]

In June of 1943 Pedro Albizu Campos left Atlanta's federal penitentiary. The road to independence now contained a gigantic new roadblock—Roosevelt Roads. It was formally commissioned in

July of 1943 and , with no fanfare at all, mothballed within less than eighteen months.

After December 7, 1941 a second Pearl Harbor suddenly seemed like a bad idea. Thus, flying into Vieques today one can easily spot the remnants of the never completed breakwater; builders gave up after less than a mile and sailors gave up after victory in the Atlantic. Since World War II never got to the Caribbean, the Navy mothballed the never-activated facility and also told the Interior Department in 1944 that it had no use for "a large portion of the acreage" expropriated from the people of Vieques.

The Puerto Ricans wanted the Navy to keep its word and give back the land. But what if there was another war? Or a future need for Roosevelt Roads? The same men who turned Puerto Rico's original military potential into Roosevelt Roads now turned Roosevelt Roads into Puerto Rico's *new* military potential. Since the mothballed base might be needed, the Navy only agreed to lease roughly 5000 of its 29,000 acres to the people of Vieques. They could farm it to survive, but the Navy still refused to pay taxes on the remaining 24,000 acres. In generously making the land available, Abe Fortas also made it clear "that these transfers do not disturb the underlying title of the United States and were made in furtherance of carefully drafted plans for the rehabilitation of the population of the island of Vieques."[20]

Without firing a shot, the people of Vieques (and Culebra) lost World War II. A U.S. victory produced the need for "rehabilitation" in Puerto Rico and, after the war, it produced the need for a "permanent" military facility in Vieques and Culebra which sailors soon called their university of the sea.

The Atlantic Fleet Weapons Range

Soldiers need to practice, but nobody wants sailors, infantrymen, marines and aviators to practice in their neighborhood. It's noisy, disruptive and not at all conducive to economic development. After the war, the Navy had Bloodsworth Island in the Chesapeake Bay, but powerful Virginia voters complained about the noise, and wildlife activists complained about the threat to fish and fowl. Thus, activists eventually succeeded in shutting down Bloodsworth Island for three months of every year. The birds needed their peace of mind.

Not so the Puerto Ricans. They didn't vote, and the islands had long been used for naval training, so, once World War II turned into the Cold War, Puerto Rico suddenly found itself—once again—at the center of U.S. military strategy. This time, instead of simply protecting the United States, Puerto Rico would help protect the entire free world. The French, the English, the Italians, the Dutch— everybody planned to use Vieques and Culebra as part of a training complex that would service the North Atlantic Treaty Organization (NATO) and the United States.

No wonder Albizu was angry. And no wonder he had significant support from Puerto Ricans of every political persuasion. Indeed, even Secretary of the Navy James Forrestal sympathized with the Puerto Ricans. "I want to assure you that the Navy department is keenly aware of the problems faced by the Insular government in its endeavors to improve the economic condition of the people of Vieques,

Culebra and Puerto Rico." But, "the Atlantic Fleet must be maintained in a high state of readiness and amphibious training and shore target exercises must be continued on an intensive and realistic basis." Thus, the Navy not only planned the "permanent use" of Vieques and Culebra, it also needed another 700 acres of the smaller island. As an admiral told the president, "this is needed for impact bombing, for the positioning of the observers, and further to be able to keep out natives."[21]

Now, the "natives" were angry. In the case of Culebra, if the Navy got the 700 acres requested, it would then control all of Culebra's grazing land; it would deprive the people of their only remaining bathing beach; and it would also add another burden on San Juan because of the Navy's tax exemption.

This issue went straight to the president's desk. He had read Admiral Leahy's memo on "real estate problems in Puerto Rico" and, like Secretary Forrestal, he sympathized with the people. But, "the detailed requirements for this additional area indicate that these requirements are related to *national defense*. There is, therefore, no objection to acquisition by the Navy Department of this 700 acres of land on Culebra."[22] (emphasis in original)

Meanwhile, on Vieques, the Navy bought another 4340 acres in 1950. That gave it control of sixty-eight percent of an island that was now split into three sections. On the western end of the island, sailors had an underground ammunition depot; aboveground, local cattlemen paid the Navy $6000 a year to graze their stock on land that was tax-exempt. The 8000 residents of Vieques were squeezed into the middle of the island while the third section—about twelve miles long—contained a maneuver and impact area. At night, ships firing from as much eighteen or twenty miles at sea sounded like thunder. They aimed for a bullseye at the tip of Vieques, and they used a mix of live and dummy ammunition—an average of 3400 bombs a month.[23]

The bombs fell on islands that are as splendid as any in the Caribbean. The ocean is always warm and blue and always surrounded by red, pink, yellow and white flowers of remarkable variety. In Vieques, you can lie on a two-mile stretch of beach any day of the week, see no one, and feel overwhelmed by the mountainous backdrop that towers over the Caribbean. An especially exquisite spot is a small house set on a ridge from which the owners carved out a stone staircase to the sea. At the bottom is a small tidal pool which never needs a filter or chlorine. The pool is protected, but a person isn't because what appear to be destroyers are pounding the corner of the island with the ammunition once housed in the cavernous armory just below the once peacefully grazing cattle.

Luis Colón Osorio was born into this surreal environment on June 29, 1950. He remembers the natural beauty but, even more, the recollections of Culebra's elders of their elders and traditions—for example, the ancestors' *bohíos*. These round or rectangular palm-thatched constructions have their cultural roots among Puerto Rico's first inhabitants, the Taíno indians. They evoke in Luis both the sacred past and vivid nightmares. Luis remembers his experiences as an eighteen-year-old Vietnam volunteer in 1968: "We were being trained to attack simulated Vietnamese villages with little wooden and thatched houses that looked like *los bohios* of our ancestors. In the houses were dummies made to look like men, women and children—all unarmed. The instructors would constantly yell, "KILL, KILL, KILL," while we attacked the dummy Vietnamese men, women and children and tore them up with our bayonets and then burned their houses—something that was not consistent with my Christian education. I felt very confused."[24]

Luis' life keeps coming back to Culebra and the warlike experiences of his childhood. At night, accompanying the setting sun, a resident heard loud sirens. This was the call to curfew; all Culebrans lived under a form of martial law because only the most courageous (or stupidest) islander went out after the Navy loudly signalled its version of "bombs away."

If Luis was theoretically safe at night, he often played a dangerous game of "dodge 'em" during the day. His first job was to tend cows near the beach, and his first near-deadly encounter with a bomb came when he looked up and saw them falling from the sky. "Often I would have to abandon the cows and run off at a gallop to save myself from the bombing...."[25]

Estimates vary, but during Luis' youth Culebra was subjected to as many as a thousand aircraft sorties each month.[26] It was not uncommon to have a bomb in one's "backyard." For Luis the experience represented a part of a world where ideals were matched by action. Men fought for what they believed in: the battle to make the world safe for democracy.

Saturday was the highlight of any week. Marines would bring a truckload of folding chairs, set them in front of the local hardware store, and, using the *ferreteria's* white wall as a screen, project free movies for the residents of Culebra. Luis probably saw every John Wayne war movie ever made. Conceivably, the Marines had a perverse sense of humor; or perhaps they subjected the residents to the only movies offered to them. Whatever the case, Luis modeled himself after the Marines in general and John Wayne in particular. He wanted to be "the Duke" on Saturday nights, and on Sunday mornings he tried to square his military ideals with the lessons taught in catechism class. In a tiny neighborhood chapel that no longer exists, Luis served as an altar boy; he wore starched white; and, for a time, he wanted to be a priest.

It was a hell of a childhood. In the United States, lucky youngsters watched *Leave It to Beaver*. In Culebra, lucky youngsters avoided the rain of bombs, and then, as if being penalized for their efforts, their families received eviction notices. John Kennedy wanted everybody to leave. As with President Truman in 1948, the Navy had convinced its brand new commander-in-chief that the island's inhabitants were an impediment to military efficiency. Thus, they had to leave Culebra. They had to leave Vieques. And they had to do it ASAP.

President Kennedy is a beloved figure to many Puerto Ricans. In homes in the mountains, one will still see pictures of the young president on a poor person's wall. He remains a revered figure, a leader whose popular image has never been tarnished by even the most controversial policies.

As soon as he assumed command, John Kennedy advocated a military strategy designed to prepare the United States for three different kinds of war: a strategic nuclear encounter, a tactical nuclear war in Europe or elsewhere, and "small" brushfire wars like the then-simmering situation in Vietnam. In theory, if the United States quickly put out the brushfires before they became full scale conflagrations, the world would never fight a nuclear war. Using forces like the Green Berets, the young president meant to aggressively put out the flames of communism wherever they erupted[27]

Puerto Rico fit perfectly into this strategy. In 1957, soldiers made the decision to turn Roosevelt Roads into the primary center for Fleet Guided Missile Training Operations in the Atlantic. Thus, as a naval aide explained to the president, the people of Culebra had to leave because of the military's need "to provide a suitable impact area for the rapidly increasing missile training of our fleet and our naval air units."[28]

Vieques was different. Soldiers meant to use it as the Atlantic Ocean headquarters of their campaign to extinguish the world's growing number of brushfire wars. As Kenneth BeLieu told the president, there is "a need for the remainder of Vieques Island, including the necessity to relocate all 7500 residents to provide a secure location for overt and covert training and/or staging of U.S. and foreign forces."[29]

Coincidentally, President Kennedy had just received a letter (dated September 28, 1961) from the Mayor of Vieques. Without telling Governor Muñoz Marín, Antonio Rivera Rodríguez wrote "on behalf of the 7198 American citizens living in Vieques who are willing to defend our freedom and our democratic way of life..." Vieques had problems. The Navy refused to turn over 80 unused acres required for a civilian airport, and it provided no jobs "to help the local government in solving the economic crisis of the Island." So, "with all respect I believe the attitude of the United States Navy is harmful for it gives the enemy of democracy a weapon to turn world opinion against us. The Vieques problem is also excellent propaganda for the separatist (i.e., the independence) movement in Puerto Rico."[30]

Like millions of other Puerto Ricans, Mayor Rivera Rodríguez had no idea what was coming. The formal eviction notice had never been received because the Navy's plans for Vieques and Culebra contained a condition reminiscent of a Dracula movie.

Roman Catholic Puerto Ricans celebrate All Saints Day by cleaning and decorating the graves of departed loved ones. The Navy viewed this sacred duty for many Puerto Ricans as potential interference with their covert operations and/or their strategic and tactical missile practice. Thus, in the plan formally approved by President Kennedy, the citizens of Vieques and Culebra not only had to leave their homes forever; they had to take their cemeteries with them. Bones, caskets, gravestones—everything had to go because soldiers wanted to be assured of perpetual freedom from the Puerto Ricans and their religious holidays.

129

President Kennedy agreed. And so—very reluctantly—did Governor Muñoz Marín. In 1959 the governor had tried to significantly "enhance" the political and economic powers supposedly associated with Commonwealth status. However, the governor had been humiliatingly put in his colonial place by Senator Henry Jackson who in open hearings aggressively stressed that Congress had absolute power over Puerto Rico and its inhabitants. Within a month, Governor Muñoz took his case to the Oval Office, but a visit with the president produced no help, and at the end of their meeting Eisenhower asked an aide to "examine into the Commonwealth question that seemed to bother the governor so much."[31]

The Republican president of the United States apparently had no idea what the Puerto Rican "Commonwealth" was. Thus, Muñoz desperately needed John Kennedy's assistance if he ever was to deliver on his long-promised enhancement of Commonwealth.

In a December 16, 1961 meeting with the president, Muñoz agreed to accept what I call the Dracula Plan: Graves and all, the people of Vieques and Culebra would leave their homes. But, Muñoz also stressed the profoundly negative public relations consequences of the Navy's proposed eviction of 10,000 American citizens.

First, it was illegal to abolish a municipality. Puerto Rico's constitution stipulated that to erase Vieques and Culebra the legislature first had to pass a law, and the people then had to vote for their own disappearance. Muñoz doubted they would do that. "The people of Vieques regard themselves as

Puerto Ricans but they also regard themselves as specifically identifiable on the basis of residence in Vieques." In fact, they had such a "strong emotional attachment" to their place of birth that even Muñoz could not guarantee an affirmative vote in a referendum. He assured Kennedy that he would work hard for the president's position, but he reminded him of this "hazard": "Not to hold the referendum would be bad; to hold it and lose would be worse."[32]

A second, equally troublesome issue was the reaction in Latin America, in Cuba and in other communist nations. "Obviously, the political and human dismemberment which the project involves will be a fundamental shock. *We know of no truly comparable action in American history. I believe it is the kind of action which arouses instinctive disapproval.*" Imagine the field day U.S. opponents would have with pictures of graves and bones being transported to parts unknown. "In Latin America, there is, of course, the danger that the project will be used to vindicate the unjust accusations which our enemies make as to the attitude of the United States towards Puerto Rico and its people." Meanwhile, "in the United Nations the project would surely be used by the Castro-Cubans and the communist block to vindicate their current charges that Puerto Rico is a colonial area and that the United Nations should include it as such."[33]

The president saw the light. "Largely on the basis of Muñoz's argument," he decided to kill the Dracula Plan. Although the people could stay, they and the Navy still needed to reach an accommodation about the use of Vieques "as a secure staging area to meet contingencies in Latin America."[34]

This last line is not the president's. It comes from a recently declassified (March, 1993) document written by Deputy Assistant Secretary of Defense Cyrus Vance in March of 1964. Through the grapevine, Muñoz had heard that the Navy once again planned to acquire all of Vieques and Culebra. Angered and worried by this news, the governor took his concerns to the White House and that prompted a "top secret" memo from Cyrus Vance.

Muñoz was both right and wrong. The Navy did not want all of Vieques. They agreed that the "social and political effects" of the grave relocations was a political hot potato. Thus, the people could remain, but the Navy did need another 1434 acres "to provide additional beach area for Marine assault and air operations and a connecting strip between the two main maneuver areas." In the event of heated opposition, this plan "could be adjusted to preclude any significant family relocation." However, "*total acquisition of Vieques is not included in the pending legislation.*"[35] (emphasis in the original)

Culebra was another matter. The Navy definitely wanted the last 4,505 acres owned by families such as Luis Colón Osorio's. The land was needed for an "instrumented target impact area," and Vance told the White House that "funds for the relocation"—graves and all—were included in the bill then *pending* before the House Armed Services Committee.

Vance saw an opportunity in the word "pending". Since Congress had not yet formally authorized the funds required for the total acquisition of Culebra and the additional 1434 acres on Vieques, "there appears to be no need to reopen negotiations with Puerto Rican officials until such time as enabling legislation is at hand." Meanwhile, "we can advise Governor Muñoz that our land acquisition plans are no different than those authorized by Congress two years ago and that we are proposing to dispose of Puerto Rican properties which are excess to Defense requirements."[36]

This last line refers to a variety of properties first acquired by the Defense Department during World War II. Twenty years later, soldiers admitted they had no need for the land, yet as with Vieques and Culebra in 1944, they were still reluctant to dispose of anything they might need in the future. Vance hoped to soften Muñoz up with a promise to break the postwar logjam, but the best indication of his and his colleagues actual attitudes toward Puerto Rico occurred in a June 11, 1965 meeting with Governor Luis Muñoz Marín.

The interview was conducted by Lee White, the White House point man on Puerto Rico during the Kennedy and Johnson administrations. White was accumulating oral histories for the President Kennedy Library, and, after Muñoz explained the "grave moral and human" significance of the Dracula Plan, White said: "In your view, was this of tremendous importance to the seven or eight thousand people on Vieques, or were they a symbol of the whole thing? *Did you think it was important enough to take the time of the president of the United States for the problems of seven thousand people?*[37] (emphasis added)

Muñoz answered "oh, yes. It was important to them; and it was important to the feeling of the people of Puerto Rico, generally. And, of course, it

133

would have been a tremendous propaganda handle for the Communists all over Latin America."[38]

And the people of Culebra? They were never mentioned in these dialogues because an administration that questioned bothering the president about seven thousand people never considered the will of seven hundred. Thus, while Secretary Vance struggled to take all of Culebra, aviators prepared for Vietnam by sending (in one year) over 6000 aircraft on 35,000/40,000 bombing runs.[39] On the island, the people tried to survive while Luis Colón Osorio, now living in San Juan, reached one of the defining decisions of his life: He enlisted in the Army, more eager than ever to imitate the valor and sacrifice glorified by John Wayne and the other Marine heroes of his youth.

David and Goliath

Speaking only Spanish, Luis went to the recruiting center. He thought he volunteered for a two year tour of duty but quickly learned that he had signed ("because I could not read English") a form which committed him to an additional year of service. When he asked the sergeant what happened, the fellow offered this reply: "Ho, Ho—we took you for a ride—you've signed for three years."

Confronted with a form that asked for his race, "I, without even thinking, filled in the only race I knew, Puerto Rican." That didn't satisfy the recruiters who, "when they read the form, they called me back and said, 'bullshit, Black.' Then they wrote, 'nationality, American, Race, Black.'"

Luis sensed the hatred, but he did not get the point. Like Rafael Cancel Miranda when he entered prison in Tallahassee, this was Luis' first encounter with Northamerican racism. If Luis used the word race at all, *la raza* referred to an ethnic group. He didn't recognize differences that stemmed from skin color, and he didn't understand the discrimination that was everyday fare during his basic training. Puerto Ricans were "spics", and the word was said in a tone of voice that indicated total contempt.

The training transformed Luis. He was conscience stricken by the order to burn *los bohios* and frightened by a side of himself he had not known. "So here I was at seventeen, eighteen, full of confusion, programmed like a robot to kill, kill, kill. I volunteered to go to Vietnam so I could use my training and let out some of the rage and frustration that were building from these experiences, the training and the discrimination. I had never dreamed such violence could dwell in my being, but this is what happened."

Luis never got to Vietnam. While he thought he would use his training in explosives and weapons to kill the enemy, he wound up in Germany. Immediately, he was isolated in two languages: English on the base, German on the outside. Luis had a nervous breakdown. "The violence that had been implanted in me would not let me live. All the contradictions were too great." He had a nervous breakdown and left the Army addicted to heroin.

Luis returned to Puerto Rico. He was promised total disability status before he left Germany, but "when the hospital in Puerto Rico treated drug addiction with more drugs, I refused this treatment and was denied my 100% disability." To this day he has been denied the benefits due a veteran with service connected disabilities.

Luis was now twenty-years-old, jobless, and a recovering addict. Two wars—Vietnam and the one in Culebra—had tried to destroy his life, like so many Puerto Ricans, he found wisdom and strength in his homeland. He identified with the poor; he worked to improve their housing; he refused to end one drug addiction by embracing another; and he returned to the church—this time deepening and extending his religious studies and meditations.

Luis struggled to make sense of his life and his military experiences while, in Chicago, a young Puerto Rican named Oscar López returned from Vietnam with an honorable discharge, a bronze star for valor, and a passionate commitment to fundamental social change.

Oscar had met the enemy and he liked them. The Vietnamese taught this "neorican" from Chicago a very important lesson: the weak could defeat the strong. David could fire his slingshot and bring down the mighty Goliath.

The Prisoners

Juan Segarra Palmer
and Luz Berríos Berríos

Oscar López Rivera

Luis Rosa

PRISONERS OF COLONIALISM

Elizam Escobar

Carlos Alberto Torres

Alejandrina Torres

The Prisoners

Eddie Cortés

Antonio Camacho Negrón

Alicia Rodríguez

PRISONERS OF COLONIALISM

Ida Luz Rodríguez

Luis Colón Osorio

Norman Ramírez Talavera

The Prisoners

Ricardo Jiménez   Alberto Rodríguez

Carmen Valentín

PRISONERS OF COLONIALISM

Adolfo Matos

Roberto José Maldonado

Dylcia Pagán

Andrés' Cap

Andrés also bought...a mutil-color cap with the colors of the Puerto Rican flag—red, blue and white...Andrés walks to the mirror; he puts his cap on, takes a close look from his forehead up, thinks about Puerto Rico and feels good.Andrés washes his cap, rinses his cap, smells his cap and he feels good."

—Leonardo Rodríguez, *They
Have To Be Puerto Ricans*[1]

One sign said Division Street; another, on the same pole, said Pedro Albizu Campos Boulevard. Was this Chicago or Ponce? The city or *el barrio*? Watching the June 5, 1993 parade in support of the Puerto Rican political prisoners the choice was not clear.

Puerto Rican flags were *everywhere*. They hung from stores and apartments, waved about on six and eight foot poles squeezed into the back bumpers of cars. Flags were on the motorcycles,helmets and black leather jackets of beer-bellied Puerto Rican (I think) Hell's Angels. The flags were in baby carriages, on hats, on shirts of every style and description, and on windshield wipers. Especially inventive supporters somehow attached flags to the rubber blades, pulled the wipers up and then turned them on. The flags waved as rhythmically as the androgynous figure leading the parade.

The fellow was dressed in white, sported a straw hat, a huge moustache, a colorful bandanna around his neck, and a flowing skirt which was attached to a female figure who had seemingly wrapped her legs around his stomach. The children loved this man who was not a man. He danced his way through a two mile parade and never once lost his smile or enthusiasm. He even got to pass on a bit of Puerto Rican culture. The androgynous figure originated in the town of Corozal; slaves brought the figure from Africa when they laid the foundation for some of the loveliest elements of Puerto Rican, Jamaican and Grenadian culture.

Behind him/her came a band and behind them a float which contained the names and large portraits of each of the political prisoners. The people chanted:"Puerto Rico will be free, drive the Yankees to the Sea." "Prison torture, we say no, Control Units have got to go." "Vieques si, Marina [the Navy] no." And, "if the Yankees do not leave, they will die in Borinquen."

As marchers shouted their open defiance of U.S. colonial authority, the parade's sponsors openly endorsed this sixteenth annual Puerto Rican Day parade. In San Juan, storeowners would hesitate, and hesitate again, before ever placing their names in a brochure that broadcast their indirect sponsorship of revolutionary activity. In Chicago nobody seemed worried. The brochures were readily available and they indicated all the shopowners who had funded this community-based parade.

Earlier in the day, other Puerto Ricans had staged a parade in the center of Chicago. Rumor had it that the "festival" was a bust; attendance was low, enthusiasm as staged as the cheers of a 1992 Clinton or Bush TV advertisement. Meanwhile, in "el barrio" people came out of taverns and the Jayuya barbershop and Borinquen Square (a supermarket) to shake the hands of marchers they knew, or, like Andrés with his cap, simply to say thank you to Puerto Ricans who made them "feel good."

One minute the parade was a celebration of self. And then, a minute later, it was an extraordinary comment about the divided city of Chicago. As the smiling marchers slowly turned off Division Street/Albizu Campos Boulevard, a gigantic mural suddenly came into view. It was two stories high; it contained caricatures of four famous Puerto Ricans; and it would never—never—be permitted on the Puerto Rican mainland. Nailed to three crosses were Lolita Lebrón, Rafael Cancel Miranda, and, in the middle, Pedro Albizu Campos. Standing in front and carrying a spear was Luis Muñoz Marín. He had cut Albizu's side, and he was responsible for the blood dripping to the ground. The twenty-year-old mural had recently been restored, and, in a neighborhood full of gangs waving spray cans, the mural was rarely disturbed. Occasionally a youngster did deface it, but on June 5, 1993 the mural was spotless— the sentiment more controversial than anything I had ever seen in Puerto Rico.

In old San Juan, right across from the U.S. federal building, the Commonwealth government had sponsored (in 1989) a museum "retrospective" about Albizu Campos and the Nationalist Party. On spotless walls, well-dressed patrons admired paintings that celebrated everything from Albizu speaking to striking cane workers in 1934, to Irving Flores firing at Congress in 1954. The exhibition was well-attended, respectful and nothing like the mural in

Chicago. The mural was in the barrio; it belonged to the people; and it challenged every standard interpretation of Puerto Rican history. In Chicago, Muñoz was Judas working for the Romans who now called themselves Americans. He had crucified the spiritual soul of the Puerto Rican people, and he deserved all the contempt the Andrés of Chicago could possibly muster.

Chicago is unique. It breeds a sense of place every bit as strong as the enthusiasm of Manuel Caballer for Ponce or Roberto Jose Maldonado for his beloved Aibonito. Chicago is a "make believe Puerto Rico," said Carlos Alberto Torres; it's something you feel, even after thirteen years in prison, and even in an antiseptic room in the federal facility at Oxford, Wisconsin.

I wanted an explanation fit for an academic; Carlos offered a story fit for a Puerto Rican. He had gone away to college. Nothing bad happened. He experienced no racism, no special dislike of Puerto Ricans. But he was still a man without a barrio. He wanted to come home and, when he crossed Division Street, "I always felt a sense of relief, of satisfaction." Out there was where *they* lived. It might be nice; it might be awful. But it wasn't Chicago. It wasn't something that made you "feel good," like waving the flag or laughing along with the she/he leading the parade.

Once the parade ended, the celebrating continued. Well into the night and early morning, cars drove through the streets, horns blared, and windshield wipers waved their one-starred reminders of Puerto Rico.

Albizu Campos Boulevard divided, not only one

part of Chicago from another, but the marchers uptown from the marchers downtown and the Puerto Rican POW's from the streets of their youth. Men like Oscar López and women like Carmen Valentín had used Albizu as their political guide. It was their work that helped resurrect Albizu as a political figure, but while he got major avenues named in his honor, they got fifty or seventy years in jail.

A cynic might argue that yesterday's terrorists often become today's prime ministers (e.g., Menachim Begin or Itzak Shamir). Give the United States a chance, and in ten years the Chicago revolutionaries also will have their day in the sun, their avenue in Chicago's North End.

Ten years is a very long time. Especially in prison. And especially on top of the thirteen years already served by many of the Chicago POW's. So, to better grasp the prisoners' world, recall that in 1956 Chicago only had 2500 Puerto Ricans. By 1970, more than 79,000 islanders lived in the North and South ends of Chicago. They had come from Puerto Rico looking for jobs.

Caracas, Anchorage, Chicago

His name was never a household word, his job never a plum for the politically ambitious, but Irwin Silverman, Chief Counsel, Division of Territories and Island Possessions, Department of the Interior, shaped U.S. policy toward Puerto Rico and its people. He was an in-house expert, the man Congress called when it wanted to examine Puerto Rico's plight and the United States' predicament.

In 1956 Silverman discussed the origins of both

147

Commonwealth government and Operation Bootstrap, the economic plan that then bore major responsibility for one of the largest mass migrations in the history of the Caribbean. During and after World War II, Congress was upset about having "to pour millions of dollars into Puerto Rico only to provide enough food to keep the people of Puerto Rico together at the lowest possible subsistence level." Something had to be done to "relieve the mainland taxpayers of direct deficit expenditures in the Territory of Puerto Rico" so Congress devised a plan: If the Puerto Ricans agreed to develop a self-sufficient economy, "Congress would be willing to grant them in the nature of a compact Commonwealth status for the first time in the history of the United States and its offshore possessions."

It was "in the nature of a compact" because, as Silverman stressed, "if it had been a compact, it would have been a treaty, and in entering into a treaty the sovereignty of the people is recognized.." That was out of the question. Congress always retained ultimate economic and political power: "I hope to God nothing happens, but, if something should happen in Puerto Rico, there is no question in my mind but that the Congress could step in tomorrow and make such changes as it saw fit."[2]

God willing, Congress could stay in the background because of the economic strategies first devised by Silverman and his colleagues in the late 1940's to offer the Puerto Ricans a bit of "bait". A federal law dating from 1921 stipulated that Americans investing in the colonies (i.e., the Philippines, Puerto Rico, Guam, the Virgin Islands) did not pay federal taxes. The absence of federal taxes along with the local tax exemption could act as a great incentive for outside investment to establish the factories that would put Puerto Ricans to work. As Silverman said, "I should point out that there is a period of tutelage, as we call it, from the time we acquired the Territory, which as a ward and guardian relationship we have to assist and help, and part of the tutelage or the fee for their learning how to handle their own affairs is this 12 years' bait."[3]

Under Luis Muñoz Marín, Puerto Rico took the bait. Muñoz and his colleagues agreed to be "wards" of the state and, in the process, they embraced a strategy with a number of inherent weaknesses which were recognized at the time. Four are especially important in terms of the mass migration of Puerto Ricans to the United States.

First was a requirement of the 1921 tax law. Instead of being able to bring home their tax free profits on a yearly basis, corporations legally could bring their profits home only when they *liquidated* the business. So, as early as 1950, U.S. corporations received this advice from Puerto Rican tax consultants: "The corporate activities of the (Puerto Rican) subsidiary should be carefully conducted with a view to liquidation rather than the continuation of operations."[4]

Operation Bootstrap quickly became a treadmill for Puerto Rican economic planners. New businesses only replaced the ones closing up shop after a "let's take the money and run" liquidation. Moreover, even if a corporation stayed after its period of local tax exemptions expired, many did it by erasing the original subsidiary, taking their profits home, and agreeing to open a new subsidiary only if the local government offered new tax exemptions. The result in San Juan was that instead of creating new jobs by using the tax revenues generated by successful corporations, the island government rarely got tax revenues. On the contrary, as places like Taiwan, Hong Kong and Singapore also tried to attract new industries, Puerto Rico had to somehow fund even greater tax incentives just to stay even. Thus, during the 1950's the island government began to pay for the buildings that would house the businesses in search of a new home.[5]

A second and even greater weakness of Operation Bootstrap was its complete dependence on the whims of the United States Congress. As Silverman told the House of Representatives: "Congress could step in tomorrow and make such changes as it saw fit." Congress had already exercised its plenary power on a number of occasions. For example, Congress had no intention of allowing Puerto Ricans to take jobs away from citizens in New Hampshire or Illinois, so, from the outset, the government in San Juan "discouraged scores of manufacturers who intended to move their facilities to Puerto Rico and close their plants in the United States."[6]

The result was a so-called "fishing net" approach to industrialization. Puerto Rico took what it could get, and that wasn't much. Or, as an internal study put it in 1957: The manufacturers who came "were small and labor-oriented and at best represented entrepreneurial mediocrity. At worst they were a motley troupe of entrepreneurial migrants...."

Haiti, the Dominican Republic, Mexico, Cuba: These manufacturers would go anywhere; *they* took most of the bait offered by Irwin Silverman, and their greed meshed so well with the tax loophole called "liquidation" that Puerto Rico became a magnet for anyone seeking a Caribbean Klondike. As a outside analyst explained it to the island's government in 1959, "Gold rush psychology is apparently still a part of the American scene and the possibility of 'making a killing' seems to be much more of an attraction than does the rather high probability of a more moderate return."[7]

Gamblers out to make a killing were never interested in Puerto Rico's long term economic health. By 1964 it was already clear that—using Operation Bootstrap—a self-sustaining economy would never materialize. A third weakness in Operation Bootstrap emerged as mainland jobs supposedly flocked to Puerto Rico, U.S. unions lobbied Congress to demand that Muñoz engineer the introduction of U.S. minimum wage laws in Puerto Rico. The governor fought this but, lacking any real power over his own economy, he watched as Puerto Rico lost jobs because it was no longer competitive with the scores of developing nations who happily took any job for any wage that was offered.[8]

The fourth and final nail in Puerto Rico's economic coffin was the government's disastrous attitude toward agriculture. The planners in Washington and San Juan put so much emphasis on industrialization that they forgot the agrarian nature of Puerto Rican society in 1950. The result was that for every 3500 jobs generated by industry, the society lost 6000 in agriculture.[9] People flocked to the cities but, given the harsh realities of Operation Bootstrap, many decided to emigrate. They left their beloved island in search of jobs.They came to the United States because they were citizens, because the non-stop flights were relatively cheap, and because men like Irwin Silverman had found no other country willing to accept what soon amounted to a million "surplus" Puerto Ricans.

Like everyone else in the Caribbean, Puerto Ricans have always been on the move. Crops like sugar were never a secure basis for employment so, as early as 1900, thousands of Puerto Ricans emigrated to Hawaii. They worked in sugar while another large group of Jamaicans and Barbadians migrated to Panama to build the Canal. Using what were openly called gold and silver payrolls, whites monoplized the best jobs in the gold mines, while blacks took what was left in silver mines.[10] In Cuba, thousands of Haitians came to cut the sugar, and they did the same thing—under conditions that resembled slavery—in neighboring Dominican Republic. Grenadians toiled as second-class help in Trinidad and, when macheteros were needed in St. Croix, Grenadians moved there or, as the years passed, to Toronto or Brooklyn.

The Caribbean has been one of the world's most exploited regions. The English, the Spanish, the French, the Dutch and the Americans built economies that satisfied their needs and accepted little responsibility for their actions. Colonial governments efficiently introduced so many changes in medicine, sanitation and engineering that they quickly produced the first phase of the demographic transition: Death rates fell, but, with birth rates remaining high, there was also a rapid increase in population.

In the case of Puerto Rico, the birth rate (per 1,000 people) was 45.7 in 1899 and 39.5 in 1950; meanwhile, the death rate had dropped from 31.4 in 1899 to 10.5 in 1950. The result was a doubling of the population. A principal reason the birth and death rates never evened out was the "parasitic" impact of colonialism: With the profits extracted from islands like Puerto Rico, the "mother country" created the conditions required for a balanced population at home while the colony witnessed more and more people searching for jobs that did not exist.[11]

U.S. officials always recognized the "Puerto Rican problem." Speaking to Congress in 1943, Secretary of the Interior Ickes outlined plans for the island's economic rehabilitation. He was guardedly optimistic but "even if all the plans suggested were put into effect and were successful, there would still be a surplus population without work. The population increased 30,000 to 40,000 each year. Puerto Ricans would be desireable additions to any nation, and many *outlets* exist on this hemisphere."[12]

Ickes never suggested New York or Chicago as an "outlet" for the Puerto Ricans. He said "the federal government should investigate the possibility of making arrangements with other American republics which might be interested in the migration, under suitable conditions, of those Puerto Ricans who voluntarily decide that they want to make their future in South and Central America."[13]

By 1948 Donald O'Connor (working on behalf of the island's government) had come up with a proposal, to send the Puerto Ricans to Venezuela. In a plan that can be found at the Truman Library, O'Connor wrote that "the imperium of Britain, France and the Netherlands is in decline...already sensing this the British Dominions have begun to participate in an "assisted passages" scheme to facilitate emigration from the British Isles." So, in the same way that President Mc Kinley modeled Puerto Rico's government after that of the British colonies, President Truman could follow Britain's lead if he assisted the Puerto Ricans to open up the "very large and virtually uninhabited tract of land that lies in the Guayana Highlands of Venezuela." Washington could provide "assisted passages" to thousands of Puerto Ricans and simultaneously "add to America's security and prosperity, to Venezuela's development...and to the pool of experience for similar projects elsewhere."[14]

One of those projects was Irwin Silverman's scheme to "settle quite a large number of them on the Alaska Railroad in Alaska."[15] However, like the proposed exodus to Venezuela, this train trip to Anchorage never materialized. Nor did Washington find a Central or Latin American nation willing to act as an "outlet" for a few hundred thousand Puerto Ricans, so, at a time when U.S. immigration laws foreclosed a mass migration of Haitians or Jamaicans, Puerto Ricans took advantage of their political status: As U.S. citizens they had the right to come to the United States whenever they pleased.

The bulk of the 1950s migrants came because of the structural economic changes wrought by Operation Bootstrap. "Recruiters" from New Jersey seeking farm labor, Connecticut looking for tobacco workers, and from Michigan seeking workers for sugar beets wanted *seasonal* labor from Puerto Rico, but the large majority of the migrants were not responding to a significant demand for labor on the mainland.[16] On the contrary, one of the tragedies of the Puerto Rican exodus was its awful timing. Puerto Ricans settled in the same cities as large numbers of African-Americans thrown off Southern farms by devices like the mechanical cotton picker. Both groups also arrive at a time when the move to the suburbs was undermining the tax base of the central city and when more and more low-skilled jobs were being automated or, even worse, "sourced out" to places like Taiwan and India.

The sheer number of immigrants is one solid indication of the failure of Operation Bootstrap. Using 1950-1960 as a benchmark, the average net migration to the United States was more than 48,000 people each and every year. The figure for the decade 1940-1950 was a little more than 14,000 and for the decade 1960-1970 it was once again 14,000.[17]

Most of the immigrants moved to New York. In 1960 fully seventy-two percent of all Puerto Ricans lived in places like Brooklyn or the Bronx, Albany or Buffalo. As the competition for work became greater, Puerto Ricans fanned out to other states. New Jersey has always ranked second to New York followed by Illinois, or more precisely, Chicago. Of the 36,000 Puerto Ricans in Illinois in 1960, over 32,000 lived in the North or South ends of Chicago. A decade later, of 88,000 Puerto Ricans in Illinois, over 79,000 lived in Chicago.[18]

The numbers alone cannot convey the human

dimensions of this "diaspora." The migration was nothing less than a frontal assault on a Puerto Rican's image of self and world. Books about the Puerto Rican culture allege that geography and five hundred years of colonialism cause Puerto Ricans to internalize a deep sense of inferiority. Their island is small, and it lacks natural resources. Thus, they must be dependent on others for their survival. The great playwright, René Marqués, even wrote of the so-called "docile Puerto Rican"—sheepish at his or her core, this islander willingly takes orders from anyone in a position of authority.[19]

Although there is a *grain* of truth in these arguments, they miss as much as they explain. In a delightful way, many Puerto Ricans are utterly single-minded: The only thing they want to talk about is their beloved island and its splendid customs.[20] These people who are supposedly inferior don't recognize the existence of anything as wonderful as their 35 by 100 mile strip of the Caribbean. For example, when I asked a Northamerican friend to read this chapter, she looked at the lines about Andrés' Cap and said, "He smells his cap? And then he feels good? What's with this guy? Has he got problems?" Yes, he does. He longs for Puerto Rico, its rhythms, its very different sense of time, and, most important, its *utterly taken for granted* celebration of everything that is Puerto Rican. POW Carlos Alberto Torres says it "goes over people's heads." They don't see it because they live it. Especially in places like Vieques and the mountain towns of Jayuya and Utuado, one lives, eats, breathes, and thinks Puerto Rican. A person's home is a shrine to the culture. The Three Kings, a flag pillow, a straw hat on the wall, a cemí (one of the Taíno Indian gods) which has been carved from a coconut shell, the smell of empanadillas. As Carlos said, it has all the everyday significance of "being an earthling." Nobody is aware of it—until they arrive in the United States.

The U.S. has not one but many ethnic groups. And, instead of a celebration of self and society, Puerto Ricans often experience a painful sense of hate and rejection. POW Oscar López tells a story from the late 1950's. One of his dreams was to go to a ballgame and see the famous Puerto Rican star, Víctor Pellot. Oscar pestered his family until, finally, an uncle took him to a game between the Chicago White Sox and Pellot's team, the Cleveland Indians. Oscar, now fifteen, searched the program for Pellot's name. It didn't appear. Then, when the announcer called out the opposing line-ups, still no Pellot. Oscar asked his uncle why Pellot wasn't playing. His uncle told Oscar to look at first base, and he would see Pellot.

His uncle was right—"the only difference was that now he called himself Vic Power. I felt betrayed and angry. Why would a Puerto Rican change his name?" Oscar had no explanation until he read an autobiographical piece in which Pellot "explained the trials and tribulations he faced, including having to find hotels where only blacks would stay because he wasn't allowed in the same hotels as the white players."

Many immigrant groups experience prejudice and a sense of rejection. Among others, Irish, Italian, Jewish, and Japanese immigrants faced considerable hardships when they attempted to assimilate into American life. The "melting pot" ideal has always been an unrealized dream for those who advocate the willing acceptance of all newcomers.[21]

However, the Puerto Rican experience is unique in some ways. Those unique factors produced a revolutionary movement in the city of Chicago in the early 1970's.

The FALN

Born in Chicago in 1953, it took Alicia Rodríguez eighteen years to find the extra money needed to fulfill a lifelong dream: a visit to her homeland. A visit to Puerto Rico.

In Chicago, Alicia only heard about the island. She also heard she was "ugly" because her features were Latin and stupid because her English was imperfect. At home Alicia grew up in a family which matter-of-factly celebrated its ancestry. Her parents always spoke Spanish in the house; they ate Puerto Rican foods; and, despite a shortage of money, they maintained an atmosphere of so much love that Alicia believes she uses the world created by her mother and father as a model for the larger extended family she calls Puerto Rico. "*Mi papito*," a janitor, would work all night but still "wake up from sleep just to prepare us lunch. And, if it was raining, he would drive us to school rather than see us get wet." Her mother, who also worked, was a model for anyone; "Fifo" Rodríguez completed only the second grade in Puerto Rico, but she finished grammar school, high school and college in Illinois. She is warm, with a soft, endearing smile, and she is also intelligent, ambitious, and a tiny tower of real strength. Alicia says that when she had a problem at school, she never thought of bringing her father. Fifo had the will; Fifo would never let her accept injustice.

That was Alicia's foundation when she and her sister Evelyn got off a plane in an airport that somehow resembled her neighborhood. With a "heart pounding so wildly I thought it was going to fall out of my chest," Alicia remembers an airport that was, and to some extent remains, organized chaos. Scores of people waited for their relatives to appear; lots of noise, lots of children, lots of packages, and an "aroma" that instantly spelled home to Alicia. She walked out of the air-conditioned entrance hall, got slammed by the heat, embraced the half of the family she had never met, and, to her, "It was like we had never separated. I had arrived."

Alicia's eyes light up when she tells this story. After thirteen years in a high security prison, the forty-year-old woman still sounds like the eighteen-year-old kid because her delight in telling about those first family hugs is as real today as it was in 1971. Alicia was home and so were all the other people who got off the plane that warm and sunny day.

Like Alicia, Puerto Ricans are always going home. In 1971, the year of Alicia's first trip to the Caribbean, 1.6 million Puerto Ricans came to the United States and 1.6 million Puerto Ricans returned to the island. It was then and is now, a giant merry-go-round. For Alicia it was a trip of self-discovery. For others, it is an admission of defeat; they never found work in New York or Pennsylvania, so they will try to find a job at home. And, for still others, the trip home is a reward for the years in exile. One fellow I know drove a New York cab for twenty-five years. He and his wife saved their money and, in their early fifties, returned to a mountain top home where they peacefully grow everything from grapefruits to coffee, from papayas to flowers.

The merry-go-round prevents the assimilation so common to other ethnic groups. My father, for example, arrived from Spain in 1916. He next returned to his birthplace in 1969. Money was part of the problem but, like Polish, Russian, French, and Italian immigrants, there was also the issue of distance and citizenship. Europe was a long way off and, once he became an American, my father was no longer Spanish. He needed a passport to enter his homeland and, if he wanted to stay, he needed an identification card to prove his identity.

Puerto Ricans need only a ticket from American Airlines. They incessantly nurture the cultural roots that always have a potentially revolutionary component because, in trying to make sense of personal and ethnic experiences, a curious person must return to the issue of colonialism. Unlike any other immigrants to the United States, Puerto Ricans come from a land that has never resolved the most basic political question—that of status.

Dominicans can fight about the injustices of a particular regime. Cubans can plot to overthrow Castro and socialism. Exiled Grenadians can reject the leadership of Eric Gairy or Maurice Bishop. But Puerto Ricans never get that far. They must first decide what they will be, and another question inevitably follows: How did we get *here*? Who is responsible for a people without a country?

Alicia explains part of her transformation with

Andrés' Cap

stories from her trip. Some members of the family tried to impress her with a visit to a fancy tourist hotel. Alicia's reaction was one of revulsion. In a tone that still contains anger and contempt, she says, "I was so mad about tourism." The Puerto Ricans had all the lousy jobs; anglos had turned once public beaches into private enclaves; and, amazingly, none of her relatives was incensed. To Alicia, the hotels were a slap in the face. "I'm finally going home, this is my big chance to see Puerto Rico and outsiders are in charge. I felt trampelled upon. It was like someone had invaded *me*."

Alicia also went to Ponce. But, instead of the beauty championed by Manuel Caballer, she went to see a cousin who lived in a poor community. The "houses" were shacks, the entrance way a maze of wooden planks that led to a neighborhood which "almost made me fall back." There were "piles of garbage," chickens with puss oozing from their legs, and children swimming in a natural "pool" that was obviously polluted. In her nightmares Alicia still vividly sees the anemic dog with three legs and she still has the same question in 1993 that she first posed in 1971: Why?

The answer is not simple. In 1971 Alicia left Puerto Rico with more indignation than direction. But her first trip to *la Patria* was nevertheless a profoundly political encounter. An exceptionally decent and bright young woman had to know what had happened to her people and so did many of Alicia's neighbors in the North and South End of Chicago.

* * *

"Chicago is a city of neighborhoods." To Carlos Alberto Torres this was obvious. We sat in prison talking about Chicago, a city that was never a whole, but rather a series of neighborhoods which accentuated your identity as a Polish, Mexican, or Puerto Rican person.

The neighborhoods were self-contained. People "hung" with their own and, for Puerto Ricans, that self-and societal segregation produced a situation which unintentionally nourished a revolutionary assessment of the Puerto Rican experience. The perpetual celebration of culture was nourished by the traveling which was nourished by the neighborhood segregation which was nourished by the discrimination which was nourished by one of the most significant social movements in the Twentieth Century: civil rights.

Carlos talks about his father, the Reverend José A. Torres, universally *viejo* (the old one) to one and all in the North End. Viejo directed the First Congregational Church of Chicago, and one of Carlos earliest memories is a trip taken by his father. One reverend was marching in support of another. Viejo went to Selma to stand beside Martin Luther King, Jr. He never took Carlos because it was dangerous. With a bit of wistfulness, Carlos remembers his disappointment, and, with a great deal of pride, he remembers his father. *Lo quiero mucho*; "I love him a great deal. He challenged us to disregard color and he taught us to accept a sense of social responsibility."

The church that Carlos remembers was as much secular as sacred, as much devoted to change in the community as to peace in the afterlife. Viejo

162

was "the mayor of his little town;" he ran a "community development agency" called Casa Central out of the church, and if Carlos "always grew with the idea that you have to help people" he also grew up in a period of intense optimism. In the late sixties and early seventies, many Americans actually thought that people could not only fight city hall, they could beat it.

Civil rights initiated this sense of optimism. But then came the women's movement, the peace movement, the antiwar movement, the student rights movement, the environmental movement, the gay rights movement, the Black Panthers, Green Peace, and the Young Lords. The decade is a series of explosions; blink and you missed the creation of another movement dedicated to promoting some of the most revolutionary changes in American history. People burned bras, draft cards and flags; they wore long hair and they reveled in the personal symbols that were always political statements. A picture of POW Eddie Cortés taken in the early seventies shows an "afro" that reached into the heavens. He was proudly affirming a sense of pride that had many of its roots in the work of a man named Malcolm X.

In his still controversial autobiography, Malcolm X said that "the worst thing white people ever did to black people was make black people hate themselves." For him this self-hatred was repeated by ads in *Ebony* where readers were told to buy the whitening skin bleaches that made them run from themselves. That was self-defeating for blacks, and, as the ripples spread across American society, new organizations like Aspira and the Young Lords moved Puerto Ricans to preach pride, learn about their heritage.To deny it was, like the skin bleaches, denial is a form of self-hate.

Carlos remembers his first encounter with Aspira, literally STRIVE. "I don't know if Viejo wanted me to learn something about Puerto Rican culture or if he was simply trying to fill up chairs in the classroom of his friend, the woman who ran Aspira in Chicago." Whatever the case, Carlos went to school. He listened to the first lecture on the Taínos, and his life instantly changed. Indeed, even though our conversation was in a prison, with one guard outside the door and another "secretly" taping our conversation, Carlos seemed to be in that Chicago classroom. "It was sheer fascination...You mean to tell me that that is part of me? That's wonderful." And simply astonishing because Carlos learned that Puerto Rico not only had a history, it had one filled with beauty—and political events that challenged the "lessons" taught in the local elementary and high schools.

* * *

POW Eddie Cortés grew up in the South End of Chicago. But South or North, the message was the same: Puerto Ricans were invisible. Eddie, already sporting his afro, and eager to learn, wanted to know why no one ever taught the history of Puerto Rico. His civics teacher answered that Puerto Rico had no history.

Eddie remained silent. Then he went to work. With help from his brother Julio and POW Alberto Rodríguez, Eddie used the books made available by consciousness-raising groups like Aspira and the Young Lords. He wrote a paper on Pedro Albizu Campos. And, "after finishing my project, I had to give a presentation before the class." The presentation had little impact on the teacher; he refused to admit either his slur or his error. But, "my presentation did have a very strong impact on the other students because they had heard the teacher say that Puerto Rico had no history."

Like Alicia and Carlos, Eddie's search still had no direction. As Piri Thomas did in his wonderful *Down These Mean Streets*, Eddie was asking more questions than he was answering. But the national and local environment still taught a lesson which has long been forgotten: We shall overcome. Or, as Oscar López suggested to his comrades in the North End, use David's slingshot to fell the mighty Goliath.

Social scientists often discount the impact of personality. It's hard to quantify qualities like charisma, dedication, warmth, perseverance and exceptional intelligence.

In a 1971 picture of Oscar López Rivera, he is seated at a press conference. The issue was a new Puerto Rican principal for the local high school, the activist a 28-year-old Vietnam veteran. Oscar was still wearing his Army jacket, had long hair, intense eyes, and the trademark moustache that still dominates his face.

The war scarred, disillusioned, changed and empowered Oscar López Rivera. "When I arrived in Vietnam I was expecting to find the Vietnemese people welcoming us and expressing some gratitude for our presence. But what I found was distrust, resentment and even hostility. As an individual, because of my skin pigmentation, my size (Oscar is 5'5" tall), and my character I was treated very well by the Vietnemese peasants. Don't forget that I was raised as a peasant too (Oscar was 14 when he came to Chicago in 1957) . Wherever I went in Vietnam I would always find Vietnemese people putting their arms next to mine and saying 'same thing.' But that was not how they perceived U.S. soldiers and the U.S. military presence."

On one patrol Oscar and his squad discovered what appeared to be a sandbar. Yet, when they peered below they discovered a long tunnel that led to a gigantic room full of every imaginable weapon. To Oscar experiences like this proved the extent of official lying and the real level of native resistance. As he identified with the Vietnemese, Oscar also compared himself to African-Americans. "Vietnam brought home to me, in a most telling way, what an earlier generation of Puerto Rican patriots (e.g., those who fought in Korea) meant when they said that we and our African American brethren were being used as cannon fodder in the white's man's wars. I was sent into tunnels and designated to lead out in mine sweeping operations, convoy protection, pacification programs, reconnaissance, and search and destroy missions. I walked around with an M-16 rifle, at least 1000 rounds of ammunition, a 45 caliber pistol with five magazines, five hand grenades, and two gas grenades. I was trained to be a terrorist; and my role in Vietnam was to bring terror and havoc to the Vietnamese, I was there shooting and trying to kill people who had not done anything to the Puerto Rican people."

The accent was on Puerto Rican. That was and remains—in Chicago, in Vietnam, and in the gulag called Marion prison—Oscar's center and it bothers him that "one thing many people don't or can't understand is how many of us Puerto Rican soldiers saw ourselves in Vietnam. We never stopped being Puerto Ricans. I remember running into this Puerto Rican with a strange design on the camouflage of his helmet. I asked him what it was, and he said it was a Puerto Rican flag. So I took a magic marker and painted one on my helmet. That was the way many of us identified ourselves. We knew the person was Puerto Rican as soon as we would look at the helmet. It was our Puerto Rican identity that made us a different kind of soldier. We would listen to our salsa music together, get high together and celebrate every moment one of us left for home. The bonding was so strong that other soldiers looked at us differently."

Like the song says, "I would be a Puerto Rican even if I was born on the moon or even if I was an alien in army of mercenaries." Oscar clung to his "puertorriqueñidad for dear life" but "as I write this letter to you I can still hear the sounds of those suction wounds, sucking a young man's life away. I can still hear the voices of my friends asking me how bad were their wounds. I can still see the face of a Chicano friend who set-off a booby trap and when I tore up his pants legs to apply a torniquet, asking me where he had been hit. His testicles were in the open and full of shrapnel, and I had to tell him a lie in order to prevent him from going into a trauma. Such a reality forces any person to question and to be critical. So when I come back to Chicago, I did what I couldn't do in Vietnam: Find out what the war was all about. And that I did. So my first conscious political act was around Vietnam."

Just before he left, Oscar called his mother. "I learned from letters that...in June 1966, when the Chicago Puerto Rican community held its first parade, the cops shot and wounded a little girl. That was the proverbial "spark." The community retaliated; some policemen got so scared they abandoned their vehicles. When I was able to get through on the telephone to my mother (arranged through a CBS television reporter who had interviewed me for a documentary) the first thing she told me was that, as a Puerto Rican, I was probably safer in Vietnam than on Division Street. In the background I could actually hear police gunfire. When I came back to Chicago my friends had many stories to tell me about what they had done to the police. Those years of pent-up rage, anger and frustration had found some release."

Oscar left one war to fight another. The Vietnamese had shown him that the weak could defeat the strong. And they also emphasized the significance of official labeling. "At no time during my Vietnam experience did the U.S. government call me a terrorist or (like today) a 'notorious and incorrigible criminal.' Quite the contrary, the United States Army gave me a bronze star, a medal for 'meritorious achievement in the Republic of Vietnam.' I was a 'good' Puerto Rican then, another one of the 250,000 compatriots who, since 1917, have been members of the U.S. armed forces. I was sent to Vietnam to do what good colonized people do; protect the economic, military and political interests of the colonizer."[22]

Oscar reached this political conclusion over time. When he first returned from Vietnam, he only carried a knapsack full of questions, the will to answer them, and a profound sense of self-respect. Oscar López Rivera was (and is) personally offended by racism and discrimination. And not because someone said he was a "spic" or a "pork chop," the hateful term used in Chicago. "In Puerto Rico we never experienced the racism we faced in the diaspora. Consequently, we weren't prepared for it. I'm not saying that racism doesn't exist in Puerto Rico. What I'm saying is that we were thrust into an environment that was very hostile and we weren't prepared for the rejection we encountered."

Oscar began to worry about the children. He visited one of the elementary schools "and found that the Puerto Rican students who didn't speak English had been assigned to the EMH (emotionally and mentally handicapped) classrooms. I was shocked and full of rage. I asked the principal if she placed the Polish, Italian or any other European ethnic students who came to the school in the EMH classes. When she said no, I asked her what rationale (one that was academically sound) was she using to justify such an injustice."

Since the principal had no answer, Oscar entered what might be called the reform stage of his political life. One of his "activities" that still brings smiles to the people on Division Street/Pedro Albizu Campos Boulevard was a tenants' strike. "There was a large apartment complex where the tenants had been left without heat in the middle of winter." There were also a number of cockroaches whom the landlord refused to evict. So, modeling his approach after a successful strike in Harlem, Oscar organized the tenants to hold back their rent. And, when that didn't work, they found out where this pillar of the community lived, they drove to the suburbs, picketed his house, and even delivered an unforgettable Christmas present: A large box of cockroaches.

Oscar (and Carmen Valentín and Carlos Alberto Torres) had come to an important conclusion: "Puerto Ricans are the by-product of centuries of colonialism. As a colonized nation or people we haven't been able to create our own structures of power. The structures of power in Puerto Rico, including the Catholic Church, represent the interest of the colonizer. So when Puerto Ricans settle in the diaspora we don't bring our institutions with us because they aren't ours."

Puerto Ricans were weak; and the way to make them strong was to create the grassroots organizations which, as they changed social conditions, opened people to the underlying causes of migration and poverty, racism and cockroaches. On the street, the Young Lords were striving for similar goals, but they sounded like Hippies when they told family-centered Puerto Ricans to live in communes; and they sounded dangerous when their paramilitary formations marched through the streets of the North End. To a *jíbaro* from Arecibo or Utuado the Lords might as well have been aliens from California; few understood their militancy because the Young Lords had never done the years of community ground work required for "average" people to generously support activists in search of social change.

Groups like the Black Panthers and the Young Lords were preaching the need for everything from a change of culture to guerrilla warfare. Meanwhile, using the message of his *Reveille For Radicals,* men like Saul Alinsky were changing Chicago by creating organizations with deep roots in the neighborhoods. In nearby Woodlawn, African-Americans had created a community organization dedicated to goals like integration and decent housing. They actively "looked for grievances that would galvanize the community" and they settled on a "great villain": The University of Chicago.[23]

In the North End, Oscar and Carmen Valentín (among others) settled on an easier target: They wanted a new curriculum at Tuley High School. Carmen explains her involvement: "From the deplorable conditions which poverty brings about, I ascended. I decided I'd have to do something with my life so that I could then help other people. So my first thought was to go to school and get an education, which I did...After I finished my education, my first and most desired thought was to go back to my people and assist them. I became a high school teacher in a predominantly Puerto Rican high school...There I worked hand in hand with the community in attempting to change the type of conditions that the students were facing, because we had a tremendous drop-out rate in that school—72.9% of the students dropped out. So I thought it had a relationship to the kinds of teaching, or the kinds of programs, curriculum, that the school had. So the first thing I decided was to get the parents involved and to try, attempt to change curriculum, change teachers, change principals."

At Tuley, the principal's name (and this is the truth) was Burton Fink. He utterly opposed the changes Carmen suggested, and she just as utterly opposed his continued tenure at Tuley . One result was a student strike. The newspaper photos show police trying to separate faculty and students, protesters and supporters (of Principal Fink), bystanders and community activists. Ultimately, the principal left, and the school even changed its name to that of a Puerto Rican named Roberto Clemente. But, after she successfully organized a permanent body for change—the Parent Council—Carmen lost her job. She believes the authorities "saw it was getting out of hand" so they moved her to a spot where she would be theoretically neutralized.

It didn't work. "From there I became actively involved in many other types of community development projects, such as health services, anti-police brutality groups, drug rehabilitation programs" and even trips to prison. As a volunteer, Carmen taught Puerto Rican history and culture to inmates at the Stateville prison in Joliet, Illinois.

"What it all starts out as is an affirmation of nationality. But then the beauty of it is it develops into a more sophisticated type of struggle. Because as you see people demanding their rights and involved in different types of struggle, you see that they have a tremendous potential, and you have awakened something in them which you all of a sudden realize that there is that potential in every human to want to change, to demand change. So then as you see this, how most of us came to realize this was when we saw that we were demanding small minor changes, small reforms within the system, and they were totally ignored. At the same time we saw a tremendous amount of fear in the system's representatives, so it gave us a sense of curiosity at the same time. Why are these small demands such a threatening type of thing? So we started to investigate and we started to realize that, yes, that's the basic steps of revolutionaries. They have to demand, and they have got to get other people to demand, and from there eventually massive types of demands will evolve, and you will have some kind of significant change."

But not without pain. Action produces reaction. Try to promote social change and others will surely try to resist it. It's a dialectical relationship that produced death, destruction, disillusionment and anger in Chicago's Puerto Rican community.

Oscar writes of a couple of successes. Cockroaches for Christmas moved the absentee landlord to repair and even repaint some of his decrepit buildings. "But we did not enjoy the complex's new look because shortly thereafter the buildings began to be mysteriously set on fire...Landlords had found a solution to the problem of pestering tenants: arson for profit." To landlords the lure of ghetto housing was the nature of the tenants. They were a captive audience, zoned out of the suburbs by everything from a lack of money to deliberately restrictive zoning regulations. Thus, landlords could use the apartments as a tax write-off and never repair them because the tenants had no other available housing.

"But, once the tenants began to organize, the landlords had trouble collecting their rents unless they were willing to make the necessary repairs. The solution was to set the buildings on fire in order to collect on the insurance. The buildings, while being torched, were occupied by living, breathing people, by babies and grandmothers—Puerto Rican and African-American babies and grandmothers. But to the landlords, these were folks who did not matter. In the fall of 1971, in East Humbolt Park, 13 innocent people—nine of them children—were killed as a result of one of these arson-for-profit schemes. The adults who died in that fire were people I had known for years, having practically grown up with them; and the children I had played with. The deaths were a tremendous blow to me. Although the Fire Department ruled the cause of the fire to be arson, that is as far as they went with any type of investigation. No one was ever charged for what was clearly a case of murder."

Like Carmen, Oscar began to ask the questions that always returned to the same points of origin: An affirmation of nationality married to a demand for "social and economic justice for our people." On July 27, 1993, in the prison at Oxford, Wisconsin, Carlos Alberto Torres quietly but emphatically emphasized this fact: "Any affront to the Puerto Rican people I take personally." Meanwhile, on July 15, 1993, in the Marion prison in Illinois, Oscar López Rivera stressed that "it's often said that Puerto Ricans in the diaspora live 'statehood' everyday. If it's true then it would be the ultimate absurdity for Puerto Ricans in the diaspora, who are politically conscious, to identify with anything which is anathema to his/her *puertorriqueñidad*. But to affirm our *puertorriqueñidad* and defend it, we have to be willing to make the necessary sacrifices. And it's easier to applaud the sacrifices others make than to make them ourselves. *And here we find a dilemma that many would prefer to avoid. It's the choice between sacrificing to achieve self-determination (which is part and parcel of our national identity) and becoming a pariah existing in a political limbo.*" (my emphasis)

Chicago had become a political limbo. Even the demands for small changes were "completely ignored," and to identify with a system which burned some youngsters, as it arbitrarily confined others to EMH classes, was an invitation to both failure and self-deprecation. Together, Carmen and Oscar, Carlos Torres and (his stepmother) Alejandrina Torres, Luz Rodríguez (Oscar's wife) and Haydée Beltrán (Carlos' wife) tried to fabricate alternative visions of social change. They ultimately decided—the words are Oscar's—that "the liberation of our homeland was the only true source of empowerment and respect" but they came to this conclusion over time, after a great deal of painful soul searching and, as a result of contact with a variety of people who had never lived in the North and South Ends of Chicago.

Vital ingredients in the transformations of these Puerto Rican patriots were: the five POW's (Oscar Collazo, Lolita Lebrón, Irving Flores, Rafael Cancel Miranda, Andrés Figueroa) then in U.S. jails, the violent resistance to the United States in Puerto Rico, the FBI's efforts to disrupt the Puerto Rican independence movement, and the cynicism of Presidents Kennedy, Johnson, and Nixon. This "melting pot" of factors moved a group of Puerto Rican patriots to formally and reluctantly declare

175

war, not against the people of the United States, but against the crime and consequences of colonialism.

The 1967 Plebiscite

On November 14, 1993 the Puerto Rican people voted in a referendum offering three political choices: Statehood, Commonwealth, or Independence. It specified none of the conditions for the results. For example, on the statehood option, there was no mention of whether the new state's official language would be Spanish or English. Most important of all, the referendum was non-binding on Congress. Nothing was promised to the Puerto Rican people.

The results of the plebiscite were a victory for the status quo. Commonwealth defeated statehood by a very narrow margin. In Washington, many congresspeople were delighted because they neither had to refuse statehood or independence to Puerto Rico. Given the arrangement of U.S. business interests with regard to the island, a victory for independence or statehood would have caused large capital flight and imposed a huge sacrifice on the people.

Governor Pedro Roselló, elected in 1992 on a statehood platform, advocated the referendum even though his position contradicts the one taken by many of his statehood predecessors. In fact, when Governor Muñoz Marín suggested a non-binding plebiscite in 1962, the island based resistance was so great that White House aides sent a memo to President John Kennedy: "After Governor Muñoz proposed this, his opposition, the Statehood Republican Party, threatened to boycott the plebiscite on the ground that it was senseless for the people of Puerto Rico to express their view if there were not some commitment from the Congress to give consideration to their choice. Governor Muñoz decided that he could not conduct a plebiscite as long as they refused to participate and now proposes that Congress express its sympathy and support for a plebiscite."[24]

The governor's request initiated a five-year process. In the end nothing changed. But to understand what happened in Chicago in the 70s, it is essential to first grasp what happened in Washington in the 60s.

President Kennedy initially backed Muñoz's requests for what was soon called "enhanced commonwealth." In Luquillo, Puerto Rico, a group of White House (e.g. Adolph Berle and Arthur Schlesinger) and island advisors fleshed out a vision which included substantially greater powers for the Commonwealth government. The president's advisors initially thought these looked "quite desirable and satisfactory." Within weeks, however, the desirable had turned into a "completely hopeless process" because Muñoz wanted something that strongly resembled independence: As his advisors explained it, John Kennedy had to agree to "the establishment of a system under which over two and one-half million United States citizens will be permanently free of substantially all legislative regulation by the United States."

On the beach in Luquillo this seemed acceptable; in Washington it was out of the question. Thus, the president privately opted for a commission to study the Puerto Rican situation; this group would take years to complete its work and, with luck, by the time the commission submitted a report Puerto Ricans would have forgotten about enhanced commonwealth. Meanwhile, the president allowed the governor to be humiliated by Congress, and, adding insult to injury, the president followed the terrible example set by Congressman Saylor of Pennsylvania.

In May of 1963 Saylor told Muñoz to remember the June 1950 words of Fred Crawford. The same man who had called Puerto Ricans subjects had also told his congressional colleagues that "we are not offering the people of Puerto Rico anything except the right to vote on a constitution to be submitted to the president of the United States who in turn is to submit it to the Congress of the United States for approval."

This was an open challenge in a very public forum; it contradicted what the governor had been telling his people for eleven years. But, not satisfied with recalling the words of Fred Crawford, Saylor added some of his own: "All of this commonwealth that you keep talking about ...are things which have been built up under your administration in Puerto Rico and have not been the intention of Congress then, and I hope not now."[25]

Muñoz answered that he had great respect for Fred Crawford, but "if he was right, then Puerto Rico is still a colony of the United States. If it is still a colony of the United States, it should stop being a colony as soon as possible for the honor of the United States and for the sense of self-respect of the people of Puerto Rico."[26]

With these words Muñoz showed that Oscar López Rivera was not the only Puerto Rican who cared about self-respect. However, as the 19-year-

178

old Chicagoan prepared for Vietnam, the governor prepared for the afternoon's hearings. He expected the president to keep his word, but John Kennedy killed Commonwealth. In Puerto Rico, the Assembly had voted to accept an "enhanced commonwealth" that was a *permanent* commitment on the part of the United States. By mid-afternoon the administration still "strongly favored the perfection of existing arrangements with the understanding, however, that actions taken now cannot and should not be considered binding for all time in the future."[27]

Seated in the audience, a young journalist named Alex Maldonado immediately grasped the significance of the administration's new position: "The Commonwealth has died."[28] Congress had yet to offer any enhancement of Commonwealth but, even if it did, without a permanent arrangement Congress could take away whatever it gave, whenever it pleased. That spelled humiliation for Muñoz, but in explaining Congress's position, Congressman Saylor said "we have 2.5 million Puerto Ricans now living in Puerto Rico under a strange status and you can find absolutely nothing in our Constitution to authorize it." Congressman O'Brien of New York was even more emphatic: "Why, then, do we need this study [i.e., the commission promised by the president]? Why not leave well enough alone? The answer is this: No one, in or out of Congress, or in or out of Puerto Rico knows exactly what the Commonwealth of Puerto Rico is."[29]

However, many people knew that Puerto Rico was a colony. Muñoz said so when he correctly interpreted the words of Fred Crawford but for the governor to face the truth was to recognize a decade of lying to his own people; and for Congress, the truth was simply irrelevant. A reading of the congressional debates makes clear that the only serious issues were to avoid letting the Puerto Ricans use the commission as a way of "opening the door to statehood;" and, equally important, something had to be done about Fidel Castro. To ward off the appeal of the Cuban revolutionary, Washington had to show the Puerto Ricans it cared. So, Congressman O'Brien first assured his colleagues that "this bill promises nothing more than a high level study; it does not prejudge anything or commit Congress to anything." However, "this study will serve to calm temporarily the winds and waves of controversy which have battered at congressional doors. Need I say that there never was a better time for a temporary surcease of controversy in the Caribbean area."[30]

The Commission was created, the winds of change temporarily stilled. But the Johnson administration played politics with the new commission. In explaining its role to a president who knew almost nothing about Puerto Rico, Lyndon Johnson was told that Commonwealth "involves the most difficult and painstaking study and review in almost every aspect of government;" meanwhile, statehood "does not seem anywhere near feasible at this point; it cannot however be left out as a possibility for political reasons. Muñoz's opposition party uses this as their chief means of holding the group together." Independence had to be "regarded as a possibility to offset charges of "colonialism" made by Castro and other Communist elements in the Caribbean and South America."[31]

Since statehood was nowhere near feasible, and independence nothing more than a ploy to appease revolutionaries like Fidel Castro, the Johnson administration settled on the "strange status" called commonwealth would win any White House referendum. But, to assure the same conclusion in Puerto Rico, the president was told that "this Commission includes congressional representation *in order to provide the Commission with some guide as to what would be acceptable to Congress and how to present it.*"[32]

The last thing the administration wanted was a repetition of President Truman's veto of the 1946 plebiscite; thus, "since it is generally agreed that the U.S. could suffer some international loss of prestige if a program supported by the administration to grant greater autonomy and freedom were defeated in Congress," the Johnson administration supported self-determination by predetermining it. The Puerto Ricans would be asked to vote only on a program that was acceptable to Congress; and, given congressional dominance in the creation of any new status plan, the administration had also neatly assured itself of "a natural body of support for it [the plan] when the recommendations were submitted."[33]

When the president finally met the members of the Status Commission on June 9, 1964, he did so because of political advantages in the United States. His friend, James Rowe, wrote a memo that said, "As you probably recall, you appointed me Chairman of the above-captioned Commission." Rowe had to call a meeting—"the press is pounding me to carry out the congressional statue which directs the Chairman to call an organizing meeting 'as soon as possible'—and another was the possible attendance of the president. Rowe thought the president should come and so did Lee White, his point man on Puerto Rico. "Presidential interest in Puerto Rican affairs could be helpful in the large Puerto Rican communities of New York City and Chicago." So, the president should personally applaud the Commission's effort but, as Rowe reminded him at the end of the memo, "Of course, you yourself would not have to devote more than 10 or 15 minutes of your own time to this, if it is politically desirable in terms of New York."[34]

Johnson went to the meeting. He underlined "the firm dedication of the United States to the principles of self-determination for all peoples;" he let photographers snap pictures which appeared in the New York and Chicago newspapers. Two years later, he was asked to do the same thing again.

James Rowe sent another memo to the president on July 28, 1966. It begins with another reminder: "As you may recall you appointed me Chairman of the (Status) Commission." The commission had now completed its work "and the question is how the president wants this handled." Rowe asked "what, if anything would a formal presentation do to *help* President Johnson?" (emphasis in original). Rowe had no specific list of pluses but he nevertheless suggested that the president attend.

"For one thing the Puerto Ricans are a formal lot, loving ceremony and ritual. They are fast becoming a balance of power in New York State politics, are a minority group which occasionally, but not often mutter about favoritism toward the

Negroes. Certainly they are not alienated today like the Mexican-Americans. But they are sensitive and proud."

So, pacify them with a ceremony and remember that "the Report itself is, I think, a safe one. It does *not* recommend to the president or the Congress that he or they *do* anything."[35] (emphasis in original) Thus, just as President Kennedy hoped, the Commission first bought time and then affirmed the status quo by recommending nothing.

However, Senator "Scoop" Jackson planned to make a statement "that Congress can act unilaterally without the consent of Puerto Rico." As Rowe explained it to the president, "this is an irreconcilable conflict between Governor Muñoz and Senator Jackson. No agreement is possible but we have 'fuzzed' it over...my own view is that this is one of those academic and legalistic arguments that are always better avoided if possible."[36]

Like his predecessor, President Johnson agreed to avoid it. But, instead of an academic argument, the issue between Jackson and Muñoz was the key to a fifteen year debate. The Senator's public reassertion of Congress plenary power proved that nothing fundamental changed in 1952. Puerto Rico was still a colony. After Senator Jackson got his shot at Muñoz, he then did the same thing to the statehooders. They would speak English if they became a state or they would remain an unincorporated part of the United States.

Senator Jackson made clear "what was acceptable to Congress." So, in 1967 some of the Puerto Rican people participated in a referendum that, as the statehooders and *independentistas* both stressed, was senseless unless Congress specified the conditions applicable to each status. Instead, the referendum simply listed the name of each political alternative. That led to a boycott of the plebiscite by a substantial number of statehood and independence supporters. They cried "farce" while, the day *before* the vote took place, Muñoz sent the White House two drafts of a presidential statement celebrating the victory of Commonwealth.

The victory statements were actually addressed to Supreme Court Justice Abe Fortas. Since his refusal in 1944 to return Vieques lands to the people, Fortas had been deeply involved in Puerto Rican policy. He was also a key advisor to President Johnson and a close friend of Luis Muñoz Marín. Fortas read and then edited the victory statement written by a shrewd politician. Muñoz had tried to slip one by the administration. He wrote that "the people of Puerto Rico have earned and deserve our fullest cooperation in the further development of their close and now unalterable relationship to the United States."

Fortas crossed out "and now unalterable." He wrote "no" near Muñoz's words, and he initialled his own changes. Thus, Congress was still in charge; the president applauded the overwhelming endorsement of Commonwealth (it received over 60% of the vote); he never mentioned the boycott, and, in another slap at Muñoz, Lyndon Johnson said "I am, of course, deeply gratified that 99.4% of those who went to the polls expressed an abiding loyalty to the permanent union of Puerto Rico and the United States *on the basis* of our common American citizenship." (emphasis added)

In this neat "fuzzing" of the colonial issue, the president closed the door on both change and the "expressed" will of the Puerto Rican people. Before the United Nations the United States loudly argued that the plebiscite fulfilled Washington's historic commitment to the self-determination of all people's. When that argument failed to convince delegates, Ambassador Goldberg told the White House that he "pulled out all the stops to block" any attempt to discuss Puerto Rico before the U.N.'s decolonization Committee.

Meanwhile, both statehooders and independence advocates criticized the "farcical" process endorsed by the White House. They openly argued that the island was still a colony—an argument that made sense to the young activists in Chicago, and meshed with an accusation then made by virtually all segments of the independence movement: The FBI had subverted the 1967 plebiscite and it was even interfering in the 1968 gubernatorial elections.

COINTELPRO

In August of 1960, J. Edgar Hoover told the chief of the FBI's San Juan, New York and Chicago offices that he "was considering the feasibility of instituting a program of disruption to be directed against organizations which seek independence for Puerto Rico through other than lawful, peaceful means." Hoover worried about the "boldness" of what he called subversive groups so he told his subordinates that "in considering this matter you should bear in mind that the Bureau desires to disrupt the activities of these organizations and is not interested in mere harassment."[37]

Within months, agents in San Juan prepared a plan which pleased Director Hoover. To produce the desired disruption, the FBI planned to use informants "to point out to one, the inefficiency of the other and in general conversation 'fan the fire' of existing friction thereby helping to bring about a factional spilt." If this didn't work, the Bureau planned to use a mix of anonymous letters and mimeographed flyers "criticizing the leadership of the organization and giving the impression that it had been prepared by another pro-independence group."[38]

The FBI used a variety of "dirty tricks." This characterization was made by an aide of President Carter who (in 1978) surveyed ten volumes of relevant FBI documents. The aide was quite disturbed by tactics which included "enlisting informant disrupters...planting stories (e.g. that one fellow was sleeping with another's wife) and cartoons in newspapers; possibly buying off a newspaper columnist; and conducting what were referred to as "aggressive interviews" of suspects." While beating people up was the appropriate characterization for this FBI tactic, what especially bothered the Carter aide was a tactical shift that occurred in 1966. A campaign that first focused on alleged subversives had turned into a scheme against the independence groups which accepted the legitimacy of the Commonwealth government.

As the plebiscite approached, a militant group called the MPI (Movimiento Pro Independencia) hoped to join forces with the Puerto Rican Independence Party. The latter had always participated in the elections but, agreeing with many statehooders that the plebiscite was a farce, the PIP planned a nationwide campaign to boycott the 1967 vote. The FBI feared that unified resistance could seriously embarrass both Washington and San Juan, so, as the plebiscite approached, it sent "informant disrupters" into an unquestionably legal political party.

"The disruption campaign was not very subtle." During and after the plebiscite, independence advocates repeatedly complained about the FBI but agents said the independentistas were paranoid as they simultaneously planned a campaign to disrupt the 1968 elections. A split in the dominant Commonwealth party opened the door to a victory by the statehooders, or, even worse, a victory by an alliance of independentistas and dissatisfied Commonwealthers. This was a possibility J. Edgar Hoover refused to countenance so, through 1968 the FBI dug into its bag of disruptive techniques to "keep the PIP from joining the dissident (Commonwealth) group."

The FBI's continued antidemocratic activities had two effects on the groups then thinking about a revolutionary posture. One was summarized by the Carter official in 1978: "The U.S. has repeatedly and pridefully declared its policy on political status to be that of self-determination. Yet here is a record of a decade of hanky-panky. Conceivably, the FBI might be forgiven for keeping a watchful eye on violence prone groups, including the MPI. What is not acceptable is a campaign of disruption of what functioned as a legally constituted party...What is most damaging is the FBI swashbuckling at the time of the plebiscite (*is that self-determination?*) and even at the time of the 1968 election."[39] (emphasis added)

Thus, one effect of the FBI's activities was to help make revolution both understandable and legitimate. Beginning in 1963 Presidents Kennedy and Johnson structured a plebiscite that was a caricature of self-determination; and then the FBI used its arsenal of dirty tricks to undermine whatever remaining legitimacy the plebiscite possessed. Where was the self-determination promised by Washington? Given Congressman Saylor's and Senator Jackson's public reaffirmation of Congress' plenary power, Puerto Rico was no less a colony in 1971 than it was in 1951.

A second effect of the FBI's activities was to "suggest" a revolutionary strategy of clandestinity. A proud hallmark of the Nationalist Party was that it wore its guns on the outside; and, in New York and Chicago, the Young Lords kept their guns hidden, but their uniforms, insignias, berets, and marches were like a gift to the FBI, saying "Here I am. Come and disrupt me whenever you please."

In the environment produced by a decade of dirty tricks, anyone inclined to adopt a revolutionary posture had to operate in small groups—to reduce the risk of "informant disrupters"—and they had to operate in clandestinity. POW Carlos Alberto Torres says that "although I am uncertain as to the precise duration, the frequency and method of the surveillance, I would say that it was frequent probably from 1972 on." That was two years before the FALN even announced its existence, yet Carlos, then only involved in efforts to remove a principal and improve the quality of housing, says "if I looked out my window I could expect to see an agent staring back at me. When I opened and closed my car door, it was as if I were in an echo chamber listening to two, three, or four other doors simultaneously opening and slamming shut. When I turned the ignition in my car, I could almost—if not actually—hear two or three different engines turning over. After a time I was also able to recognize the different cars and faces of the agents...My family members, relatives and friends were approached and asked to participate in and collaborate with different facets of the investigation...In some cases old family friends and some relations actually lent themselves to the lowly and philistinic practice of collaborating with the police for praise or profit. In some cases, uncooperative family members and friends were accosted by police agents, sometimes quite brutally."

The FBI helped produce the FALN and so did the example set by a number of young Puerto Ricans who were resisting U.S. authority in a variety of new and traditional forms. POW Elizam Escobar writes that "this was the mid-sixties: the Vietnam War, compulsory military service, struggle against the ROTC presence on campus—in short, the most militant period of student activism in Puerto Rico and around the world. I was incarcerated for one day the first of three times I refused to enter the U.S. Army."

Elizam opposed the "Blood Tax" and so did a number of the activists who would later join *Los Macheteros*. Roberto Maldonado, Jorge Farinacci and Hilton Diamante Fernández all participated in the anti-draft efforts that produced serious confrontations with island and federal authorities. In September of 1969, for example, students at the Rio

Piedras campus of the University of Puerto Rico took over the ROTC building. They burned part of it, hauled down the stars and stripes, and, with only the Puerto Rican flag flying, 3000-4000 students proudly sang *La Borinqueña*, the national anthem of Puerto Rico.

This was a mild disturbance compared to the efforts of a new revolutionary organization: CAL, or Comandos Armados de Liberación. In February of 1968 CAL announced its aims, which were nothing less than "the national liberation of Puerto Rico through armed action; an end to the monopolistic control of industry and commerce in Puerto Rico by U.S. firms; and the expulsion of all U.S. firms from Puerto Rico." Within a week CAL had set off eleven bombs throughout the island (including the Shell Oil pipeline) and within a year it had issued this warning: "We will not lose sight of the real enemy: The Yankee imperialists. Therefore we undertake the commitment, which today we renew before the patriotic people of Puerto Rico, that for each young Puerto Rican jailed for refusing to serve in the U.S. armed forces, we will execute one Yankee."[40]

This was not an idle threat. When, on March 4, 1970, Antonia Martínez Legares was killed during an anti-ROTC demonstration at the university, CAL "executed [the next day] two U.S. Marines in San Juan in retaliation for the murder of Antonia Martínez." CAL also bombed U.S. banks, department stores, and on September 12, 1971, CAL set off a bomb at the U.S. governors conference at the El San Juan Hotel.

In Washington, officials argued that the three years of violence reflected the sentiments of a lunatic fringe; meanwhile, in San Juan, the union feared by J. Edgar Hoover had already taken place. Revolutionary and "legitimate" independentistas joined forces to stage one of the largest anti-American demonstrations in the island's history. Estimates varied, but on September 12, 1971—the birthdate of Albizu Campos—between 30,000 and 100,000 Puerto Ricans took to the streets to protest any U.S. governors conference on Puerto Rican soil. Governor Luis Ferré might have wanted statehood, but a substantial body of "average" citizens openly expressed their indignation when he tried to treat Puerto Rico as if it was a part of the United States.

Those demonstrators would have been even more angry if Luis Ferré had leveled with his own people. In public he claimed influence in Washington; in reality he had trouble getting the president to notice his existence. On July, 30, 1969 for example, White House aides said that "the governor of Puerto Rico is getting ants in his pants for an appointment with the president." His prestige was "on the line" so President Nixon agreed to a five minute encounter but Ferré had to "understand that this will be a quick picture-taking session ...."[41]

By May 1971 Ferré wanted another five minutes of the president's time. If nothing else, three years of anti-american demonstrations had taken their toll, so he wanted to show that Richard Nixon still supported both Luis Ferré and his statehood ideals. On May 28th, 1971 the governor got almost twenty minutes in the president's presence but White House aides once again emphasized that this was "a courtesy meeting with very little substance involved." This was a "quick Puerto Rican photo opportunity." Selected media from island could snap shots while President Nixon, "got some film in the can for 1972 for targeted media advertising in Puerto Rican areas."[42]

The last scene in this drama occurred in November of 1971. More anti-american demonstrations in San Juan, Culebra, and Vieques moved Ferré to request yet another batch of photos. In the handwritten response to the governor's request, President Nixon's assistant said this: "Ferré already *has had* a meeting with Pres in the pictures of May 28, 1971. A new picture would help Ferré—he has been loyal—only marginal help for Pres. in Puerto Rican and Spanish districts: Recommendation: Only if the president has time. Not a high priority."[43] (emphasis in original)

Ferré knew the truth. A memo in the Johnson Library—dated July 18, 1968—notes that "Ferré talked to 11 or 12 members of Congress and found a general ignorance of Puerto Rican problems which amazed him." From 1969 through 1971 the governor had to have ants in his pants just to get five minutes of the president's time and even then he only got the second photo opportunity so that Nixon could use Ferré to get votes in New York and Chicago.

Washington's cynicism might have changed the mind of a less devoted statehooder. Ferré simply deceived his people. Ferré lost the 1972 elections. His successor was Rafael Hernández Colón, a strong advocate of Commonwealth status, and by any political definition, a centrist. However, the White House thought of him as such a "radical" that even George Bush (then Chairman of the Republican National Committee) couldn't get Hernández Colón an appointment with the president. Bush agreed that the new governor "made a mistake in getting too political. He went to the Democratic National Convention. He backed McGovern." However, Hernández Colón was repentant. "I talked to Colón at the governor's dinner at the White House. He reiterated his willingness to cooperate and to stay out of domestic politics. He was attending a dinner for Congressman Badillo but emphasized it was strictly because Badillo is Puerto Rican."[44]

A critic with a sense of humor noted that Puerto Ricans were citizens but they also had to stay out of domestic politics. Hernández agreed to follow orders but the White House still refused him an appointment. A March 16, 1973 memo from the National Security Council noted that "a presidential meeting is not called for because we do not know what the governor wants. Furthermore, the governor is apparently surrounded by various nationalistic advisors—some of whom allegedly advocate independence—which could embarrass the president. From a foreign policy standpoint, there is no need for the president and the governor to discuss Puerto Rico as a colonial issue in the UN."[45]

Although the United States supposedly favored self-determination, even an "allegation" of independence sentiment meant the governor of Puerto Rico was a radical who deserved no White House appointment. Hernández ultimately settled for a status commission that would discuss—with no promises from Washington—the enhancement of Commonwealth. When that Commission met Hernández Colón offered many of the exact same suggestions made by Muñoz Marín in 1959, 1962, and 1966. Ever the optimist, Hernández not only hoped for success, in April of 1974 he asked Senator

Henry Jackson to visit Puerto Rico. At a news conference called by the governor, Hernández said Jackson
"was the man with the best knowledge of Puerto Rico
in Congress." He was also the one with the most
power and in a public statement the senior Senator
from Washington offered this assessment of Puerto
Rico's past, present and future: The island had
become "part of the U.S. by an act of conquest." The
United States wouldn't allow it to be independent. It
might consider statehood if English was the dominant
language. But, since even that seemed unlikely,
"Puerto Rico must remain a colony."[46]

The governor asked his legislature to censure
the senator. Actually all Jackson had done was be
brutally honest. He told Puerto Ricans what Muñoz,
Ferré, and Hernández refused to publicly concede:
The arrogance, indifference, ignorance and imperialism of Congress and the White House.

While Hernández went back to the bargaining
table, in the United States a new revolutionary
group announced its existence on October 26, 1974.
The FALN—the Armed Forces of National
Liberation—took credit for the September 28 bombing of the Newark, New Jersey Police Headquarters
and City Hall. In their communique, the FALN said
that "we have opened two fronts, one in Puerto Rico,
the other in the United States, both nourished by
the Puerto Rican people...."

The FALN was deliberately imitating the actions
of the Nationalists in 1950 and 1954. Puerto Ricans
were making war on the symbols of U.S. imperialism
because revolution was the duty of any patriot who
refused to accept a future that mirrored the past.
Despite Senator Jackson, Puerto Rico would not
remain a U.S. colony.

Revolutionary Violence

"Until we found our own means of manufacturing substantial quantities of explosives—the main weapon in the struggle for liberation—...the major part of our T.N.T. was acquired from Arab suppliers."

—Menachim Begin, Prime Minister of Israel, 1977[1]

As a close aide of President Jimmy Carter, Hamilton Jordan met with pro-statehood Governor Romero Barceló in the summer of 1977. During the meeting the governor "raised the situation of the 5 prisoners who have been in jail for the shooting in the House of Representatives during the Truman administration." Jordan knew nothing about the prisoners, but he was told that President Ford "offered them a pardon if they would accept some blame." They refused to do so. Meanwhile, "the governor says it is a continuing problem in Puerto Rico and wanted to know what our position might be...I simply told the governor we would look into the situation without any promises."[2]

By October of 1977 one decision had to be made: Andrés Figueroa Cordero still refused to ask for a pardon but he had terminal cancer and "we have been told he has a life expectancy of four to eight weeks." In the "options memo" prepared for President Carter, Jordan wrote that the four Puerto Ricans have become "a rallying point for pro-independence groups in Puerto Rico, who see them as political prisoners. Puerto Rican terrorists, namely the FALN, have thoroughly exploited this theme and have linked numerous bombings in this country with demands for the release of these 'freedom fighters.'" However, "in spite of this...four former governors, the current governor, Puerto Rican Bar Association, the Council of Catholic Bishops, numerous congressmen and other prominent leaders have called upon you to commute his sentence. Should Cordero die in prison, he may become a martyr for the cause and it could place a powerful propaganda weapon in the hands of the FALN given their apparent willingness to use force. Further loss of life (such as the New York bombings) may result in retaliation for his death."[3]

Andrés Figueroa would not cooperate. "The Justice department guidelines for commutation of a sentence require the prisoner to request consideration. Figueroa has refused to apply because he regards himself as a political prisoner." Thus, the president had three options. He could require a request for a pardon. "We [Hamilton and his White House colleagues] recommend disapproval" because "everyone agrees that it is virtually certain that he will not apply and therefore he will die in prison."

The president could "direct the Justice Department to consider clemency for him on the merits without his petitioning." That option was rejected because it would set a bad precedent, and, as Attorney General Griffin Bell stressed in a separate memo, "to allow Figueroa to die in prison would make him into a cause celebre and incite further terrorism on the island. To free him would blunt

these same terrorist activities...It should be noted
that presidential intervention in Figueroa's case
could be based solely on <u>humanitarian grounds</u> and
should not be viewed as a precedent for the release
of the other four Puerto Rican nationalists."

③ Finally the president could release Figueroa "on
purely humanitarian grounds." This option was recommended because it would not set a precedent
since "this is a unique case where a man for ideological reasons will not apply for a commutation,
but who is terminally ill."[4]

Andrés Figueroa received a pardon the day after
the president read a memo of purely political considerations about an allegedly humanitarian gesture. The cynicism is noteworthy for an administration that celebrated its concern for human values.
Further, Andrés Figueroa's death could not place a
"powerful propaganda weapon" in the hands of the
FALN unless the claim of political prisoner resonat-
ed in the minds and hearts of the Puerto Rican and
Latin American peoples.

The other four prisoners who, by mid-1978,
threatened to become serious political liabilities,
offered no easy solution like Andrés's approaching
death had done. In White House memos, the four
prisoners were now "Puerto Rican Independence
Fighters." Presidential Assistant Al Stern recognized
their political status and he also worried about the
perception of others: "I have heard that Amnesty
International plans to list them as 'prisoners of conscience' sometime next year. Therefore, early release
would save us all embarrassment."[5]

However, none had cancer and if "they are
released as part of a larger swap arrangement, there

is no doubt that that would be perceived as an admission that they are and were political prisoners which we have heretofore strenuously denied. I am not confident at all that denials of that status or as motivation for the release will be plausible to anyone concerned."[6]

By August of 1979 Zbigniew Brzezinski wrote the president a memo about "the four Puerto Rican Nationalists." There were "*compelling humanitarian, foreign policy and political reasons for releasing from prison the four Puerto Rican nationalists.*" (Emphasis in original)

An examination by staffers showed that "in recent times *only three inmates have served more time in federal custody than these four.*" (emphasis in original) In fact, while the principal charge against the Nationalists was aggravated assault, the president learned that the average time served by life-termers for murder was slightly more than 8.5 years. As of August 1979, each of the four had served more than 24 years. Oscar Collazo was in his 29th year of incarceration.

Releasing the prisoners was thus a humanitarian gesture with significant political benefits. Again the president was told that: "*Release of the prisoners will remove a propaganda issue from the agenda of various international fora which is used each year against us and is increasingly used as an example of the inconsistency of our human rights policy.*"

"*The release of these prisoners will be welcomed as a compassionate and humanitarian gesture not only by virtually everyone in Puerto Rico, but also throughout Latin America.*" (emphasis in original) Thus the four were not political prisoners but they should be released for "compelling" foreign policy and political reasons.

Another complication was that Fidel Castro had privately agreed "to release six U.S. citizens being held in Cuban jails as political prisoners. But, in order to avoid any implication that the Nationalists are 'political prisoners' consideration of their petitions has thus far been entirely independent of the release of the American prisoners. Should you commute their sentences we would make clear publicly that your action was *not* part of a prisoner exchange."[7]

But it was part of a prisoner exchange. And the president knew it. However, to face the truth was to place revolutionary violence in social and historical perspective and, even more threatening for the president, to admit the legitimacy of a comment made by Congressman Benjamin Gilman. He wrote a letter asking the president to free the Nationalists because "successful efforts of the administration in freeing a group of Soviet dissidents has served to focus attention on the Puerto Rican nationalists—who are, of course, dissidents within our own country."[8]

President Carter first fudged the issue in his September 6, 1979 grant of executive clemency—he released the four because of "diverse and good and sufficient reasons." He then called the FALN a terrorist organization at the same time he negotiated the Camp David Accords with a man who had only recently lost these political labels: terrorist, murderer, fanatic, barbarian.

In the 1940s Israeli Prime Minister Menachim Begin headed an organization called the Irgun. Both the British and Israelis called Begin a terrorist because, besides robbing more than a score of banks to fund his cause, he also boasted (in *The Revolt*, first published in 1950 and reissued in 1977) that his organization "destroyed bridges, tore up railway lines, demolished stations, blew up trains, mined roads and sent armored cars flying."[9] TNT was in fact the "main weapon in the struggle for liberation" and the Irgun did not hesitate to use it on the King David Hotel in July of 1946. The Hotel was a military target—it housed the British High Commissioner's Secretariat's offices—with a multitude of civilians always in the building. Begin's group warned people to leave but, when they did not, over 200 civilians were killed or wounded. In *The Revolt* Begin wrote that "our satisfaction at the success of the great operation was bitterly marred."[10]

Critics suggested that in negotiating with Begin, President Carter was unhappily proving a terrible truth: Yesterday's terrorist is today's prime minister. However, Begin himself wrote that, besides judgments based on politics or ideology, there were internationally accepted laws of war. Indeed, "the education which we gave our soldiers throughout the years of revolt was based on the observance of the traditional laws of war. We never broke them unless the enemy did so first, and thus forced us, in accordance with the accepted custom of war, to apply reprisals."[11]

Begin had a point which applies to Puerto Rican political activists. Like the Nationalists, the women and men now incarcerated are Puerto Rican Independence Fighters. Like the Nationalists, their freedom will be decided on the basis of "compelling" foreign policy and political factors. Still, it must be recognized that *the label terrorist is as much a political term as it is a characterization of groups who violate internationally accepted moral and legal norms.* As the Carter memos show, in Washington the Puerto Rican prisoners have always been judged from the shifting perspective of U.S. colonial politics; so, to more fairly analyze the contemporary prisoners actions we need to consider at least six issues.

Delicate Balance of Terror

First, it is hypocritical and inaccurate for U.S. officials to call the Puerto Rican political prisoners "terrorists." If the essential feature of modern terrorism is the severing of the link between the *target* of violence and the *reason* for the violence,[12] the origin of modern terrorism is in the military establishments of England, Italy and the United States. It was Western soldiers who argued that the way to win World War II was to destroy "the enemy's will to resist." In practice this included "paralyzing the organic industrial, economic and civic systems that maintained the life of the enemy nation itself;" and it also included "*attacking the people themselves, especially those concentrated in the cities.*"[13]

This was openly called obliteration bombing in Italy, England and the United States because the deliberate idea was to systematically terrorize the civilian population. Exposed to bombardment from thousands of planes people would surrender rather than live under a fiery barrage.

After World War II, obliteration bombing became an institutionalized part of American life. In

201

the 50s the grand strategy was labeled "massive retaliation;" in the sixties the Defense Department used the initials MAD as shorthand for a strategy called Mutual Assured Destruction; and, all the while, analysts spoke of the delicate "Balance of Terror." Since either side could potentially exterminate the other, each had the difficult task of deliberately creating so much fear that no opponent would ever risk a nuclear attack. In the movie "Dr. Strangelove," Stanley Kulbrick satirized a crazy man's device called the Doomsday Machine. In reality, this was a notion seriously broached in congressional hearings. If the Soviets ever threatened the United States, Washington would hold them off with a machine capable of destroying the world.[14]

The Doomsday Machine carried postwar insanity to its ultimate conclusion: End war by ending humankind. The theories of terror bombing severed—totally and completely—the link between the target of violence and the reason for violence. Some analysts call this state terrorism but, whatever the label, the soldiers who deliberately burned civilians in WW II[15] and the civilians who maintained the delicate balance of nuclear terror during the 50s, 60s, 70s, and 80s must bear primary responsibility for creating societies in which the deliberate and systematic slaughter of civilians was the *axis* of national defense.

It is, therefore, hypocritical for Washington officials to condemn terrorism when the intentional obliteration of innocent men and women has been— and remains—an elemental part of U.S. military policy. Obliteration bombing was an essential part of President Bush's Desert Storm campaign in Iraq.

The American public even watched the "live action" footage on CNN; meanwhile, many of the Baghdad civilians deliberately killed by U.S. bombardment not only had nothing to do with the reason for the war, they were opponents of Saddam Hussein.

Second, as Senator Henry Jackson stressed, Puerto Rico is a colony. For the United States to judge the actions of Puerto Rican revolutionaries is to have the colonizer decide what is and is not acceptable anticolonial resistance.

The American revolutionaries protested "transporting us beyond Seas to be tried for pretended offenses." And so did Haydée Beltrán when she told a U.S. court in 1980 "my case can truly be heard in front of an international court...this country and this court cannot stand here and judge me against what they call crimes because there are no crimes. There have been no crimes committed."[16]

Third, a willingness to use violence is *not* the essential issue when the Puerto Ricans are condemned by U.S. authorities. As Alejandrina Torres told a federal court in August of 1985, "the U.S. Government labels me a terrorist because I am willing to engage in armed struggle to free my nation. Yet, if I were a mercenary who fought with the contras in Nicaragua, President Reagan would call me a freedom fighter. Clearly the issue is not how I am fighting but what I am fighting for and who I am fighting against."

Fourth, the latest definition of terrorism offered by the FBI is so expansive it eliminates the legitimacy of any revolution, anywhere on earth. To the Bureau terrorism "is the unlawful use of force or violence against persons or property to intimidate or force a government, the civilian population, or any segment thereof[17] in further of political or social objectives."[18] By this definition the FALN and the *Macheteros* are terrorists, but so are the Nicaraguan contras and so, too, Samuel Adams and the Mohawks when they used force against the British government during the American revolution.

⑤ *Fifth*, instead of the black and white assessments of the FBI, any overall judgement of revolutionary violence is fraught with ambiguities and colored by political sympathies. One analyst says to think of it in terms of a continuum. On one side the target of and reason for violence are the same, e.g., the Nationalist attack on President Truman or the Nationalist attack on the House of Representatives. On the other end of the continuum is the Palestinian attack on the *Achille Lauro*. When group members threw a handicapped man overboard they exploded the link between grievance and target. It repelled so many of us because we saw no connection between the man in the wheelchair and the Palestinian struggle in the Middle East.

In real life many revolutionary acts are hard to judge: they fall in the middle rather than at either end of the continuum. Thus, fair assessments of any revolutionary group can never disregard the ambiguities which characterize so many acts of anticolonial violence; and, just as important, those assessments must also recognize the *political* factors that shape the words and actions of U.S. or other government officials. For example, President Clinton invited Yasir Arafat to the White House in September of 1993. The same man who was a moral leper in January was suddenly an invited guest at

Washington's "best" parties and the nation's best rated TV talk shows.

Sixth, any revolutionary group must be judged ⑥ in relation to *all* its actions. To single out one or two uses of violence is to judge the whole by the part; indeed, when governments do it they often focus on the target of an action only as a way of avoiding the reason for the action. That may be "good" counter-revolutionary politics; it is not a fair way to make an overall assessment of the actions of the FALN or, in the next chapter, *Los Macheteros*.

The FALN and Revolutionary Violence

The first public announcement of the FALN's existence came on October 26, 1974. In a communique made available to the press, the organization indicated that "today, commando units of FALN attacked major Yanki corporations in New York City. These actions have been taken in commemoration of the October 30, 1950 uprising in Puerto Rico against Yanki colonial domination. These bombings are also to accent the seriousness of our demands for the release of the five Puerto Rican political prisoners, the longest held political prisoners in the hemisphere: Oscar Collazo, Lolita Lebrón, Rafael Cancel Miranda, Andrés Figueroa Cordero, and Irving Flores; and for the immediate and unconditional independence of Puerto Rico."[19]

This communique openly and deliberately tied the FALN to Albizu Campos and to the then 75 year struggle against U.S. colonialism in Puerto Rico. It stressed that the bombings were part of a two front war—one in Puerto Rico, one in the United States; it proudly labeled the FALN a Marxist organization, and it ended with these words: "The FALN supports the demonstration at Madison Square Garden on October 27 in support of the independence of Puerto Rico. We view this as a significant step in the formation of an anti-imperialist front in the United States."[20]

In defining the FALN, even a harshly critical report issued by the RAND Corporation stressed that, "although verbally committed to Marxist Lenist lines" the FALN "seems more devoted to Puerto Rican separatism than to socialism."[21] Nobody missed the essential thrust of the FALN's aims but, instead of focusing on the reason for violence, or the legitimacy of the FALN's claims—e.g., Senator Jackson's statement in April of 1974 that Puerto Rico must remain a colony—critics poisoned the political atmosphere by using the word terrorist. While this label helped create the hatred and fear which produced seventy year jail terms in 1981, it did nothing to seriously analyze the reasons for the FALN's resort to violence.

As the RAND corporation noted, "The FALN's first operation was the fire—bombing of five New York City Banks on October 26, 1974. *Subsequent symbolic bombings*—operations that caused no loss of life but were designed to cause extensive damage and thus attract attention—were directed against entities that the terrorists perceived as representing U.S. capitalism and imperialism."[22](emphasis added)

By 1981, the FALN had assumed responsibility for 120 separate bombings. And the RAND study stressed that "historically the independentistas have tended not to strike at individuals. Indeed, given the number of bombings, very few people have died. The deaths that have occurred (five human beings had been killed) have been deliberate, not the accidental consequences of bombings; most have been carried out in retaliation for what the terrorists believe is violence against jailed separatists."[23]

The bombings were generally "symbolic," they focused on property, and very few people died, none accidentally. But the FALN was nevertheless labeled a terrorist organization.

This political use of the term was necessary because to employ other labels—e.g., revolutionary, dissident,—was to honestly confront reality, in the form of a claim made by Oscar López: "The evidence will show you that we have a deep respect for human life, that we care for human life."[24] To Oscar the proof was in the result of the bombings: How could the FALN violence be characterized as "indiscriminate" if, in 120 bombings, "very few people have died." Obviously, when it attacked banks, recruiting centers, or military installations the FALN could have slaughtered people if it chose to do so.

Throughout its existence the FALN consistently maintained a close connection between the reason for violence and the target of violence. However, of the five people who died as a result of FALN attacks, four lost their lives (and scores were wounded) in the *first months* of the FALN's existence. This is the period in which any social movement receives what is often a *permanent* public definition of its aims and activities; sometimes that definition changes but even then the group always works against the public conclusions which were initially lodged in people's minds.[25] In the case of the FALN, government officials shaped the public's first impressions on the basis of attacks that were not characteristic of the FALN's resort to revolutionary violence.

As one of its first actions, the FALN planted a bomb (on December 11, 1974) and deliberately directed police officers to its location. The rookie officer who found the bomb—Angel Poggi—suffered severe injuries; he lost an eye and was permanently disabled. In the communique issued by the FALN the group noted that it "assumed responsibility for the dynamite attack on members of the New York City police force, on Wednesday, December 11, 1974, in El Barrio." The attack was in retaliation for the "brutal murder of Martin Tito Pérez" by local police officers. "By this action the FALN wishes to make it known that racist attacks against Puerto Rican, Black and other Third World Communities, as well as attacks against Puerto Rican liberation fighters and militants will be met by the armed resistance of the people...For each repressive act taken upon our people and fighters for Puerto Rican independence the FALN will respond with revolutionary violence."[26]

This attack deliberately and clearly linked the reason for and target of the violence. It was thus a revolutionary rather than a terrorist act; however, it was also ambiguous because, instead of trying to retaliate on the—admittedly unknown—officers who brutally murdered Tito Pérez, the FALN chose to attack any officer who picked up the bomb. I do not believe that is an acceptable form of revolutionary behavior; attack the murderers or attack property but not an officer whose only offense was being a part of the police force.

Revolutionary Violence

Objecting to this attack does not make it a terrorist act; on the contrary, it only underlines the terrible moral ambiguity which acts of revolutionary—and state—violence normally contain. For example, when the United States fired missiles against the intelligence headquarters of Saddam Hussein in July of 1993, General Colin Powell reluctantly admitted that "stray" bombs had killed many civilians. Powell argued that these deaths were regrettable but critics noted that, given the central city location of the target, they were also predictable. Thus, given the likelihood of many dead civilians, should the United States have refrained from the attack? Or, like General Powell, mourn those who died but justify their deaths on political grounds: The Clinton administration wanted to send a threatening message to Saddam Hussein and the people of Iraq.

In the January 24, 1975 attack on Fraunces Tavern—only three months after the FALN announced its existence—the Puerto Rican revolutionaries severely strained the link between the reason for and cause of violence. Indeed, it is this one attack which still moves people to judge the whole by the part, 120 revolutionary acts on the basis of one very terrible act of retaliatory violence.

On January 11, 1975 a number of people were quietly eating dinner in a Mayagüez (Puerto Rico) restaurant. Suddenly a bomb exploded; it killed its targets—two young independence activists named Luis Chavonnier and Eddie Ramos. It maimed ten civilian diners, and it also slaughtered a six-year-old Puerto Rican child. No one took credit for this bombing but the FALN (correctly) blamed the CIA and it decided to engage in an act of retaliatory violence.

The attack had a simple aim: an eye for an eye. Or, as the communique which accepted responsibility for the attack noted, "we warned the North American government that to terrorize and kill our people would mean retaliation by us. This was not an empty warning." Presumably the FALN believed that because Fraunces Tavern was located near Wall Street, it was also frequented by many rich and powerful businessmen. Thus, organizers supposedly calculated that when the bomb exploded during the busy lunch hour period, it would necessarily kill its intended target: Corporate executives. In fact, four people died and over sixty were wounded. However, not all were executives and most knew nothing about Puerto Rico.

In Puerto Rico, supporters approved the attack because "the scene of the explosion was the center of Yankee finance capital;" but those same supporters never confronted what I believe is the basic reason to strongly and unequivocally condemn the attack on Fraunces Tavern: Retaliation against, or imitation of, the CIA is not an acceptable moral basis for blowing up a restaurant. It was—and is—understandable that the FALN sought to retaliate for the death of the independence activists and the six year old child; it was also understandable—and perfectly appropriate for a legitimate anticolonial organization—to send a message to Washington: "Seventy-seven years of colonialism is enough. We will no longer peacefully tolerate the repression and murder of independence activists."

But, the FALN severely strained the link

210

between the target of and reason for violence when they attacked Fraunces Tavern. For example, as in Mayagüez children could have been in the room and neither Puerto Rican nor Northamerican youngsters deserve to be injured for the behavior of their parents.

Many government officials, not to mention revolutionaries, would never support my strong criticism of the Fraunces Tavern bombing. Former U.S. Secretary of State Robert Lansing believed "that almost any form of atrocity is permissible provided a nation's safety is involved."[27] And, as Menachim Begin stressed, the Irgun only violated internationally accepted standards when the British or other enemies of the Jewish people did it first; thus, he and many other revolutionaries would argue this was acceptable because "in accordance with the accepted customs of war," it is legitimate to "apply reprisals." For example,, when the British failed to commute the death sentences of four captured members of Begin's group, he immediately killed two British sergeants. They were first hanged in a factory; "their bodies were then carried in bags and strung up in a wooded area surrounded by mines; the bombs were then detonated, the bodies blown to pieces and the British presumably got the message about the meaning of reprisals for actions against Jewish 'freedom fighters'."[28]

The retaliatory side of the Fraunces Tavern bombing makes it much harder to judge. However, no matter what conclusion a reader draws, it is still one act out of 120; the group has always been judged by this very uncharacteristic bombing because that is the best way to avoid focusing on the *symbols* which were the characteristic targets of virtually every FALN bombing.

On October 27, 1975 the group bombed a variety of locations in New York, Chicago, and Washington. Citibank and Chase Manhattan—two corporations which then (and now) dominated the island's banking industry—received damaging assaults on their facilities; in Washington the FALN placed bombs near the State Department and in the shrubbery alongside the Bureau of Indian Affairs; meanwhile in New York the attacks focused on the U.S. mission to the United Nations.

In the communique issued after these attacks the FALN commemorated the 25th anniversary of the 1950 revolution in Puerto Rico; it also demanded the release of the five Puerto Rican Nationalists; and it celebrated the first anniversary of its existence "by launching a simultaneously coordinated attack against Yanki government and monopoly capitalist institutions in New York, Washington and Chicago."

Toward the end of the communique, the FALN made what appeared to be an exaggerated comment: In the United Nations "the yanki gorillas were forced to expose their claws to the world by resorting to fascist arm twisting of their own allies in order to prevent a committee (i.e., the UN Committee on Decolonization) discussion of the case of Puerto Rico."[29]

The FALN was correct. It then had no way to document its case, but the files of the presidential libraries indicate that "arm twisting" was a tactic of long standing. In November of 1964 a White House memo notes that a Decolonization Committee report failed to include Puerto Rico because "USUN prevailed on its friends to get any mention of Puerto Rico deleted." Unfortunately, a report of a committee working group did mention Puerto Rico. "It appears that USUN tried very hard but got outvoted by the less developed countries. *When colonial issues arise, even the Latins desert us.*"[30] (emphasis added)

And, in 1968, UN Ambassador Goldberg had "come to the conclusion that we can downgrade this troublesome (decolonization) committee by removing ourselves from it. " As an aide noted in a confidential White House memo, Goldberg "has recommended removal to the secretary and has been authorized to take soundings with friendly governments prepatory to a final decision. One of the soundings is with the government of Puerto Rico. There are recurring efforts to put the Puerto Rico question on the committee's agenda—*efforts which we pull out all the stops to block.* Goldberg's view is that we can continue to be effective in this regard off the committee."[31] (emphasis added)

Finally, files from the President Ford library indicate that shortly before the FALN attack, "Cuba proposed a resolution to the UN Committee on Decolonization which would have recognized the Puerto Rican National Liberation Movement as representing the legitimate aspirations of the people of Puerto Rico for independence. The resolution called for PRNLM non-voting observer status in the UN. Only after we had made *extremely strong* demarches in members' capitals did the Committee adopt a procedural motion to postpone consideration of this resolution until 1976."[32]

These documents are especially significant

because a focus on the target of violence runs the risk of neglecting the reason for the violence. The White House knew Puerto Rico was a colony, but, nevertheless, used "extremely strong demarches" to deny, distort, and avoid reality. The FALN thus sought to call attention to hypocrisy at the United Nations and the presidential documents thoroughly support their contentions. As the Interior Department put it in a memo to President Ford dated December 30, 1975, "admittedly the argument can be made that this (Commonwealth) is continued "colonialism" and falls short of full self government and self-determination; but we do not believe that the constitutional mechanism exists to do more without admitting Puerto Rico as a State of the Union, or granting it its independence."[33]

That admission was all the FALN wanted, but, given Washington's refusal to honestly confront its own contradictions, the FALN continued to engage in a variety of symbolic bombings. In March of 1977 it exploded devices near the FBI's offices in New York; in August of 1977 it attacked Department of Defense facilities (also in New York) and in November of 1979 it bombed military recruiting centers in Chicago as well as that city's Naval militia building. In each of these symbolic attacks the aim was to call attention to an old enemy—the Blood Tax—and a new spirit of resistance. On Vieques many islanders had engaged in non-violent "beach-ins;" they tried to close down the Navy's University of the Sea so the FALN tried to echo what was then happening in Puerto Rico.

In 1980 the FALN also invaded the Chicago campaign offices of President Carter, but a much more common target was the corporate headquarters of organizations with serious economic interests in Puerto Rico. Marshall Field was an absentee landlord with substantial holdings on the island so his store received a number of symbolic attacks. So did Sears, oil companies like Mobil (one person died in an August 3, 1977 attack), and a variety of banks. In each instance the aim was to call attention to the colonial exploitation of Puerto Rico's resources. As the group noted in its communique of August 3, 1977, "these corporations, which are part of Yanki imperialism, are the cause of the problems of the Puerto Rican people on the island and in the United States; since they are the ones that strangulate us with their colonial yoke."[34]

Mainland critics argued that this was a form of Marxist overkill; the FALN could never substantiate such ridiculous allegations. However, not only were the charges true, they were a matter of public record. Testifying before the House Ways and Means Committee in July of 1975 the Commonwealth government's Resident Commissioner, Jaime Benitez, testified "that no place under the American flag has been more dismally affected by the inflation, recession, and the quadrupling of oil prices than Puerto Rico." Indeed, after almost thirty years of Operation Bootstrap, it most ardent supporters came to this conclusion: "Puerto Rico is essentially a trading post where we import what we consume and export what we produce."[35]

Benitez argued for a change in the tax laws. Because a "possession's corporation" could not bring home its profits at once, since 1948 "the present denial has forced a U.S. subsidiary to place

215

this investment abroad until such time as the company is liquidated or until such time as it can be returned to the United States. *These investments are not available in the United States or Puerto Rico while they are outside of both countries.*"[36]

Benitez was right. And so was the FALN. For thirty years the possessions corporations had banked the lion's share of their profits abroad, used them to develop Europe, and, in the meantime, they had provided so few meaningful jobs that by 1975 Puerto Ricans began to use food stamps as a means to survival.[37] Instead of independence and self sufficiency, the Puerto Rican people had embraced an even greater degree of abject dependence on Washington (food stamps were introduced by President Nixon in 1974) while Congress changed the tax laws in a manner that made it even easier to exploit Puerto Rico and its people. To the FALN this was the final degradation.

Introduced in 1976, the new tax laws had a new number: 936. Congress now allowed corporations to bring home all their profits at once and a June 1978 memo in the Carter library explains why: "Having at first contemplated repeal of the section which exempted the income of possessions corporations from federal taxation, Congress rejected this idea out of the conviction that repeal would lead to plant closings, accelerate Puerto Rican unemployment—which was approaching 20% of the labor force—and compel many Puerto Ricans to move to the United States to find work."[38]

Congress wanted no more Puerto Ricans in the United States so it created this situation: "Increasingly the typical possessions corporation

216

has become a pharmaceutical company with high profit margins and *minimal* labor requirements... In one possessions corporation the federal tax expenditure (i.e., the taxes never paid) exceeded $500,000 per Puerto Rican employee. The average for pharmaceutical companies was $34,873, more than three times the average compensation of employees in that industry. *Corporations whose federal tax savings per employee exceeded $10,000 a year received 71% of the total tax saving while employing 15 percent of all possessions corporations' employees."*[39]

The final tax incentive to the possessions corporations was arguably the most controversial of all: If a corporation took its profits and invested them in island banks, the interest paid on the deposits was also free of federal taxes. This quickly created such a bonanza for the banks and the corporations that Citibank—one of the FALN's primary targets—published a book entitled *The 936 Market: An Introduction.* Three Northamerican financial institutions—Chase Manhattan, Citibank, and the Bank of America—held over 55% of the already (by late 1979) three *billion* dollar 936 market but, instead of allowing that money to be invested in Puerto Rico, the companies made short term "rollover" deposits. Sixty percent of all funds (in 1979) were invested for six months or less; and another 15% for 6 to 12 months.[40]

There was no way the money earned in Puerto Rico could be used for the *long term* development of the island's resources and that, of course, was the whole point of the FALN's focus on corporate targets. Multinationals were using Puerto Rico as a banking warehouse while Congress helped the corporations because they were lobbied to do so; and because Congress wanted to keep Puerto Ricans in the Caribbean.

In its 120 bombings the FALN generally focused on political targets because gaining independence for Puerto Rico was at the center of Oscar López's or Alejandrina Torres' life; because they wanted to preserve the island's culture; because they hated the dependence fostered by colonialism and symbolized by food stamps; and, because they agreed with Pedro Albizu Campos that an indispensable basis for any self-sustaining economy was political power. Without the latter even the best plans for industrialization contributed, not to the well-being of the Puerto Rican people, but to their continued dependence on investors who would remove their rollover deposits as quickly as the 936 exemptions disappeared.

Different Planets

The clerk said "80 CR 736, *United States v. Carlos Torres, et.al.*; on trial."

It was the morning of February 13, 1981 and after the prosecutor said, "Good morning your honor, Jeremy Margolis and Walter Jones for the United States," Judge Thomas Sullivan asked "Is there anyone representing the defendants?" There was no answer so the judge said, "well, I guess we will have to bring out the defendants by themselves, individually, then."

Judge Sullivan: "Are you Ms. Alicia Rodríguez?"

Alicia: "Long live the progressive revolutionary forces! (Whereupon the defendant converses in Spanish.")

Judge Sullivan: "Wait a minute Alicia. Just a minute. Now calm down. Turn around (Alicia was then talking to her supporters in the gallery) and let me ask you—(Whereupon the defendant converses in Spanish.)

Alicia: "I want to be removed from here. I have already told the people that are here who are my supporters what I wanted to say. I wish to be removed."

Judge Sullivan: ."..I do not understand Spanish. Do you want to participate in the trial like a lady or do you want to be returned to the lockup? Which do you want to do?

"You have a right to stay here and participate in the trial. You have a right to talk to the jury. You have a right to interrogate witnesses."

Alicia: ."..I wish to be removed from this place. I no longer want to be present."

Judge Sullivan: "All right, under Rule 43 you are entitled to absent yourself from the trial, so you can go back to the lockup. You are going to have an amplification system so you will know what is going on at all times."[41]

Alicia went back to the lockup. Even behind bars the handcuffs were never removed as she and the other defendants were forced to listen to an amplified broadcast of the *U.S. v. Carlos Alberto Torres.*

Judge Sullivan: "Carlos Torres. All right. He is the first named defendant." (Defendant Torres speaks in Spanish).

Judge Sullivan: "Are you Carlos Torres? (Defendant Torres Speaks Spanish).

Judge Sullivan: "Mr. Torres I can't understand Spanish. If you wish to speak—if you wish to say something in English? (Defendant Torres speaks Spanish.)

The next defendant was Elizam Escobar. He also started in Spanish so the judge said, "if you want to say something say it in English. We cannot understand Spanish."

Elizam: "We can make believe this is a trial. I can make believe you are a judge, a fair judge. But we understand what this is already. We have told you many times that we don't recognize the jurisdiction of the United States... I don't know why you still say that we have the right to participate. We have the right to defend ourselves only at a tribunal which is international in a fair hearing of our case, of our struggle for liberty, our struggle for justice, of our struggle against every oppression of our country, of our people. We are not here—and we don't want to hear words like we are in any case uncivilized people because we are very civilized people. We can show you that."

Judge Sullivan: "I respect your rights Mr. Escobar."

Elizam: "We have a civilization older than this civilization."

Judge Sullivan: ."..You have a right to excuse people from the jury."

Elizam: "We are already guilty. We have been found guilty because we have the guts to fight the most powerful imperialism in the world."

Judge Sullivan: "Mr. Escobar, you have a right to help select the jury."

Elizam: "We Puerto Ricans are very proud of

what we are. We are not better than anyone and we are not worse than anyone. Those that say we aren't anyone, we're going to prove that is not true. We have been proving that."

Judge Sullivan: ."..do you want to stay here and participate in the trial?"

Elizam: "Do you know that a little country like Puerto Rico is fighting for independence? Do you know that?"

Judge Sullivan:."..All right you can go back to the lockup with the rest of the defendants and you can listen to it over the speaker system."

(Defendant speaks Spanish)

(Defendant Escobar taken out of the court-room.)[42]

The next day, with the proceedings piped into the shackled defendants, prosecutor Margolis told the jury about seditious conspiracy. The FALN used "terror and violence, such as explosives and incendiary devices planted in various government establishments" to achieve the independence of Puerto Rico. The defendants "proudly" conspired in an "insidious" plot to overthrow the government of the United States. "You (the jury) will see evidence before you, far more than you see before you now...You will see their weapons. You will see their ammunition. You will see their intelligence files and dossiers ...you will see ...."[43] Irrefutable evidence that these men and women were revolutionaries. But, the jury would not see the government documents which fully supported the arguments made by Elizam Escobar and Dylcia Pagán, Carmen Valentín and Luis Rosa. In Chicago the defendants refused to participate in the judicial proceedings.

But, before an international tribunal, any of the defendants would have happily made several points.

First, Congress forced U.S. citizenship on the Puerto Rican people. As Secretary of War Garrison told Congress in February of 1914, "as I understand the situation there is no sentiment whatever in the United States that the island of Porto Rico should be an independent sovereignty. There is no suggestion that it should not be connected with the United States Government for all time and that we should not in the fullest measure be responsible for it as we are for any other thing that is under our flag. If I am right on that premise—and I do not know of any contrary opinions held or expressed *in the United States*—then it seems to me to follow that it would be unwise to foster the idea in anybody's mind by whatever we might do that a contrary course down there could be properly pursued."[44]

As in 1945, in 1914, too many Puerto Ricans wanted their independence. So, as Congressman William Jones, Chair of the House Committee on Insular Affairs put it, "do you not think that, in as much as the sentiment in the United States seems to be practically unanimous that Porto Rico is to remain permanently a part of the United States, in order to put an end to all agitation of this question there [i.e., independence] we ought to declare at once that the people of the island are citizens of the United States ...is that not the best way to remove this question from Porto Rican politics."[45]

Puerto Ricans disagreed. In fact, as soon as these hearings ended the only democratically elected body in Puerto Rico—the House of Delegates—*unanimously* asked that the island's inhabitants not

222

be made citizens against their will. Puerto Ricans didn't want to foreclose their status options. But in 1917 the Jones Act made Puerto Ricans U.S. citizens in spite of their wishes.

This history that never came out in the 1981 trial. Because they only accepted the legitimacy of international tribunals, the defendants remained silent while the judge said, "If it [the death penalty] were authorized under the statues I wouldn't have any hesitation in imposing that sentence." However, Judge Sullivan also said, "I understand it is a colony," and "I don't object to the movement. It is the way in which you are attempting to achieve those objectives that are violations of our laws."[46]

OUR LAWS. The entire case was in those two words. U.S. colonial laws, dominated Puerto Rico and its people so if the judge couldn't kill the defendants—"I think that would be the appropriate penalty"—he would give them sentences which meant that "you are not going to have freedom for a very long time."[47]

Elizam Escobar—60 years

Ida Luz Rodríguez—75 years

Ricardo Jiménez—90 years

Luis Rosa—75 years

Adolfo Matos—70 years

Carlos Alberto Torres—70 years

Dylcia Pagán—55 years

Carmen Valentín—90 years

Alicia Rodríguez—55 years

The average sentence for the FALN POW's was 70 years. In the same year that these sentences were imposed the next highest average sentence in all federal jurisdictions was 41.2 years. And, between 1966 and 1985, the longest average sentence for all persons convicted of homicide was 22.7 years; for rape 12.5 years; and weapons and firearms violations similar to the charges against the POW's, 12 years. *Only 12% of all federal prisoners have sentences of more than 20 years.*[48]

In response to her sentence Carmen Valentín offered this assessment (on February 18, 1981): "Revolution doesn't get accomplished by mere thought. Action must lead the way, and that is what the FALN is. The FALN is action on behalf of the millions of Puerto Ricans who have been victims of colonialism and exploitation. This action has to take place because without it our territory will not be free. Guns and bombs, guns and bombs imply death or life imprisonment. They also imply revolution and freedom for our country.

"The right of the Puerto Rican people to self-determination was once more reaffirmed at a conference of non-aligned nations of the world. Ninety-six nations gathered two weeks ago in India and once more urged this imperialist government to comply with the United Nations resolution and colonization.

"It is unfortunate that the mandate of the international community receives little recognition by this government. It is because of this continuous disregard of the people's desire (e.g., in 1914, 1945, and in 1981) and of the international arena demand, that we are forced to meet this government with ongoing resistance and ongoing revolutionary justice...Today we faithfully reaffirm our commitment to serve our nation until final victory."[49]

Pork Chops

Oscar López went underground in 1976. On May 29, 1981 he was arrested. "I made a turn. I made the wrong turn. I was lost. He [the police officer] saw two Puerto Ricans, two Puerto Ricans in a car. And he followed us. The first thing that he said when he stopped us was, "what are you guys doing around here?" I handed him a driver's license, a phony driver's license. Soon after that he was joined by another patrolman. Soon after that they asked us to step out of the car. Soon after that the second patrolman joined him, went into the car and started looking through the car. All this time we're standing right there with the patrolman and he is talking to us about what we are expecting to rob in that particular community. He was just telling us what we were expecting to steal from that particular community.

"The patrolman did not realize it was a phony driver's license...it took him an hour and a half, an hour and a half before they realized. And I had been arrested. And I had been slapped. And I had been called a porkchop by the same patrolman, a porkchop. And Puerto Ricans know what that means when you are called a porkchop, when you are called a spic.

"And this same man, this same man then tells me about how we can fight for freedom and justice, how democracy really works...."

The officers ultimately discovered who they had actually arrested, Oscar was quickly tried on charges of seditious conspiracy, and subsequently sentenced to 55 years in prison. At the very end of his statement to the court, Oscar said, "Just one more remark, a very simple remark. Mr. Margolis [the prosecutor] has said there are ways to fight in a democratic manner, to fight and get things done. But he forgets to tell you I have a history of that, that I have marched.

"I have marched. I have demonstrated. I have asked and I have begged. I have a history, something that has not come out here. I have marched with black people in this country for their rights. I have marched for jobs. There is a history of that. I have marched for housing and there is a history of that. I was in Vietnam. I am a veteran of Vietnam. There is a history of that.

"There isn't such a thing as your enemy dictating to you how it is that you are going to wage your struggle. Mr. Margolis intends to do that. He stands here. He has the gall to tell me how to wage my struggle. He doesn't know. Mr. Margolis doesn't know how it feels to be black in this country. He doesn't know how it feels to be a Puerto Rican in this country. He doesn't know how it feels, the indignity, the indignity that we feel when a policeman, the man who is supposed to uphold law and order, calls us 'pig' or 'nigger.' And after you are called those things—and I have been to my face—people spit in my face in this country. People have spat in my face, yes. And I have been arrested for demonstrating peacefully, legally. So ...If I stand here, if I stand here it is not because I have not had the courage to fight. It is because I have the courage to fight. I will attest to this and I affirm this, that Puerto Rico will be a free and socialist country."

Los Macheteros

> "Los Macheteros will always take responsibility
> for our actions. As a revolutionary army we
> respect the lives of all innocent people that we
> understand are victims of the oppressive system
> ...but we will be implacable with those that
> exploit and deceive our people,and with those
> that intend to prevent our revolutionary work."
>
> —Los Macheteros,
> Communique #2, October
> 6, 1978

The banner headline read: "Robbers take
iremite and large quantities of other explosives from
a warehouse in Manati." The year was 1978 and virtually no one knew about a clandestine army called
Los Macheteros.

Trying to calm any worried citizens, the front
page story said that the superintendent of Puerto
Rico's police flew to the scene in his personal helicopter; he and his "best" agents were on the job,
ready to pounce on the "terrorists" who "dared" to
steal from the government.[1]

Steal was an understatement. *Los Macheteros*
probably needed an eighteen-wheeler to load their
explosive cargo. They took 17,500 feet of primacord
and more than five hundred pounds of ammonium
nitrate to help detonate the 53 dynamite cartridges,
112 Iremite cartridges, and 988 blasting caps also
removed from the government warehouse.

To the police superintendent the robbery was "a
tremendous threat to the country." To *Los*

227

Macheteros the "operation" was a military action that required a political explanation. Three days after the robbery *El Ejército Popular Boricua - Macheteros* (the Boriquén Popular Army) told the Puerto Rican people that "the success of the operation was total. After mocking the vigilance and all the security measures of the objective...our combatants took possession of all the material stored in the warehouse with the exception of two sacks of ammonium nitrate that were abandoned due to the poor condition they were in, with no casualties of our forces nor for the enemy."

"Combatants. Casualties. Our forces. The enemy." In all *Machetero* operations group members told the Puerto Rican people who was responsible, what was the objective, whether there were casualties, and, if so, why. The group always stressed that it was accountable to the Puerto Rican people and that the only enemies of *Los Macheteros* were the colonial government of the United States and its representatives. Thus, occupying soldiers were a special target for the *Macheteros* because they wanted to send this message to the Puerto Rican people: "Coño Despierta! Boricua." Wake up! An organized people can end colonialism, especially if their struggle is rooted in the sense of dignity and Puerto Rican identity *Los Macheteros* hoped to inspire.

Puerto Rico bore (and bears) little resemblance to the Chicago of Oscar López and Carmen Valentín. No Puerto Rican stands out in Rincón or Vega Baja. No Puerto Rican living in Fajardo or Ponce needs to seek out their roots. Every islander walks around with a five hundred year history of colonialism strapped to his or her back. Reactions to the weight

228

of history vary, but the typical response is to accept colonial authority like the sun in the morning or hurricanes in late summer and early fall.

Los Macheteros wanted to explode the chains which locked up people's minds. Thus, any operation included real and symbolic objectives. The bombs blew up buildings, but, even more importantly, they created cracks in the mental walls that had to fall if a small army of revolutionaries was to help end *half a millennium* of Spanish and U.S. colonialism.

Los Macheteros appreciate the value of symbolism. After they cleaned out the warehouse at Manati, they left a calling card: A small machete with a red flag bearing the initials EPB and a machete. The flag helped satisfy United Nations requirements for anticolonial combatants while the machete instantly linked them to the Puerto Rican masses and to a century of anticolonial resistance. Well into the 1950's, thousands of campesinos wielded the long knife (usually made in Connecticut) as they cut the cane of absentee owners (who often lived in Connecticut or New York); and to this day public workers trim the miles of plantings along Puerto Rico's expressways using the machetes which are now a national symbol.

The pitirre is another national symbol appropriated by *Los Macheteros*. A modest-sized member of the mocking bird family, pitirres are celebrated in Puerto Rican art and music for a fierce collective defense of their territory against much larger birds. *Cada guaraguao tiene su pitirre,* is a popular saying which, roughly translated, means that "every colonial invader (bird of prey) has its small, persistent enemy."

For *Los Macheteros* Pitirre One occurred on March 13, 1980. As two cars drove along on a San Juan street, passengers in one car fired at the car containing Colonel Charles Tucker. No one was killed from the seven shots fired and Colonel Tucker, head of ROTC at the University of Puerto Rico, quickly assured reporters that he would stay on the job. "There is no change in my feelings toward Puerto Ricans. I know it was done by a minority."[2]

That minority immediately assumed responsibility for "Pitirre I." *Los Macheteros* announced that its combat units had issued a warning: "No Yankee soldier ought to feel secure trampling (*pisando*) on Puerto Rican soil." One reason for the attack harked back to the complaints made by Pedro Albizu Campos in 1948 and Lolita Lebrón in 1954: "Our youth is once again menaced with being drafted into the United States Army." To *Los Macheteros* this profound injustice was as intolerable as the ubiquitous presence of American soldiers. "In Puerto Rico you can find military bases of every branch of the United States armed forces. Our right to life and liberty is constantly violated by the bombings and landings which take place on our beaches by the United States Navy and their NATO allies...and all our people are threatened with literal nuclear extermination because of the presence of bases like Roosevelt Roads."

Pitirre Two took place on January 12, 1981 and, according to members of the group, this "military action brought international recognition to the EPB." Pitirre Two "was the most serious blow given to the Yankees in Northamerican territory since Pearl Harbor and outside the territory since the TET offensive [in 1968] in Vietnam."

But, unlike Pearl Harbor and Tet, it was carried out without airplanes and heavy artillery. As the *Macheteros* later explained, eleven men and women worked diligently for 7 minutes and 49 seconds to blow up nine National Guard planes sitting on the runway in the military-only area of the San Juan airport. The planes were supposed to train Puerto Ricans as part of the United States military commitment to help the Salvadoran army in its battle against the Frente Farabundo Martí para La Liberacion Nacional (FMLN). They planted bombs on every plane and by the time the iremite exploded—shortly after midnight—most members of the unit were on a light-colored boat motoring down to a nearby landing dock. The combatants soon disembarked and, when police inspected the site in the morning, all local residents remembered was a landscape full of fire and the maybe five people who marched off into the night.

This time *Los Macheteros* added a new twist to their propaganda campaign. Besides a communique, they made a videotape which was sent to a TV reporter. She played it on the 10 PM news, and Puerto Ricans saw a Puerto Rican flag and a machete with the *Machetero's* symbol waving in the night. After this opening shot the silent tape panned to several figures, all armed with M-16 rifles and all masked by black cloth drawn tightly over their faces. Some of the *Macheteros* wore berets, others sported GI caps, and all seemed to be diligent soldiers as they prepared to blow up—on the evening

231

news—portions of a U.S. military base.

The tape served its purpose: to inspire confidence in the ability of Puerto Ricans to mount an effective assault on the colonialism "which is trying to stuff our people with assimilation against everything that defines us as a people and a nationality and a culture." In the long communique that accompanied the attack and the tape, the combatants denounced "the murderous regime of the bullying colonial Governor Carlos Romero Barceló," urged islanders to support the 11 jailed members of the FALN, and, in a comment that again focused on public enemy number one, *Los Macheteros* expressed "solidarity with the anti-government forces fighting in El Salvador."

U.S. imperialism was the issue that linked every Machetero action and comment. In destroying the planes that trained American soldiers, the Boriquén Popular Army told the world that, as far as it was concerned, the United States could no longer use Puerto Rican soil as a military bastion for the repression of Latin American peoples.

In focusing on military objectives Los Macheteros always made a very tight link between the target of an attack and the reason for the attack thus making the terrorist label quite hard to employ because, *living in the colony*, *Los Macheteros* chose to attack targets that symbolized the essential nature of the United States' colonial government. In Chicago, the FALN often attacked the corporate targets that bore significant responsibility for the migration of the Puerto Rican people and their simultaneous exploitation at home and in the diaspora.

232

In Puerto Rico, *Los Macheteros* also perceived the exploitive impact of the U.S. corporations; but, the root of those corporations economic power was the massive military and political presence of the United States. So, instead of attacking economic targets, Los Macheteros fired bazookas at the federal building in San Juan (in January of 1985) and fired bullets at sailors when the Navy held its Ocean Venture maneuvers in 1982.

Ocean Venture represented one of the largest concentrations of military force ever assembled in the Caribbean. Over 500 airplanes, 60 destroyers, and no less than 45,000 troops used Vieques and its surrounding waters as a base for military maneuvers that ran from April 27 to May 16, 1982. Before Ocean Venture began *Los Macheteros* issued a warning; hold the maneuvers and we will retaliate. On May 16, 1982 the group attacked four sailors returning to the USS Pensacola, an amphibious assault ship used in Ocean Venture. One sailor died instantly and three were wounded when passengers in an automobile fired on the sailors. The car sped off into the night but *Los Macheteros* soon issued a communique.

Pitirre Three occurred because "the armed forces of the United States have usurped the right of our compatriots in Vieques to have their lands, their waters, and their peace and tranquility." Except for poverty, Vieques had no future. Besides Ocean Venture, an additional reason for the attack on the *white* sailors was the use of Fort Allen to hold the Haitians who, escaping their nation's poverty, had tried to enter the United States in 1980. It was crime enough to train troops for El Salvador but *Los*

Macheteros protested the use of their nation's land to militarily imprison the "Haitian brothers" with whom we share "the same past of slavery and oppression." If Puerto Rico was free, no one could use it as an instrument of U.S. policy. Because it was a colony, *Los Macheteros* attacked the white sailors who turned Boriquén into a prison colony for the poorest people in the Hemisphere.

Pitirre Three was a military action; however, it also attacked agents of authority who held no real military power. Rather than bearing responsibility for Ocean Venture, these young sailors were simply available targets. International law would justify the attack because the targets were uniformed members of an occupying army. A stricter code of ethics would argue that the only "legitimate" targets are those individuals who hold real colonial power. These sailors were "swabbies," not admirals.

Despite my criticism, *Los Macheteros* were always revolutionaries, never terrorists. They tried to destroy colonialism, and they rarely lost sight of a compelling and important fact: They were accountable to both history and the Puerto Rican people.

Who becomes a *Machetero*? What sense of history, values and early life experiences give rise to such a deep sense of indignation and commitment? In a group that contained over 300 full time members, generalizations are difficult if only because membership was and is secret. Nevertheless, there are characteristics which typify the men and women who, despite different backgrounds and personal histories, eventually appeared for a trial in the United States of America.

The first "portrait" describes a gentle, middle

aged man who is also an acknowledged founder of Los Macheteros.

Two Macheteros

Filiberto Ojeda Ríos was on the line calling from prison; would I accept the charges? When I agreed, Filiberto—a man I hardly knew—asked if I was ok. He had read my newspaper piece about his treatment in prison and worried that the accurate details about the nature of his "white torture" would move the authorities to harass me. I thanked him for his concern but to this day I remain amazed by that call. He was in a maximum security hell; I was in a comfortable chair in an even more comfortable home yet the prisoner worried about the free.

Such concern is characteristic of the man. He is uncommonly decent because it is a demand of his culture; and because it is one way he shaped himself based on the experiences that shaped him.

He was born near Naguabo, Puerto Rico in 1933 and he recalls that "my grandparents, on both my mother's and father's side, were farmers. Their land and agricultural properties were lost and businesses ruined when the established system of production changed hands and the North American sugar monopolies took over the Puerto Rican economic structure."

Because of that structure, Ojeda grew up in a decade "in which many thousands of *macheteros* [sugar cane cutters] were enslaved by Northamerican absentee companies. These companies controlled all productive agricultural land in Puerto Rico. The wages paid to the Puerto Rican people guaranteed nothing but abject poverty and misery."

As one response to that misery, Filiberto's father enlisted in the Cadets of the Republic. He became a Nationalist because he could not escape the effects of the Depression and then the war. By 1944 conditions were so bad that "when I was 11 my mother emigrated to New York. It was then that I was confronted for the first time in my life with all the elements of racism, social discrimination and social oppression that characterize the life of Puerto Rican migrants to this day.

"I went through my Junior High School years in different schools in Manhattan and Brooklyn, returning to Puerto Rico in 1947. This was due mainly to my inability to accept and adapt to a degrading and humiliating system ...."

Filiberto returned to the island. He graduated high school and entered the University of Puerto Rico "during the years of great struggles by the Puerto Rican students for the adoption of the Spanish language as the vehicle for education. I also enrolled in the Puerto Rican Free Schools of Music starting what would later become a professional musical career." In fact, the FBI files indicate that Ojeda later played trumpet with a number of the best bands in New York and taught some of the most popular Cuban trumpeters. He was a talented musician who, "during the early fifties worked in factories in Manhattan and Brooklyn while I continued musical studies."

The factories transformed Filiberto Ojeda Ríos. He was already a nationalist in the making but, with a reaction strikingly similar to that of Oscar López twenty years later in Chicago, Filiberto says that "it was this contact with brother Puerto Ricans in the factories which finally helped me understand the true nature of exploitation, racism and colonialism. I understood what life in the ghettoes meant ...I was able to establish the connection between workers' exploitation, and the predominating economical system, including colonialism.

"This understanding led me to oppose the forced military recruiting of Puerto Ricans to be utilized in their wars of aggression. I had the misfortune of losing loved family members and receiving others spiritually and emotionally harmed in a war they neither understood nor condoned. I refused to be drafted during the Korean War."

In 1959 Filiberto joined the just founded Movement For Independence. This organization tried to revive the spirit of nationhood evoked by the Nationalist Party; it was inspired by Albizu, by the success of the many former colonies then winning independence, and by the achievements of the Cuban revolution, an example that showed how a small Caribbean nation could potentially transform its future.

By 1961 the call of Cuba's example was irresistible to Ojeda. He went to Havana and, for a time, represented Puerto Rico at the office of the international anti-colonial solidarity movement. Through this work Ojeda met the many men and women active in national liberation struggles throughout Latin America and Africa. During the day he told others about the colonial condition of Puerto Rico and its people; at night he earned his living playing trumpet at the Tropicana and other fashionable nightclubs.

237

Accused by the United States of being an agent of the Cuban government, Ojeda replied: "I can say with pride that I hold great respect and esteem for the Cuban revolution. And this respect and esteem emerge from the fact that this revolution taught me the values of self respect, independence, and the enormous value of pride in being Puerto Rican. It has not been a lesson of dependency, but rather of the need to break away from dependency and follow a true path of restoration of dignity...No, your honor, I am not a Cuban agent...but I have personally experienced the Cuban revolution. I have lived in that country, worked amongst its people, cut sugar cane, helped construct schools, studied, and raised my children. My activities in that country were very far from anything that could be connected to the government...."[3]

Filiberto Ojeda Ríos is Cuba's brother but Puerto Rico's son. In 1969, he returned to his homeland a committed revolutionary. He went underground in 1970 and, in the late seventies, he helped found *Los Macheteros*. The idea was to involve Puerto Ricans in a popular struggle for decolonization; a clandestine army was part of the strategy for at least two reasons. First, international law (e.g., UN General Assembly Resolution 33/24 of December 1978) recognized "the legitimacy of the struggle of people's for independence, territorial integrity, national unity and liberation from colonial domination and foreign occupation by all means available, particularly armed struggle."

Second, armed struggle was especially important in Puerto Rico because of the need to destroy what Ojeda terms the institutionalized "myth of impotence, of the supposed incapacity of the Puerto Ricans to exercise their inalienable rights."

Ojeda exploded that myth when he helped create *Los Macheteros*. And he destroyed another when, instead of behaving like a violence crazed fanatic, he behaved—through four years of court proceedings—like a man with such a passionate regard for people that he melted in the presence of children and other innocents.

The passionate revolutionary and the gentle, tender man are one; they are as impossible to separate as arrogance, U.S. colonialism, and the question Ojeda posed in 1988: "What gives the United States the right of subjugating the Puerto Rico people and imposing on us the onerous colonial system of exploitation? The era of manifest destiny is long gone and we, the oppressed, are claiming our right to live in freedom, peace and self-determination."

* * *

Defense attorneys, the rest of the defendants, jurors, those of us in the gallery, the prosecutors: We all stood up whenever Judge Emmet Claire came into Hartford's federal court. Only one man refused to stand, a *jíbaro* from Yauco. Antonio Camacho Negron refused to show respect for federal authority and it cost him. The jury resented Antonio; you could see it in their eyes. They could not fathom the experience of a man who lived in the mountains without a telephone, a man who represented (and represents) an aspect of Puerto Rican culture as foreign to the jury as a Marxist on Wall Street.

Antonio is a farmer. He has also studied psychol-

239

ogy and law and worked as a counselor in the Puerto Rican government's program against drug addiction. His family has lived in the coffee growing region of Yauco for generations, and, however unintentionally, Antonio and the other residents of this small pueblo use the mountains as a shield against both colonialism and acculturation. The roads are narrow, the pace of life as slow as a McDonald's is fast. People linger in Yauco; they have time for family; and they proudly nurture the "simple" customs that manifest a profound and deep respect for the gifts of nature.

In a story called "The Gringo's House," Antonio writes about mangos, or more specifically, "pineapple mangos." They are called that "because they look like a pineapple. When they are young they are violet and when they mature they become bright red and yellow. They are bigger than all the other mangos and they are also the latest to mature. Their scent is sensual and irresistible to every Puerto Rican." However, at the *gringo's* house, they rotted on the ground. Nobody is allowed to touch them. So, "for twelve years, going and returning from school, I passed in front of that house and when summer vacations ended and I returned to class, a strong odor permeated the air; a rug of pineapple mangos lay on the ground, rotting into the soil of Puerto Rico."

Antonio is a man who cannot be understood apart from Yauco and apart from his family.

"In Puerto Rico colonialism and 'modernism' have not destroyed strong family ties...the big family—although not as big as in the past—continues to have meaning in Puerto Rican society, particularly in the interior of the island. Even under the most adverse conditions our people continue to think that children are the only capital.

"The Puerto Rican family drags along with it the customs and traditions of agricultural society: The respect and the veneration for adults is unquestionable. Although these are only words, it is still common to hear adults ask for a blessing from their aunts and uncles. The younger children learn to show respect for, and subordination to their older brothers and sisters; and in case of death or the temporary absence of the father, the older children care for and sustain the rest of the family.

"For me the family occupies a very special place. I would say that a great part of my life has revolved around the family. I come from a large farm family and I still nurture extremely strong ties with all my many family members. I had the responsibility, after the death of my mother, of becoming head of the family and 'father' of two very young sisters. This experience was the prelude to my own marriage, where I was not only the provider, but from the moment of my sons' births, I was an active participant in their care, their education and their recreation...."

Antonio is also political. He *is* a *Machetero*. But, instead of the facts and figures offered by academics, Antonio writes of islanders returning from New York with "shiny watches, chains and suits." In a story called "The United States," he says "How much we admired them! Our dream was to imitate them. It hurt me. What a way to hide their poverty—and not only their material poverty. What a way to deceive themselves. Many even get to the point of denying their origins. They want to be something other than Puerto Ricans. Sometimes I don't know if it is sadness or disgust that I feel...."

Antonio perfectly grasps the social psychological power of colonialism. He knows about Franz Fanon's *The Wretched of the Earth*. But, this very Puerto Rican man *feels* the pain; and he is both angered and amazed by the *gringos* who, as they call him (in another short story) a "spic," expect him to submit to federal authority. It's as out of the question as not eating a ripe pineapple mango.

Aquila Blanca

GO FOR IT! The T-shirts screamed out that slogan under a picture of 25-year-old Victor Manuel Gerena. According to the newspapers, the young Wells Fargo guard robbed over seven million dollars from a local branch of his own company on September 12, 1983. He was an instant hero in the center of the Puerto Rican community—and even in the halls of the West Hartford police station—because everyone understood the temptation of handling so much money. It was as if the entire city said, "Grab the gusto! Enjoy life in Rio de Janeiro and sip a *grande* piña colada for me kid."

Perceptions changed when "the *Macheteros* did it." The same young man who was smart as a whip when he acted alone was suddenly a dupe of political fanatics. He was a fool to work for men who, "pulling a Jimmy Hoffa," had already buried Victor and the money he so artfully robbed.

Victor Gerena took the money as a *Machetero* and because, like Filiberto Ojeda Ríos in the factories of New York, or Oscar López on the streets of Chicago, he wanted to make sense of a life that pulled him in two different directions. He grew up in

Hartford, raised by a very remarkable woman. Gloria Gerena is a soft, intelligent, ambitious, and dedicated member of the Puerto Rican community. Politically, she is an *independentista*; professionally, she is a social worker, a woman who continually deals with the social and economic consequences of life in the diaspora.

Víctor lived in *el barrio*; he also lived in the United States. In his first year of college students placed shit on the door of his dorm room; he was a spic who spent most of his college time on the telephone talking with friends and family. He was lonely, he certainly understood that he was completely out of place in the world of white, upper-middle-class America. He went home, he married, he became a father, divorced, went back to college, and looked for a direction, a way to add significance to a life that was on hold—going nowhere and everywhere at the same time.

The *Macheteros* approached Víctor. They needed money, and, sensing a chance for a spectacular haul, they tentatively planned their first operation outside of Puerto Rico. Víctor became a Wells Fargo guard, he read history, that markedly increased his sense of political commitment, and he simply waited for the right moment.

That came on the birthday of Pedro Albizu Campos. The Wells Fargo routine was to have five or ten million dollars in the vaults on a Monday night. Víctor knew that he and his boss would be alone with the money. When he returned from an armored car run to Bridgeport, he tied up his boss (and another guard who was not supposed to be there) and in two hours he squeezed over seven million dollars into a 1974 Buick which he had cleverly parked inside the vault area.

Outside were the *Macheteros.* They and Victor disposed of the car immediately after the robbery occurred and, while he went in one direction, the money went in another. Meanwhile, the authorities looked for a lone Puerto Rican who had long ago disappeared into the night.

After conducting more than two hundred interviews, the police and the FBI had no clues, no idea where Victor went or why he took the money. The trail led nowhere until *Los Macheteros* made a mistake, not in the United States, but in San Juan.

On October 30, 1983 the group fired a Law (light anti-tank) rocket at the federal building in Hato Rey. While this represented yet another symbolic attack on the agents of colonial authority, agents found significant clues when witnesses provided them with the license number of one of the vehicles used by *Los Macheteros.* It was a Chevrolet Blazer, found about a mile from the federal building. Members of the group had wiped the car clean of fingerprints and registered it to a fictitious person at a fictitious address. When the FBI searched motor vehicle department files for a José R. Almodóvar Ramírez, they came up empty handed. No such person, no such license.

However, after they obtained a search warrant, agents found a small section of a traffic ticket squeezed into the vinyl pocket of the driver's side door. The ticket was issued to a Pedro Almodóvar Rivera, a man who also lived at a fictitious address. But, the license came with a photograph and that promised to be of some assistance—if and when

244

agents discovered the identity of the middle aged man pictured on the license.

Agents found out who Almodóvar was when they followed other suspected members of *Los Macheteros*. Since at least 1981 the Bureau had secretly bugged the offices of men like attorney Jorge Farinacci. Those wiretaps provided links to Farinacci's associates, and in late 1983, one of those associates led agents to a nondescript apartment in Levittown, Puerto Rico. The man who lived in the apartment matched the photograph of Pedro Almodóvar. And, even more significantly, for a man with a phone in his home, "Almodóvar" used the pay phones in front of his apartment with unusual regularity. Agents removed the receiver from the pay phone, replaced it with another, and sent the original to Washington for fingerprint analysis. The fingerprints matched those on file of Filiberto Ojeda Ríos. It was December, 1983. Ojeda had been underground for thirteen years.

At times, the FBI had six cars following Ojeda Ríos. That made any efforts at evasion fruitless. Agents followed the revolutionaries by wiretapping their cars, wiretapping their apartments, wiretapping the public telephones in front of their homes, and even wiretapping people when they made love in the shower. Years later even conservative newspapers like *The Hartford Courant* would agree that agents had illegally satisfied their "prurient interests"[4] but, in 1984, those interests, were still allowed free rein.

Agents made no attempt to arrest Ojeda or other alleged members of *Los Macheteros*. In order to find out about the entire network of Machetero members, they simply watched, taped, photographed, and waited. This paid off in a thoroughly unexpected manner when group members began to talk about "Aguila." This was Víctor Gerena's code name so when agents put two and two together it added up to seven million dollars. That was serendipitous for the FBI, which quickly realized it had two golden opportunities to find the money and to prosecute *Los Macheteros* in the mother country. Since the not guilty verdict obtained by Albizu Campos in 1936, federal officials never willingly trusted a Puerto Rican jury. But, a trial of "terrorists" in a Hartford federal court would certainly produce the guilty verdict desired in Washington.

In the United States, agents followed Juan Segarra Palmer. He was a Harvard graduate who played a key role in the Wells Fargo expropriation. From Boston, Segarra helped organize the robbery and purchased a van used to transport the money. Throughout 1984 agents kept a close watch on Segarra's movements to and from Boston, Puerto Rico, and Mexico. Antonio Camacho became part of the story when he allegedly helped transport part of the money still stored in the United States; and Attorney Roberto Maldonado incriminated himself when agents spied him crossing the Mexican border at the same time as Juan Segarra Palmer and the money laden van.

In January of 1985, *Los Macheteros* staged a "Three Kings Giveaway" in Hartford, Connecticut and Bayamon, Puerto Rico. Members of the group—which had announced its responsibility for the robbery in October of 1984—used Wells Fargo money to provide gifts for poor Puerto Rican youngsters. It was a propaganda coup for the group but also a victory for the colonial authorities who, at each stage of the Three Kings planning, knew who was and was not participating. Thus, Norman Ramírez Talavera became a suspect when he helped organize the giveaway in New York and then participated in the purchase and distribution of toys in Connecticut.

By the middle of 1985 *Los Macheteros* confirmed—through their sources in the Justice Department—what they had long suspected: The FBI was about to arrest them. Members responded in a variety of ways: some fled, some went underground, and Filiberto Ojeda Ríos acted as if nothing was about to happen. He decided to fight colonialism in a public forum, but he never suspected that, in arresting eleven members of *Los Macheteros*, the FBI would simultaneously prove the group's charges of U.S. colonialism.

Long before dawn on August 30, 1985 roughly two hundred agents assembled in the San Juan offices of the FBI. Wearing camouflage uniforms, bulletproof vests, and "war paint" they prepared to arrest *Macheteros* in many parts of the island. Teams, accompanied in some cases by helicopters, showed no warrants as they stormed through doors and grabbed everything from a Donald Duck video cassette (at the home of Jorge Farinacci) to antinuclear war poetry (at the home of attorney Roberto Maldonado). In some cases agents broke down doors when frightened family members asked for identification; and in an example that typified the entire operation, men in bullet proof vests made a ten-year-old boy use the bathroom with an agent at his side and a shotgun at his head.

For the FBI, the arrests were a criminal matter. For Puerto Ricans of all political persuasions August 30th immediately represented a military assault on the *dignidad* of the Puerto Rican people. Representative Severo Colberg, a member of the Commonwealth party, said that "the FBI acted like the marines when they invaded Latin American countries." And Miguel Hernández Agosto, president of the Puerto Rican Senate, indignantly criticized the "humiliating" methods employed by the FBI. It was an "unpardonable omission" that the FBI never even informed, much less consulted the Puerto Rican governor about what one mainstream journalist called "the most flagrant outrage to democracy" ever witnessed in Puerto Rico.[5]

In *El Nuevo Dia*, owned by the founder of the statehood party, Rafael López Rosas spoke of "the master's courtesy." He was ridiculing Puerto Rico's governor who, when asked if the FBI told him about the raids, said they had not extended that courtesy. For López, the nature of the arrests indicated that the master had no faith in his slaves. Thus, islanders should instantly "rescue their political dignity by establishing a patriotic and revolutionary organization of all Puerto Ricans."

In a less impassioned but more insightful piece (also in *El Nuevo Dia*) Juan García Passalacqua—a deservedly distinguished political analyst who was once an assistant to Governor Luis Muñoz Marín— laid out the political nature of the problem. He took it for granted that the arrests proved that the United States was "an imperial power with a colony called Puerto Rico." However, the United States refused to face reality and the authorities in San Juan were both decadent and impotent. Thus, he saw a vital role for *Los Macheteros*. "The key questions are, of what are they guilty? Of robbing Wells Fargo? And was the robbery committed to advance an anticolonial ideal? The *final* trial would depend on the future of the anticolonial ideal."

García Passalacqua asked his readers to remember Menachim Begin. When Israel was an English colony he robbed numerous banks; today he received the Nobel Prize. Thus, the victor not only received the spoils of war, he received the fruits of peace. Likewise, if the United States faced the truth, the arrested revolutionaries would be free men in a free society. If not, they would be criminals in the halls, not of justice, but of the imperial power.[6]

As the shackled and handcuffed defendants entered the courtroom of Judge Justos Arenas on Friday, August 30th, their attorneys had one over-riding goal: Keep them in Puerto Rico. Only a week before the arrests occurred, Puerto Ricans debated the fate of Juan Juarbe Juarbe, formerly the personal secretary of Albizu Campos. Juarbe exiled himself in 1936 because he refused to accept any form of United States authority; for the last 20 years he had lived and worked in Cuba, e.g., as a foreign service officer for the Castro government. Now dying, Juarbe wanted to return to Puerto Rico and even the English-only *San Juan Star* said "One does not have to agree with the viewpoint of the Nationalists to know they are a rare breed of *patriots*, almost an extinct species in their unrelenting clinging to principle."[7] (emphasis added)

The defense had a chance in Puerto Rico; on

the island any trial of the *Macheteros* meant a real and serious discussion of U.S. politics. That was the last thing Washington wanted so it pressed for removal of the defendants before any decision on bail. The defense countered with a request for five days to prepare for the bail hearings and the prosecutors readily agreed. After all, since the removal hearing took place on Sunday, by the time the defense returned to court the eleven defendants would be in the United States.

The defense got the point. They agreed to immediately proceed with the bail hearings and that moved federal prosecutors to ask for a recess. An hour later—after they consulted with officials in Washington—prosecutors reversed themselves. When the proceedings began they wanted the bail hearings to occur that afternoon; now they wanted a "three day continuance" and everybody knew why: The stall gave the federal government a chance to take the defendants to the metropolis.

In a final attempt to stop the FBI juggernaut, defense attorneys pointed to the arrest warrants: They were blank. No names, no addresses, no docket numbers, no signature of *any* judicial official. Judge Arenas agreed that the legal code clearly stated "that a warrant shall be signed by the magistrate" and "these are not signed by a magistrate, I realize that." However, he also realized that he worked for the federal government. The judge asked for a recess; he studied his law books and then told all assembled that the warrants contained no "fatal" defect. The prosecutors thus got their continuance and the defendants got what they expected. As Judge Arenas summed it up, "In a way if these gentlemen are removed, I am putting them in a place where they don't have ties to the community and I realize that. That may be one result of my granting the motion of the U.S. Attorney and unfortunately that will have to be taken up in another court. My decision stands."[8]

On Sunday, the defendants were flown to Hartford. And when they finally entered a Connecticut courtroom on September 3, 1985, authorities shaped public opinion in—for Hartford, Connecticut—a totally unprecedented fashion. Main Street looked like Beirut or Bosnia. Dogs, machine guns, sharpshooters, flak jackets, and one fellow wearing as many bullets draped over his chest as Rambo in Vietnam. To enter the courtroom spectators passed through two metal detectors, and, in sharp contrast to the casual attitude at an airport, burly courtroom officers checked everything.

Defense lawyers cried foul. How could anyone get a fair trial when, as in Chicago in 1980, the authorities first labeled the defendants terrorists and then created an atmosphere that was far more frightening than anything Hartford had ever witnessed?

In answer, the defendants were immediately denied bail. At this point, the *Macheteros* had an important strategic and political decision to make. Should they declare themselves prisoners of war? Should they try to find a way to convert the illegitimate courts into a forum in which to denounce the crime committed against their people by the United States? And, could the group follow a unified strategy, or would the personal problems that caused political divisions within the organization be reflected in differing legal tactics as well?

While the eleven defendants eventually chose to follow different strategies, the initial, united decision to *not* boycott the federal proceedings surprised many court watchers. In sharp contrast to the POW position of the FALN, the *Macheteros* marshalled a small army of lawyers, constitutional scholars, and international personalities to forge a novel "legal/political" defense.

The Strategy

In 1936, Albizu Campos certainly denied the authority of the federal government, but he nevertheless participated in a federal trial in a federal courtroom. Some scholars suggest this decision was a consequence of Albizu's profession and eminence; he was a distinguished lawyer who had used his intelligence to defeat the system on a number of occasions. So, why not try again?[9]

Many of the *Macheteros* were influenced by Albizu's example—and by the trials of the FALN. Men like Ojeda Ríos and Colón Osorio applauded and supported the FALN's unwavering commitment to principle; but, by taking a POW position, no open debate about the nature of U.S. policy ever took place. Like Alicia Rodríguez in Judge Bailey's Chicago courtroom, the defendants were silenced as soon as they tried to make a point about international law or the rights of anticolonial combatants.

The *Macheteros* chose to fight *before* the case went to a formal trial. They vehemently denied the jurisdiction of federal courts with a variety of provocative motions to the court.

In June of 1986 the Macheteros asked for a

change of venue in a motion that summarized the history of U.S. involvement in Puerto Rican society. When the defendants presented witnesses who testified to the degree of prejudice Puerto Ricans experienced in Connecticut, Judge Claire cited President Eisenhower. Hadn't he offered Puerto Ricans independence if they chose it? Therefore, the United States wasn't to blame if the Puerto Ricans wanted to remain under U.S. authority.

Although they never realized the actual degree of cynicism and duplicity practiced by the Eisenhower administration (see Chapter Two), the defendants nevertheless called the president's offer "fraudulent at best." However, Judge Claire refused to accept an argument made by the Chief Justice of the Puerto Rican Supreme Court. In his *Historia Constitutional de Puerto Rico* Judge Trías Monge closed his two volume treatise by arguing that "regardless of the profuse expressions of the United States in favor of self-determination, Puerto Rico has never had that right recognized except rhetorically...the people of Puerto Rico have practiced without success all kinds of gestures, tricks, and pirouettes before the negligent Sphinx of the North to provoke its attention and solve the (colonial) charade. All has been in vain. The gates remain closed and the Sphinx mute."[10]

Judge Claire was never mute. On the contrary, he reaffirmed his faith in President Eisenhower as he simultaneously denied the validity of the legal arguments made by Supreme Court Justice Trías Monge. The change of venue was denied, but the defendants claimed a moral victory because their nation's real history was now a matter of public record.

Trying another tactic, the *Macheteros* argued in December of 1986, that the court had no jurisdiction because "the United States Constitution prohibits colonialism." This eloquent brief by law professor Arthur Kinoy relies upon the outraged dissent of U.S. Supreme Court Justice Harlan in 1901: "The idea that this country may acquire territories anywhere upon the earth, by conquest or treaty, and hold them as mere colonies or provinces—the people inhabiting them to enjoy only such rights as Congress chooses to accord them—is wholly inconsistent with the spirit and genius as well as with the words of the Constitution."[11]

But, was Puerto Rico a colony? Prosecutors argued it was not and the judge agreed, making the defense right about the Constitution but wrong about its own nation. The trial would proceed, and Juan Segarra and Filiberto Ojeda Ríos would remain in administrative detention. After two years in "the hole," the two defendants had undergone *over three thousand* searches of their bodies. They sometimes received four to six "investigations" a day but, in the summer of 1987, correction officers suddenly made a new demand. After a strip search, the political prisoners now had to place their fingers inside their lips and pull them up and down. For both men this was a final indignity which they adamantly refused to accept. They went back to their cells rather than allow officials to, as Ojeda noted, treat them like "horses."

The lip searches finally stopped. But Juan Segarra spent more than two years in pretrial detention, and when Filiberto Ojeda Ríos was given bail after an unprecedented 33 months in the hole, his treatment—and the court's disregard of the venue and constitutional motions—might have moved some to question the efficacy of the new legal approach. Nobody seemed to be listening. The facts didn't matter. So, why continue?

One reason was the nature of the FBI's evidence. Many defendants thought they could prove the FBI flagrantly violated the law in pursuing the *Macheteros*; if they succeeded, the defendants would not only go free—for lack of usable evidence—they would show the people of the United States and Puerto Rico how the FBI actually did business.

Of particular importance to both sides was the June 1987 hearings which focused on the FBI's allegedly illegal search of the *Machetero* safehouse. One attorney described the safehouse—actually a two room suite in a San Juan office building—as an "independence movement archive." It contained an enormous quantity of everything from original *Machetero* communiques to strategy planning documents to papers outlining the internal organization and hierarchy of the *Macheteros*. For the prosecution, discovery of the safehouse was serendipitous; for the defense it was a "black bag" job reminiscent of the FBI's worst offenses during COINTELPRO in the 1960s. After all, agents had been following the *Macheteros*, including those in charge of the office, for weeks; yet they wanted the court to believe that their surveillance had nothing to do with the discovery of the safe house.

This was hard to swallow, especially after the FBI presented a group of witnesses who told their story: When Gary Alonso went to his office on the morning of April 2, 1984 he immediately discovered that someone had robbed his suite. Alonso wasn't surprised—this was the fourth robbery—so he called the police (according to the official records the call was received at 8:47 A.M.), an officer arrived, and, as they walked to Alonso's third floor office, it was obvious that the thief also visited other third floor offices. But, as Patrolman Diaz told Alonso, he could neither enter nor prepare a report on the other suites because the owners of the offices were not present. Police protocol specified that if "there wasn't somebody there presenting a complaint about what had been taken," an officer could neither enter nor search the premises.

Roughly five hours after Alonso's call to the police, Miguel Elvira arrived at his third floor suite. No one had contacted him during the day so, once Elvira discovered the robbery, he immediately went outside to find a police officer. Official records say Elvira first approached Officer Eugenio Colón at 4 P.M. Colón already knew about the robbery: because it occurred on his beat, and colleagues told him about it when he went to work at noon.

As Colón accompanied Elvira to his office, the officer noticed that the door to Suite 302 was open. And, according to his sworn testimony, he suspected that the thief might still be in that office. However, despite his suspicions, he went down the hall with Mr. Elvira, they chatted amiably for 25 minutes or so, and then they both returned to the suite that supposedly housed the thief.

Since defense lawyers found it hard to believe that Colón waited 25 minutes to confront the thief, or that he thought the burglar was still around seven hours after the police's first appearance, Attorney Leonard Weinglass probed his state of mind. Did he think the robber might be armed? "Correct." Did Colón call for a backup? "No." Did he announce himself as a police officer? "No." As he entered the office, was Mr. Elvira standing right next to him? "He is near me, yes." An unarmed civilian? "Correct."

Many observers found Colón's testimony hard to believe. Still, he had only been on the force three months. Perhaps he was just flustered by what could have been his first criminal investigation.

Now inside the suite, Colón—and Elvira, who was still tagging along—sensed "in about a minute" that the office was empty. However, he continued to search the suite, and, to his surprise, he discovered a bomb. Supposedly it was located in a cherry red shoebox "in plain view" of anyone entering the office. But, when Colón was asked in court to look through a series of FBI photos of the office's contents, he said the clear photo of the red shoebox represented an item he either had not seen, or could not remember seeing. At first he didn't remember the color of the bomb, but, eventually, he settled on white and he never mentioned the cherry-red shoebox produced by the FBI as the bomb's receptacle.

This confusion about the bomb—which was the FBI's main justification for its search of the office—upset the defense. Did the device really exist? Or had the police and FBI made up the bomb story to justify their search of premises which had already been entered illegally? Colón said the bomb—or what he thought to be a bomb—existed, but Elvira said the officer made no mention of a bomb as they

257

searched the suite. More important to those examining the evidence, Officer Colón testified that once
he saw the bomb, he and Elvira casually walked
back to Elvira's office, Colón called his superiors,
and then, in an office right next to the one with the
bomb, Colón and Elvira sat around gabbing for the
fifteen minutes it took other police officers to arrive.

As Attorney Weinglass incredulously asked
Colón, "You just engaged in small talk, passing the
time of day?" "Yes, we chatted." "With a bomb in the
office next door?" Officer Colón: "Correct."

If, after listening to Officer Colón's sworn testimony, it was hard to believe that a bomb ever existed, the story became even more far-fetched when
FBI agent Joséph Reyes took the stand. At first he
said he had seen a nine-volt battery—used to
explode the bomb—in the office. Later, under cross
examination by the defense, he admitted that was "a
mistake;" what he had actually seen was a nine volt
battery connector. And then, even though a judge
gave permission for a search because Reyes assured
him that the dangerous device—which needed the
battery to explode—"would pose grave threat and
danger to human lives and property if these devices
were not removed as soon as is practical," Reyes
admitted that no police or FBI official evacuated the
office building, the school across the street, or the
senior citizens facility also nearby. Indeed, to prepare the affidavit required to obtain a proper search
warrant, Reyes left the supposedly dangerous
premises for six hours, and no one evacuated the
area, not to mention the office building itself.

Given the testimony of Officer Colón and Agent
Reyes, there are only two plausible interpretations

of the seven volumes of sworn testimony: Either the authorities discovered a bomb or bombs but they were so unbelievably incompetent they saw no reason to protect themselves, the aged, and the children in the school, or, the Puerto Rican police and the FBI fabricated the bomb story to justify their seizure of materials which—without the presence of a bomb to justify their search—would never be permitted as evidence in a court of law.

To the defense, the search of the safehouse represented a repeat of the illegal entries conducted by the FBI during the Hoover years. They fully expected the judge to believe the FBI's incredible story but, for the historical record, they had once again made a point about the nature of the colonial authorities and the methods they employed to repress meaningful resistance to federal authority.

A final pretrial controversy centered around the evidence accumulated through wiretaps. Defendants believed they could show how Washington had once again disregarded the dignity of Puerto Rican people.

In the United States, the specter of Big Brother casts a shadow over the use of any wiretap, so the law is generally quite explicit about what the agents of authority can and cannot do. To obtain permission to engage in "electronic monitoring" police officials must normally submit sworn affidavits which contain the following types of information: the basis for assuming that a person is involved in criminal activity, the activity, the length of time the wiretapping will last, the assurance that other forms of surveillance (e.g, following the person) are impossible or fruitless, and the promise to "minimize the interception of communications" which have nothing to do with the criminal activity under investigation.

Even with their authorization to eavesdrop in hand, the agents of police authority are still required to maintain the strictest control over every tape recording they obtain. The possibility that the tapes may have been tampered with raises the most significant legal problems concerning their admissibility as evidence. So, to protect the *prosecutor's* case as much as the defendant's rights, the law is exceptionally clear: The tapes must be literally sealed—usually with an adhesive—"immediately" after they are obtained. With the seal in place, all concerned have a much greater assurance that what a jury hears in court is also what officials heard when they first taped the conversation.

In the Wells Fargo case, the FBI apparently encountered what one fellow called "a severe shortage of tape adhesive." In the recordings compiled at Levittown (at or near the home of Filiberto Ojeda Ríos) the FBI waited more than eighty days to seal the monitoring evidence. And in the tapes accumulated at Vega Baja (at the residence of Juan Segarra and Lucy Berríos) federal authorities waited a minimum of sixteen days to seal the evidence.

When the defendants discovered the taping gaps, they argued that the judge would have to disallow the government's recorded evidence.

Anywhere but in a court of law, "immediately" means right away. But in a federal court, in a political case, the judge has enormous discretion in interpreting the meaning of words. So, as the judge reached a judicial definition of immediately, he had two possible choices at his disposal. In the Second

Circuit Court of Appeals—Hartford's circuit—case law said that "immediately" meant two days. However, in the First Circuit—the one for Puerto Rico—no one had yet arrived at a specific definition of "immediately."

The judge used the First Circuit's lack of a specific standard as his standard; this meant he would allow the prosecution to use the sixteen-day Vega Baja tapes but the eighty-day tapes from the residence of Ojeda Ríos were excluded. The prosecution appealed because they needed the tapes to win in court; the case of Ojeda and five other defendants was severed from the rest; and in the fall of 1988 five *Macheteros*—Juan Segarra, Roberto Maldonado, Antonio Camacho Negron, Carlos Ayes Suárez, and Norman Ramírez Talavera—went to trial on charges stemming from the robbery of Wells Fargo.

Despite losing on the sixteen-day tapes, some defendants claimed three victories. The FBI got caught violating its own laws. The judge got caught in a major contradiction: To permit the tapes as evidence he changed circuits for one of the first times in the court's history. Equally important, the judge argued that the defendants would be tried in Hartford because the robbery occurred in that circuit's jurisdiction; but, when he needed a way to use evidence, he used another circuit's law to make the government's case.

The last contradiction was the most significant of all: Puerto Rico's constitution explicitly forbid *all* forms of wire tapping. The tapes were utterly illegal even if agents sealed them two seconds after completing a tape. But, Puerto Rico's constitution obviously meant nothing to the mother country. That was a truth few could now reasonably deny so defendants felt they had once again used the law to underline the colonial status of Puerto Rico and its people.

The judge made certain that political issues never became a part of the judicial proceedings. The jury only heard the evidence relating to the robbery and the safehouse documents, and a variety of very incriminating witnesses. Juan Segarra was ultimately sentenced to 65 years in prison. On appeal that was reduced to 55 years but a political revolutionary was treated like a common criminal. Juan paid a great price for his political beliefs, and so, too, Antonio Camacho Negron. He received maximum sentences for minimum charges (i.e., helping to transport the money) and—this is my opinion—it was his open refusal to accept federal authority that moved the jury to convict him even though the evidence against Antonio left room for a good degree of reasonable doubt.

Was the attempt of the Macheteros to use the legal system any more effective than the POW stance of the FALN? Not if by effective, one means changing the system. In 1981 and 1989, authorities in the metropolis refused to honestly confront the colonial realities of the Puerto Rican nation. In both instances, officials denied that Puerto Rico was a colony as they simultaneously called American firms operating in Puerto Rico "possessions corporations." And, in Hartford, a judge authoritatively cited President Eisenhower as an example of an American committed to self-determination even though this president was not only cynical, he was demonstrably disregarding the expressed will of the

Puerto Rican people.

The record indicates that the courts are an expression of the North American government. That government sometimes admits—e.g., in the remarks of Representative Fred Crawford in 1952 or Senator Henry Jackson in 1974—that Puerto Rico is a colony, but it always incarcerates those who struggle to eliminate a terrible contradiction: The United States, the oldest representative democracy on earth, owns Puerto Rico, the oldest colony on earth.

America's Gulags

"Nationwide, most correctional officers acknowledge that a court can implement remedies, but believe that unless it is done prudently, prison administrators will have to sacrifice autonomy to comply with the Constitution—a sacrifice they would prefer not to make."

—Scott Styles, Federal
Prison Journal, 1991[1]

This warden refused to lie. In discussing the pretrial incarceration of Alejandrina Torres, Edwin Cortés, and Alberto Rodríguez, Warden Dennis Luther told the court why they were being treated differently. "The sole reason" was a dossier provided by the FBI. "That information can be summarized as follows: Petitioners are members of a disciplined, well organized, international terrorist organization dedicated to achieving political goals through violent means...."[2]

After their arrest on June 29, 1983, the three Puerto Ricans were immediately placed in "administrative detention." Their cells contained a bed and a toilet bowl. In the early days of their detention they received no utensils to clean either themselves or their cells. They received no visitors, no showers, no change of clothes. The solid steel doors were bolted at all times and the small "portholes" in the door were also kept shut. As Alberto explains the impact, "when the chuckholes are closed we are completely isolated and cut off from all external stimulation. The cell is virtually soundproof; the air does not circulate and becomes stuffy, stale, and suffocating; the room temperature rises to an uncomfortable level; and the level of stress increases substantially. The only way to communicate with anyone, for example, to ask an officer for pencil and paper, is to bang on the door and scream."

The guards didn't hear a thing, not even the complaints of a woman in the man's wing. Chicago's Metropolitan Correctional Center has a floor reserved for women, but, given Alejandrina Torres' political status, she not only was housed with the men, but her cell contained a window which made it impossible for her to even use the toilet "except in view of male guards and prisoners." Ms. Torres—a grandmother and the wife of a minister—was forced to listen as other prisoners made every lewd comment imaginable; meanwhile, her requests for privacy got this response from the guards who were willing to talk: "The terms of their custody had been inflexibly ordered in Washington."[3]

Although prison regulations stipulate no limitation on the amount of time a person can spend in administrative detention, a review committee is supposed to reassess each prisoner at least every thirty days "and a psychologist should make a 30-day evaluation to ensure that the inmate is not deteriorating."[4] The potentially traumatic effect of such intense sensory deprivation is universally recognized. Thus, the prisoners' families and a group of attorneys first protested the nature of their incarceration, and, when that produced no changes, the attorneys took the government to court. The three Prisoners of War had been found guilty of nothing, yet they were subjected to "cruel and unusual punishment." To the attorneys, "the conditions of their present confinement at M.C.C. Chicago amounted to deliberate physical and psychological torture, apparently designed to pressure and 'break' the prisoners, and to intimidate and terrify their families, their community, and the internationally recognized political movement of which they are a part."

Judge Paul Plunkett rendered his decision on July 11, 1983. He agreed that politics was at the center of the case: In deciding to use administrative detention Warden Luther considered the seditious conspiracy charges against the prisoners and the special information he received from the FBI—information that was secretly submitted to the judge by the warden and not released to the prisoners, their attorneys, or the general public.[5]

The judge also agreed that the FBI's dossier moved the Warden to make the prisoners' administrative detention even more restrictive "than that of prisoners normally held under that status." Alberto Rodríguez was correct in arguing that other administrative detainees who had tried to escape—including one who had shot two marshals in his attempt to flee—enjoyed full telephone and unmonitored visiting privileges. Nevertheless, each of the Puerto Ricans was permitted telephone calls only to their attorneys. Alberto Rodríguez described family visits. "One guard sits at the table with us and takes notes on our conversations, often interjecting himself into the visit. At times a second guard has also monitored the visits from behind the visiting room window."

The judge acknowledged that this constituted special treatment for "special management detainees." It was, therefore, unusual by the standards of any prison in America, but it was not the cruel punishment forbidden by the Constitution because it was not punishment. Judge Plunkett wrote that "in determining the constitutionality of treatment of pretrial detainees, the United States Supreme Court has held that this court must determine whether those conditions amount to the punishment of the detainee." Since the three revolutionaries had been found guilty of nothing, the judge not only agreed that it would be unconstitutional to punish them before a trial occurred, he also stressed that "courts must be vigilant to protect the rights of those who espouse unpopular causes because inroads into our liberties most frequently occur in such a situation."[6]

However, the court also had to consider the sealed FBI dossier and the charges of seditious conspiracy. The "allegations" against the prisoners were "directed against the very fabric of society" and the FBI said the prisoners might try to escape. Thus, "we conclude that the Warden's decision to place Petitioners in administrative detention was not punitive in nature but rather was based on legitimate prison objectives—to prevent escape or unauthorized entry, to prevent the introduction of contraband and to protect the institution's security."

The admittedly unusual conditions of confinement did not constitute punishment because this form of administrative detention was justified by the FBI's secret information charging political terrorism. Moreover, the prisoners had to remember that their detention would end promptly "because the length of any pretrial confinement is substantially limited by the Petitioners rights under the Speedy Trial act" (theoretically ninety days).

Edwin Cortés disagreed. Almost a year after the judge 's promise of a speedy trial, he was still in administrative detention. It was still "very difficult to breathe in the cell when the chuckhole was closed (for 23 hours a day), and, after Eddie complained "to a physician's assistant of stomach pains, he gave me medication through the chuckhole in the cell door without ever examining me."[7]

The pain soon produced such pain that Eddie cut short a much cherished family visit. This convinced the authorities to take his complaints so seriously that he was first taken to the MCC medical unit and then to Mercy Hospital. "A physician told me that in one hour he was going to operate to remove my appendix but the U.S. Marshall refused to allow me to telephone my family or my attorneys, even after I expressed my desire to obtain a second opinion. He eventually relented and allowed me to phone my wife."

The surgery was postponed. Eddie stayed on intravenous feeding for a day and then the doctors ordered 24-48 hours of observation. "After an hour and a half of this, the U.S. Marshall, refusing to allow me to consult with a nurse or doctor, took me out of the hospital and back to the sensory deprivation cell, chuckhole tightly closed, in administrative detention at the MCC. "

Eddie wanted a doctor. Two days later one appeared, but "I was not seen in the medical unit, nor were any tests done...my own doctor was not allowed to examine me after I had been taken back to the MCC. I have tried to make telephone calls to my attorneys, and each time the staff has refused to respond. As a result the last legal call I made was November 4, 1983."[8]

Eddie's statement is dated March 5, 1984. He and the other prisoners remained in administrative detention for over two years. Alejandrina Torres received a visit from her daughter. Afterwards, Alejandrina submitted to a strip search and then a cavity search. When this was over the guard said to do it again. Alejandrina questioned the necessity of another search, suggesting that this second intrusion was nothing more than harassment. This prompted the guard to call her lieutenant but, instead of telling the truth, the guard said that Alejandrina had refused to be searched.

"Lieutenant Lewis came into my cell, handcuffed me from behind and took me to a small room. Besides the Lieutenant, there were four female guards (one was Lewis' wife) in the small enclosure. They removed the handcuffs and sat me on a milk crate near the door. When I realized that they had blocked the door I questioned the presence of the Lieutenant...he didn't answer but ordered me to be quiet. I said that I would not submit to a strip or cavity search in his presence."

After more than a year in administrative detention, Alejandrina knew the regulations. Strip searches were to be conducted by a member of the same sex "although in an emergency, when there is imminent likelihood of escape, assault, or serious contraband being introduced, this condition does not apply."[9]

The Lieutenant didn't care. "He grabbed my hands and ordered the guards to search me. I said that he was not going to do this to me. He took my wrist and began to squeeze and twist it...I shouted in desperation asking that they did not violate me in such a fashion. He didn't pay attention and the others did nothing. When I got a hand free they handcuffed me again and threw me to the floor while I continued asking that he leave...I asked the four women that they stop him from searching me. I said that I would submit to a search by them. The four said nothing, not even the Lieutenant's wife. They used their feet to apply great pressure to my neck. My body was bent over my knees. I felt a punch in the ribs and they pushed my face against the floor, causing me great pain. They forced my legs apart and on the Lieutenant's orders they did a cavity search without the least consideration to my constant pleas."

The warden's response to this incident was to place Alejandrina in the hole, deny her the ability to telephone her family to report the abuse, convict her of being insolent, and, before her trial, the guards covered their tracks by sending the judge a false report of the incident. They said it was Mrs. Torres who provoked the incident and it was her fault that the Lieutenant needed to use so much force that Alejandrina lost the use of her arm for two years.

Such is administrative detention. It's not punishment but a means by which the authorities maintain pretrial order against the political prisoners who "threaten the very fabric of society."

The Cardinal Unit

Haydée Torres says "we were put to the test when we came to prison... I spent over 2.5 years on the tenth floor which is the equivalency of 20 stories up in San Diego, California. I was locked up in that building with no sun, no air, and with no access to the ground for 2.5 years. My system began to break down. I had to give up eating meat. I had a complete breakdown in my system. I cannot tolerate bacteria. Meat is something that makes me physically sick now. Anything that has an excessive amount of bacteria will put me in bed. Now they know this. They knew this, because I was progressively getting worse and worse. What did they do with me? They transferred me to Alderson, West Virginia."[10] It was called the "Cardinal Unit," a presumably cute phrase for a prison within a prison—two cells both reserved for Puerto Rican prisoners of war.

Haydée and Luz Rodríguez arrived before construction of the "control unit" was completed, and lived through a tear down of asbestos filled walls. Noxious fumes temporarily overwhelmed both women, but they produced permanent damage to Luz. "I developed nasal polyps. Also serious sinus infections which have plagued my existence ever since."

Each cell contained the following items: A bed bolted to the floor, a sink bolted to the floor, and a table—with no chair—also bolted to the floor. Each cell also contained one window; it was permanently shut and made of a glass which distorted any view of the outside. The cell's first door was made of steel bars, the second of wood; the first was a lock, the second a coffin-like seal. As Haydée says, "there was no air conditioning in Alderson because it's a very old prison. So if they shut the door—there was a window down the hall they would open for air—so if they shut the door your air is gone...we do not see any other prisoner. For all we know no one existed in the world, just us. This was a sound proof room."

Outside was a guard. Twenty-four hours a day. Every day of the year the two women spent in the Cardinal Unit. Luz says that "every sound and whisper was subjected to scrutiny. Daily logs were maintained of all our activities, including what and how much we ate at each meal, when we menstruated, how many sanitary pads we asked for, when we slept, exercised and showered, how often and with whom we spoke on the telephone, with whom we corresponded, as well as the content of our letters...."

The women received no explanation for their new "placement." Haydée, already quite ill from her incarceration in San Diego, was placed in the cell and told "this is where you are going to spend the rest of your life. Have some fun." When Haydée asked to speak to her attorney she was told "we'll see if we can get around to it." And that's it. "The warden says this to me. Lucy arrives, and they tell Lucy, 'You cannot see Haydée.' We're next door to each other. 'We're going to shut the door whenever we take one of you out of the room. The other one cannot see. You cannot see each other. You cannot talk to each other. You are not to have attorney visits together. You're not to have anything together. You are never to have any contact with each other.'"

The exercise room was another cell. It contained an old exercise bicycle, a floor mat and a toilet, also bolted to the floor. "We were allowed one, ten-minute phone call per week. We were not permitted to dial the number nor to speak in private. At least three guards would be present making us aware that our conversations were being strictly timed and monitored."

Handcuffing was a constant. Before the woman left the cell three guards appeared. Haydée or Lucy would then turn their backs against the steel door, slide their hands through an opening, the cuffs were locked on, the hands came back through the slot, the door opened, and the women walked the ten feet to the "exercise area" or to the shower.

Within six months the handcuffing procedures were somewhat relaxed. What never changed was the "suffocating nature" of family visits. The rest of the population saw their loved ones for an entire day, "outside most days of the week. Each one of our visits with family members took place within a small room downstairs from the unit, and always in the scrutinizing presence of a guard. Under those conditions we were allowed to visit for two hours."

Luz recalls one visit with her mother. "After the visit was terminated, my mother was asked to remain seated until a guard escort was available to take her to the front gate. Meanwhile I was taken to a bathroom a few feet from where my mother sat and there I was strip searched by an arrogant female guard who resented my political views and proceeded to voice it, aware that my mother was within hearing distance and aware of all that was happening. I was forced to internalize my anger because I didn't want to add to my mother's anguish and loss of power to protect her daughter."[11]

Protests finally forced the Federal Prison Bureau to close the Cardinal Unit. But, in answer to the question, "what is the meaning of the control and manipulation?," Luz says, "By dehumanizing the living conditions of prisoners of war and political prisoners in general, the State attempts to instill fear and a sense of impotence in the hearts and minds of those who dare to resist...for example, in today's highly technological world strip searches are not necessary to impede the introduction of weapons and drugs into the prison. Prison bureaucrats lie when they make claims to the contrary. Strip searches constitute a form of rape, a violation of the individual's human rights. It's sexual abuse and harassment to wear down the resistance and morale of the individual."

The New Penology

Alicia Rodríguez needed surgery. She received a strip search—flashlight and all—before she left for the hospital and, once she was dressed, guards locked handcuffs on her wrists and shackles on her legs. She was accompanied by a prison "apprehension team" and they were accompanied by state troopers carrying a variety of large and small weapons.

When the army of officers entered the emergency room Alicia waited while guards explained procedure to the hospital staff. "I was put in a room with a guard and not allowed to leave for a moment. I was handcuffed when they removed my clothing. To get my pants off they removed the shackles from my feet but they left them on my hands. They chained me to the table when I had x-rays taken and the nurses didn't want to come into the room for fear I would kill them. They gave me an enema with the cuffs on. The doctor relaxed the technician but not the guard who stayed with me throughout my preoperative examinations."

In the hospital room "my bed was chained to the wall and I was chained to the bed." A sergeant and lieutenant, both armed, stood outside my door while inside there was a female guard who called the prison every twenty minutes. The nurses did not want to enter my room. Outside they had two police cars patrolling the area twenty-fours hours a day. They had plainclothes police in the hospital and at each entrance. No privacy. The door was never closed."

In prison, the warden had given permission for Alicia to call her mother and sister. This was revoked at the hospital. "Not even a legal phone call. The doctor was in contact with the lawyer giving general information but no details whatsoever. The doctors took pictures of what they removed from my body because they were not allowed to take me to the laboratory. The operation was at 8 AM, and I was waking up by 11 AM or so. One of my most vivid memories is of the guard in the recovery room. He was there all the time and when I was just regaining consciousness, he came over to my side and shook the chain which locked me to the bed. The chain was intact so he walked back to the door."[12]

Alicia's story underlines the essence of what is today called the "New Penology." From the outside it looks like a fatal dose of security overkill; from the inside it's a new approach to penology, an approach which can best be seen in the treatment of United States political prisoners in general, and Puerto

Rican prisoners of war, in particular.

To correction officers it's a question of professionalism. Call the federal penitentiaries at Marion,
Lewisburg, or Oxford and a business-like voice
always asks, "Is this call in relation to an inmate?"
If so, one must provide a name and a nine digit
number. If not, one can be efficiently connected to
anybody from the warden to a unit chief. It's always
a matter of procedure, always a matter of deperson-
alizing—as institutional policy—everything from a
phone call to the cavity searches that symbolize life
in America's gulags.

"Spread cheeks" is an order burned into the
brain of all the Puerto Rican political prisoners but,
read the Department of Justice's *Guidelines For the
Development of a Security Program* and a strip (or
the "successively more intrusive" cavity) search
looks like a procedure as devoid of life as an auto or
appliance repair manual. "Whenever possible the
written consent of the inmate should be secured
before attempting the cavity search." Use disposable
gloves. All inspections should be "conducted only by
a member of the medical staff" and "these searches
should be *restricted* to digital intrusions and the use
of instruments such as an anascope, otoscope, vagi-
nal speculum, nasal speculum, tongue blade, and
simple forceps." (emphasis added)

This dead language hides a disturbing fact: An
anascope is a machine that uses a snake-like tube
to crawl around the rectum. Meanwhile a technician
looks through a microscopic device or at a "tv
screen" to see what can be seen.

However unnerving, strip and cavity searches
are still only the most graphic illustration of an ide-

ological response, not only to Puerto Rican revolutionary movements, but to an explosion of the U.S. prison population. From 330,000 prisoners in 1980, the number of people who may now receive a strip search has jumped to 823,000.[13]

The numbers (and the Puerto Rican revolutionaries) demanded a response. It is called the "New Penology." The old way of thinking focused on rehabilitation and crime control; it stressed things like fault, responsibility, intervention and treatment. The New Penology focuses on professionalism in the service of incapacitation. The idea is that the United States is so criminally out of control that correction officials have neither the time, the resources nor the energy required to rehabilitate inmates. So, prison planners lowered their aspirations and created a penological ideology: to "detain offenders for a time and thus delay their resumption of criminal activity."

In today's prisons, correction officials seek "variable detention depending upon risk assessment." Corrections officers must never allow prisoners to "disrupt the orderly operation of the institution." Indeed, following the adage "a place for everything and everything in its place," the federal prison system has turned into an organization which uses "actuarial language" to "identify, classify, and manage groupings sorted by *dangerousness*."[14] (emphasis added)

Prisons are rated from one (Community Security) to six (Super Security), and prisoners from one to thirty-six. In theory officials objectively classify their "clients" on the basis of seven numerically weighted variables and, with his or her "security score" in hand, an individual is sent to the numerically correct institution. Thirty or above sends you to level six. In the case of a revolutionary like Alejandrina Torres, the nature of the factors considered assures a score which is at or near the highest security level. Her sentence is 35 years, thus a three on a "projected length of incarceration" scale of three. Her offense is serious, therefore a seven on a "severity of current offense" scale of seven; and, because she is a revolutionary, on the "history of violence scale" she also rates a seven on a scale of seven.[15]

In theory, an individual can be downgraded to a lower level prison. There is another chart—labeled "custody scoring"—and another set of seven numerically weighted variables. For example, a person who has served 91% or more of their sentence gets a six, while 0 to 25% of a sentence rates a three. Since the average sentence of many of the Puerto Rican political prisoners is 70 years, the custody chart doesn't do them much good. In fact, even if they scored a virtually impossible 28 of 30 (the highest score) , they still only get 1 point subtracted from their *original* security score. So, if one had a security total of 33 and the custody score permits the subtraction of one, the score is still 32, or, in English, Super Security.

This outcome is intentional. The "custodial continuum does not design penal measures for the particular needs of the individual or the community. Rather it sorts individuals into groups according to the degree of control warranted by their risk profiles."[16] Thus, the Puerto Rican revolutionaries are centrally monitored; only high level officials in

Washington are empowered to make the ultimate decisions about their fates and this extra special form of (personal plus numerical) classification assures that their initial security score is like the rock of Gibraltar.

The New Penology proudly uses the tools and language of science to develop what purport to be professionally objective criteria for its staff and inmates. In theory, few would quarrel with an objective approach. However, security/dangerousness/risk cannot be objectively measured. Once they became the axis of the federal system, officials taxed logic and reason to their ultimate limits. When they perceived even the remotest possibility of escape—and, by definition, a political prisoner like Alejandrina Torres or Oscar López Rivera or Ida Luz Rodríguez could or might or would try to escape—they used all the managerial tools at their disposal to create a unit so secure it had no place on the bureau's security continuum. The control unit at the federal prison in Lexington Kentucky was off the charts, so managerially "perfect" that its human significance is best grasped only when this special brand of administrative segregation is compared to "traditional" torture .

Lexington was slow, invisible torture. It bore no resemblance to the "normal" torture experienced by political prisoner Luz Berríos when she was detained in Mexico .

On August 30, 1985, U.S. officials arranged for the arrest of Ms. Berríos-Berríos, and her two children (then ten and five), in Cuernavaca, Mexico. She was allegedly a member of the Puerto Rican revolutionary group *Los Macheteros*. The Mexican authorities were asked to hold her until U.S. officials could arrange to take custody. Normally, the U.S. does not have the power to arrest in Mexico, and U.S. citizens lawfully in Mexico can only be returned to the U.S. by means of extradition. However, since Mexico has a long history of upholding international law by refusing to extradite Puerto Rican political prisoners, the FBI had to negotiate the release of Ms. Berríos and her children.

Luz was swept up and hustled into a truck, her children following in another vehicle. She was blindfolded, beaten enroute, and finally locked in a room, in an unidentified building, with the children. They ate in a "filthy" cell, without utensils, and, playing a game of awful versus despicable cop, the Mexicans told Luz to cooperate because "the next guards who were coming on were not nice." The "good cop" warned the children "he would blow their heads off if they were not good." According to Luz's sworn declaration, "he seemed to enjoy terrorizing the children. He continually told me that it didn't matter to him that I was a woman, or that there were children involved. He repeated the expression about 'breaking' or 'tearing out' the mother in me."

Two days into her nightmare, Luz and the children were separated. Three men interrogated her and, while one asked questions, another beat her. She could think of nothing except the fate of the children. "They told me it all depends on you. Finally, although I could hardly bring myself to say the words, I said, "you wouldn't kill them?" The man refused to answer." The Mexicans interrogated Luz about her husband Juan Segarra Palmer, about Filiberto Ojeda Ríos, about her friends, and about her entire history in the independence movement. When it was all over they made her sign a variety of documents. One was a waiver of extradition.

After four days, Luz was flown to Florida by the FBI. However, before she left, the Mexicans made her pay for processing the paperwork required for her release. In a perverse way, it was a fitting end to four days of physical and personal agony.[17]

This is "traditional" torture. One of its roots is hatred, and a love of pain is often an elemental part of the torturer's personality. Yet, however despicable, what happened to Luz Berríos is humanly comprehensible. Anyone can understand hateful people doing hateful things.

But, what about efficient prison professionals who house people in a sealed-off basement where the walls, ceilings and floors are high gloss white? Nothing is cleaner and nothing is more likely to create an environment so deliberately dead that the bright, artificial lighting seems appropriate. In the 8 foot by 10 foot cell where prisoners often could spend more than 23 hours a day, the furniture includes a single bed, a metal watercloset, a metal shelf, a metal stool, a metal cabinet. If they are lucky, there may be a color TV. Only an inspection by outsiders moved officials to install a small cork bulletin board (suitable for photos) and even the women's underwear is government issue and not the right size. The oversized overalls hang on their bodies while the earrings and bracelets permitted to women convicted of large-scale drug dealing, bank robbery, and murder are forbidden to the political prisoners. Indeed, like Ms. Torres' grandchildren, who were denied access because they were *not* immediate family, *nothing* personal easily enters this subterranean tomb because the essence of administrative segregation is total dehumanization in the service of total control.[18]

Luz was terrified and bloody; Alejandrina, apathetic and clean. Indeed she had such open shower privileges that the twenty-four hour a day TV surveillance allowed both male and female officers to monitor her every shower. In Lexington, they didn't beat you with their fists, they beat you with a managerial system that officials perceive to be amoral. Administrative segregation is a form of torture that allegedly takes the weapon out of the officer's hands. As one of the political prisoners at Lexington put it, "they're trying to kill us. But they'd rather we kill ourselves."

I don't think so. Nobody is trying to kill the prisoners. *It's worse than that.* What Alejandrina Torres (and others) endured is so terrible because at Lexington suicide (or the ever present depression, claustrophobia, hallucinations, and heart palpitations) would be nothing more than an "it should be studied" byproduct of social conditions specifically designed—not to kill—but to incapacitate. In this system any sign of humanity is such a functionally irrelevant variable that it must be trained out of any potentially susceptible officer.

"Don't talk to the prisoners." That was the standing order to staff who rigidly maintained social distance by keeping conversations to a minimum and by dutifully maintaining a written log of each and every conversation. Want to know how many tampons a prisoner requested in June or December of 1987? Check the log. Two or three sanitary napkins might be used to somehow subvert the system so, despite heavy periods, a prisoner received one napkin at a time, one humiliating request at a time.

Meals became an ordeal. Delivered to a small room at the end of the cell corridor, the food was passed through a slit in the wall and, before organizations like Amnesty International investigated, the rules stipulated that all meals should be eaten in the day room. This was a perfectly clean environment, with one terrible drawback: The endless TV surveillance made it impossible to even chew in private. Thus, the prisoners often ate alone in their cells rather than expose themselves to the literal Big Brother on the wall.

When outsiders began to complain, officials contradicted the prisoners. Don't believe their lies about a lack of facilities. Look. They have a clean room in which to eat, a shower in which to bathe, and a recreation area for physical activity. It's all there for the asking.

True, except for any appreciation of human factors. Originally, officials permitted only one prisoner in the recreation area at any point in time. Weather and staff availability permitting, a prisoner could stay outside for an hour. However, despite the TV cameras in the yard, despite the perpetual presence of a guard, and despite a rule forbidding the political prisoners to use the yard when either workman or prisoners from the main facility were even close to the yard's fence, every time the women went out they still received a strip search.

Therefore, rather than face yet another humiliating and unnecessary search, the women stayed inside. Lexington thus had a perverse effect on the prisoners. Instead of using their "privileges," the women increased their sense of isolation as the only means of assuring some degree of privacy and humanity.

Alejandrina Torres is the wife of a Protestant minister, the mother of five children, and a very typical Puerto Rican. Family is at the center of her existence; she would have a hard time defining herself apart from the extended family that is the social unit of Puerto Rican life. Yet, despite the Bureau of Prisons written policy about keeping prisoners near their families,[19] virtually all the Puerto Ricans are deliberately placed in prisons very far from their loved ones. And, in the case of Ms. Torres, the definition of immediate family was so restrictive it excluded one generation (the grandchildren) from seeing another. While this is spiritual death for a Puerto Rican, it is only another security precaution in units that house the nineteen political prisoners.

At Lewisburg Eddie Cortés received a visit from his paralyzed brother. Julio Cortés was confined to a wheelchair because of a car accident that had occurred while he was on the way to visit Eddie in Lewisburg; thus it was torturous for Eddie to imagine this first visit with his now handicapped brother. However, because Lewisburg had no facilities for the handicapped, Eddie had to see his brother in a non-visitors area. The result was that both men were then paralyzed, Julio by his accident, Eddie by the handcuffs on his hands and the shackles on his legs.

By the middle of 1988, complaints about the conditions at Lexington had finally reached the courts. Judge Barrington Parker (U.S. District

Court, District of Columbia) first tried to distinguish between the ideal and the real. It was true that the Federal Bureau of Prisons had pages of regulations specifying the prisoners rights; for example, the Unit Team did include a Psychologist and the team "did perform quarterly reviews of each prisoner's adjustment to the Unit and their assignment status."

But, "as detailed as this procedure appeared, it is misleading." The judge noted that "the written report produced after each review session is a mere one-page form with the inmate's name, the date, a few checked boxes, and occasional cryptic comments such as: 'Requests transfer—no change in criteria for placement.' Nor is there any indication, after a review of plaintiffs' quarterly reports, that any serious consideration was ever given to the matter."[20]

Alejandrina Torres already knew this and another fact which the judge carefully verified: The women were in Lexington because of their political ideals and beliefs. Barrington Parker had read all the denials written by Bureau officials but, "as the assignment criteria were disseminated among the Bureau's wardens and regional directors, the focus on an inmate's political ideologies became obvious." As one of the Bureau's officials noted when he discussed putting other Puerto Ricans in segregated units, "the offenses for which these individuals have been sentenced were the result of their *committed alliance to terrorist-oriented ideals and politically revolutionary organizations.*"[21] (emphasis is in the judge's published decision)

The judge refused to interfere. He wrote that

"the court is greatly troubled about the previous conditions within the Unit and the defendant's (i.e., the Federal Bureau of Prisons) gross insensitivity and belated response to those conditions. The Unit at best meets the bare Eighth Amendment standards prohibiting cruel and unusual punishment, but at times the treatment of plaintiffs has skirted elementary standards of decency. The exaggerated security, small group isolation, and staff harassment serve to constantly undermine the inmates morale."[22]

Amnesty International agreed with Judge Parker: It concluded that "the conditions of confinement and the transfer of prisoners to the HSU unit on the basis of their political beliefs constitute cruel, inhuman and degrading treatment in contravention of Article 5 of the (United Nations) Universal Declaration of Human Rights."[23]

The judge nevertheless let the prisons police themselves. He followed the "hands off" approach of his judicial predecessors and that produced a sigh of relief from many wardens. As a Bureau official succinctly put it in a 1991 issue of the *Federal Prison Journal*, "For more than 60 years the Federal Bureau of Prisons has succeeded in avoiding major judicial intervention to correct conditions of confinement in its facilities...these measures have made it difficult to prove that conditions of confinement in Bureau facilities are unconstitutional."[24]

While judges refuse to intervene for a variety of reasons, a major factor is the typical interpretation of the words "cruel and unusual punishment." Courts have held that the drafters of the U.S. constitution only wanted to proscribe torture and other barbarous methods of punishment.[25] Thus, if Luz Berríos had been beaten in a U.S. prison the treatment she and the children received might have qualified as cruel and unusual punishment. But, when she was whisked from a Florida airport to serve 18 months of pretrial detention at New York's Metropolitan Correctional Center, that wasn't cruel and unusual punishment. It was simply the way the U.S. system deals with Puerto Rican revolutionaries and other dangerous people.

For the Puerto Rican political prisoners, the New Penology represents a form of institutionalized inhumanity; control units like the one at Lexington are unusual by definition and cruel in practice because they justify anything in the name of risk management, even a system that deliberately trains its professionals to see numbers instead of people, risk-profiles instead of political prisoners, charts instead of human beings.

Marion: The Concentration Model

Lexington was an experiment. Marion is an institution. Created as the successor facility to Alcatraz, Marion represents an attempt to achieve "super security;" it is the only level-six facility in the federal prison system and, in what correction officials call the "rapid growth" environment of the eighties, Marion is the New Penology's "concentration model" for incapacitating "its relatively small number of disruptive inmates."[26]

Amnesty International writes that at Marion "there is hardly a rule in the (United Nations) Standard Minimum Rules for prisoners that is not infringed in some way or the other. The reason has to do with the purpose of Marion. According to the Standard Minimum Rules, treatment of persons shall have as its purpose encouraging self-respect and developing a sense of responsibility amongst inmates. The purpose of Marion, however, is security. All other considerations are secondary."[27]

Prison officials boast that since 1983 the average stay at Marion "has been only 35.6 months." As of late 1993, Oscar López has spent over 84 months at Marion, almost all of it in a control unit that promises security by practicing what the head of the federal prison system calls a "permanent lockdown" of virtually every man in the facility. In the case of Oscar López, he has been in his cell for 22 1/2 hours a day, every day, for the last 2555 days.[28]

In 1984 Norman Carlson (then director of the Federal Bureau of Prisons) told Congress that "as far as Marion is concerned I really don't know how to handle the extremely violent and dangerous offenders. The longer I am in this business, the less I know how to handle them."[29] Despite his lack of knowledge, Carlson nevertheless instituted a complete lockdown of Marion prison. The facility had recently experienced a number of assaults and murders so, "it is not a long-term solution but at least in the short term I think we have demonstrated that it is effective in reducing violence, which is our primary objective."[30]

When prisoners and lawyers, ministers and psychologists complained about Marion, Congress commissioned a study. It offered a variety of suggestions for change and at least one thought-provoking statistic: Of the 343 prisoners housed at Marion only 20% were rated at Level Six. The remainder of the prisoners were at Level 5 or 4, and two were at Level 3—medium security anywhere in the country.[31]

Marion thus represented an institution which severely punished the overwhelming majority because of the threats offered by a small minority. Still, the short term solution became a long term institution because, lacking knowledge, prisons officials made life easier for themselves by creating the concentration model of inmate incapacitation. The mere threat of being sent to Marion is enough to keep most prisoners in line.

Two federal officials who worked at Marion note that the prison system had two choices: Disperse the inmates or concentrate them. Dispersal had its benefits. No one institution was required to deal with "problem" cases and, with many prisons holding a few inmates each, fewer "security related resources" were required overall. But, the inmates "could not be confined indefinitely in detention or segregation units." The U.S. Constitution gave them rights so, while detention "briefly arrests their activity, it does not free the institution from their influence; neither does it prevent them from resuming their activities when they are put back into the general population."[32]

To federal officials the "correctional beauty" of the concentration model was that it put all the problem cases under one roof and provided a theoretical rationale for what had become a perpetual lockdown at Marion. In essence, even though only 20% of the prisoners were at Level Six, and even though the director of the system testified that he didn't know what to do, officials began to argue that

Marion's population overwhelmingly contained "predatory individuals" who could be well managed in the one facility that used "extremely refined" and "heightened security procedures." For example, in its cavity searches Marion officials employ forced rectal probes. Since inmates can easily store contraband out of a finger's reach, the main purpose of these probes appears to be degradation and intimidation. Leave the cell, go to court, try to use a library and you may very well experience what the prisoners call a forced rectal probe: rape.

By 1989 Congress questioned the legitimacy of the Marion lockdown. Congressman Charles Kastenmeier of Wisconsin said that "it would appear that maintaining security is possible without the sort of permanent in-cell lock-down as practiced at Marion." The congressman also questioned the "sincerity" of prison officials. He thought that Marion "serves not a temporary" purpose but that it was "part of the permanent deterrence and control strategy of the federal system."[33]

In response, Michael Quinlan (then the new director of the Federal Bureau of Prisons) offered a retraction. "I would like to correct a statement that I apparently made that I did not intend to, Mr. Chairman. When I talked about Marion as a temporary measure I was talking about the original efforts that were made in 1983-84 to lock down the facility. At the time it was believed to be a temporary measure. But, because of the effect that that measure had on the institution and the decreasing violence that occurred and on the rest of the system it became a permanent part of our system and we now term it a high security operation and it is a permanent part of our system."[34]

In truth, Marion was the prison system's ultimate deterrent. It could not be justified in terms of its population—even in 1984 only 20% were at Level 6—and it could not remain open with such a small number of incorrigibles. So, officials locked down everyone and then used Marion as a threat to any potential troublemaker. As Oscar López put it in a letter to prison officials in 1990, "Let's not forget that when I first arrived in Leavenworth, I was told by officials that where they really wanted to lock me up was in USP-Marion. Five years later their endeavors paid off and their wishes were fulfilled."

By 1990 Oscar had spent 43 months in "total segregation." That was already seven months more than the average stay at Marion and in the worst conditions at the nation's worst prison. No access to institutional programs, no use of the library, minimum association with all human beings, no contact visits with family, arbitrary interruption of interviews, severe restrictions on correspondence, no furniture in the cell, a dual purpose sink/toilet, and a bed which has a thin mattress on a concrete slab.

Even the officials worried about the effect of these conditions: "One concern raised about the closely controlled operation at Marion is that inmates may begin to experience detrimental mental health effects. This is premised on the belief that inmates have very few programs and activities, and are held in cells that create the equivalent of sensory deprivation."[35] However, most inmates didn't stay "indefinitely" and officials made sure no one went out of their mind by "touring the units regularly and providing counseling and other advice as necessary."[36]

This 1991 rationale was the same one offered in 1988 when Judge Barrington Parker harshly criticized the oversight procedures maintained by the Federal Bureau of Prisons at Lexington: It was all form, no content. Prisoners asked for help or change but there was no indication that anyone ever took their requests seriously.

In the case of Oscar López, "I was the only person that without ever having received a single incident report was held in D-unit (i.e., total segregation) for 43 months before being transferred to C-Unit." Hopefully this was Oscar's first step on the road to "freedom": a regular maximum security facility. However, "as soon as I arrived in C-unit, on two different occasions I was told by Counselor Rick Ellet that I wasn't B-unit material. Why such comments?"

Oscar suspected political motivations. "Members of the administration have openly stated that I had to stop being an outspoken critic of USP Marion's program and policies otherwise I wasn't going anywhere." Oscar refused to remain silent. Indeed, if he had been permitted to read it, he would have agreed with a 1991 Supreme Court decision written by Justice Byron White: Wantonness, brutality, and sadism were not the keys to a finding of cruel and unusual punishment. On the contrary, "Inhumane prison conditions are often the result of cumulative actions and inactions by numerous officials inside and outside a prison, sometimes over a very long period of time."[37]

Marion's lockdown was ten years old in 1993 and it was especially cruel and unusual punishment because the "concentration model" assures everything from sleeping on a cement bed to perpetual sensory deprivation. It is a generally depersonalized form of white torture which was increased in intensity when Oscar allegedly broke the rules. In a 1990 shakedown of his cell, officers said they found contraband. He was hiding a knife and that meant he had to return to total segregation .

Oscar refused to defend himself. "As a matter of political principle I don't recognize the jurisdiction of the U.S. government or any of its bureaucracies, including the Bureau of Prisons, over me...however I'm submitting this statement with the hope that you read it and enter it into the records.

"It's crucial to consider the fact that this incident defies all logic. I was the unit orderly. I had access to empty cells and to every nook and cranny that exists on the second floor of B-unit. Since I has access to all that space why should I be so blatantly stupid and put my contraband in the cell that I lived in? Since I've been in prison, I"ve been the object of constant surveillance and shakedowns. Knowing this, it would be a stultifying and puerile act on my part to leave any contraband in the cell where I live or in any place where I could be held responsible for it. Thus, the allegations that have been lodged against me not only militate against my behavioral patterns but also against the most basic logic.

"Another suspicious and questionable move occurred on the day that the shakedown was conducted. For the first time since I had been working in B-Unit I was asked to go down to the first floor while the shakedown was taking place. What is curious is that the order was not issued until all the officers were inside the cell. What caught my attention was that Officer Hood went directly to cell C-12 without even looking in cell C-11. In all previous shakedowns I had never been asked to leave the floor. When the shakedown crew came into the unit they saw me working. Why didn't they ask for me to step out then? The pattern was that I would remain on the floor while they conducted the search.

"Looking at all these facts I can only conclude that the powers that be have opted to commit another injustice in order to keep me in this concentration camp...In this situation truth and justice can prevail only if an impartial entity conducts a thorough investigation. Therefore it is incumbent upon those who love truth and justice to investigate this matter."

> This statement is not meant to be interpreted as an expression of disrespect...It's a political statement that seeks the truth and wants justice to prevail,
>
> "For those who understand, no explanation is necessary,
>
> For those who don't understand, no explanation is possible."

The Sign Said TS

On August 26, 1988 Filiberto Ojeda Ríos was rearrested after 96 days of "freedom." He had already spent more time in preventive detention under the "Bail Reform Act" than anyone else in U.S. history, but, when officials formally charged him with violently resisting the FBI on August 30, 1985, the new charges started a new clock. No one knew what happened when Ojeda was taken from Hartford and brought, not to Puerto Rico, but to the military base at Roosevelt Roads.

In San Juan U.S. Attorneys argued that "Ojeda was being detained under unusual circumstances for his own protection." Gregorio Lima questioned this assertion. He had just been appointed by the court to represent Ojeda and he wanted an answer to this question: "Protecting him against who? You—the U.S. Attorney's Office, this court, the FBI and the marshals are his enemies."

The magistrate got the point. This was Puerto Rico. Ojeda had substantial support in the community so the judge complied with Lima's request: He asked the marshals if Ojeda could be removed from Roosevelt Roads. They asked for a fifteen minute recess "to make a couple of phone calls." When they returned from checking with headquarters in Washington the marshals told the magistrate that "Ojeda could not be removed from his detention site for security reasons." Attorney Lima then said that "the marshals decision confirmed his client's status as a military prisoner of war; this is a case where the local people have no control; the master said 'no' and you have no control over that. Washington is controlling this case," argued Gregorio Lima.[38]

For disrespecting what he saw as a colonial court, Lima was removed from his legal responsibilities the next day. Meanwhile, Filiberto Ojeda Ríos was not removed from the military base. In fact, when a cardiologist told the magistrate that Ojeda's heart problems could prove fatal, Jesus Castellanos ordered Ojeda removed to a hospital but never considered the treatment the prisoner received. Ojeda was put in the military hospital on the military base but, since he could conceivably walk around the hospital ward, marshals used a six foot chain to link Ojeda to his bed.

In the hospital, the prisoner said "The ultimate hypocrisy [of the bail hearing] was the show of feigned humanism on the part of Magistrate Castellanos who declared that he could not bear to have my death in prison on his conscience and then permitted me to be chained to a bed in a military hospital. With such false and cliched statements designed to satisfy nothing more than a need for propaganda, this colonial lackey washed his hands of all responsibility."[39]

Of responsibility perhaps, but not substantial criticism. In the newspapers and on the radio and television Puerto Ricans heard what was happening to Ojeda Ríos. The Magistrate even received a call from his own mother who asked how he could do this to another human being? Ojeda went on a hunger strike to protest the conditions of his incarceration. Washington ordered the marshals to play politics. They reduced colonial tensions by secretly whisking Ojeda from Puerto Rico but they increased his personal stress by placing Ojeda in a cell in New York for 24 hours a day.

On September 9, 1988 Ojeda was transported to the United States. He landed at La Guardia airport and was taken, in a roughly 20-car caravan, to Manhattan's Metropolitan Correctional Center. The East Side Drive, one of the main arteries into one of the world's largest cities, was closed for Ojeda's solitary drive into a new period of pretrial detention.

"The minute I arrived ...everything was immediately familiar. I could also recall having seen, during the few times I was allowed to go outside for recreation, one isolated wing, completely sealed off with bullet proof glass. This, other prisoners told me, was the wing where they kept those in 'protective custody'—informants."

On this, his second stay at MCC, Ojeda was locked in the glassed-off wing. In fact, "when I was brought to MCC this time, I was locked inside the last cell of this wing. It is, of course, the cell that no one sees. Here I remain 24 hours a day. The cell is small, like all those in United States prisons. It contains a steel bed two feet wide; a metal table fifteen inches wide by two feet long, and (just like Oscar López's "room" in Marion) a toilet with a small washbasin attached...On the front door to my cell hangs a sign indicating my classification and restrictions. It reads: 'TS,' or TOTAL SEGREGATION. It further specifies that I am not allowed to talk to another prisoner, am to be locked into my cell 24 hours a day, am not allowed to make telephone calls, and must be forced to wear handcuffs for showers.

"I have been denied all access to my lawyers and every other basic right of pretrial detainees. In spite of extremely precise information about my medical condition (i.e., the triple bypass heart surgery) in the records of the institution, it insists upon doing the opposite of everything prescribed. The food is inadequate (I rarely get more than 1200-1500 calories per day that I can eat) and inappropriate (greasy meats, hot dogs, and chocolate pudding for a low fat, no cholesterol diet)...I have been denied exercise despite the fact that an exercise bike is parked in front of my cell."

Sleep was made impossible by what jailers labeled a "suicide watch." A man who complained about too much cholesterol was apparently going to kill himself so, each and every half hour, guards shined bright lights in the prisoner's face.

When he was awake, "a guard is stationed just outside the door of my cell, recording my every movement in a book. When I have heart palpitations, problems breathing, or am nauseous, he writes it in his book instead of calling a doctor...I have been denied all reading material since they took from me the few books I brought from Puerto Rico and they will not allow me to have any magazines or newspapers. Nor will they allow me to clean my cell. But the height of arbitrariness is revealed in the refusal to give me the forms on which prisoners must use to file complaints and grievances. In a similar vein, they refused to provide a notary public to execute a sworn affidavit."

"I am presenting this reality to the people of Puerto Rico today because it is absolutely imperative that we unmask the government of the United states and show the world that it is deceitful, hypocritical, and the worst violator of human rights in the world today. Its colonial policies and the treatment of people jailed for political reasons is the best illustration we can offer of its reactionary inhumanity."

Filiberto Ojeda Ríos remained in total segregation for nearly a year. Finally, in June of 1989, he was returned to Puerto Rico. Since the alleged attack on the FBI occurred in Puerto Rico, the proud head of *Los Macheteros* would be tried in his homeland, by his people.

Ojeda welcomed the opportunity. He acted as his own counsel because he is very intelligent, because he accepted responsibility for his own actions, and because "women and men, members of the jury. You are Puerto Ricans, as I am. I trust you absolutely ..

The trial began on June 27, 1989. And, as the next chapter argues, it was an historic encounter between a determined revolutionary, federal prosecutors, and the Puerto Rican people.

The Will of the People

"I do not wish to raise the expectations of the people of Puerto Rico...while we can assure through this legislation that a winning status will be considered by both Houses of Congress, we cannot ensure enactment or that the bill will be precisely what the winning political party-would prefer."

—Representative Morris Udall, "Puerto Rican Self Determination Bill," Congress, May 9, 1990

In 1986, Ojeda came into a Hartford federal court room wearing a blue suit, white shirt and conservative tie. He strode to the podium, stood next to his attorney, and in a respectful, but determined, tone, Filiberto Ojeda Ríos refused to speak English. He was a Puerto Rican, he wanted to be judged by his peers, and, if a federal court refused to concede that right, Mr. Ojeda refused to compromise his principles. Spanish was his language, Puerto Rico's independence his openly admitted goal.

In April of 1989, he came into a San Juan federal courtroom wearing a blue suit, white shirt and conservative tie. He had not showered because the marshals demanded that he bathe with his hands cuffed behind his back. As in 1986, Mr. Ojeda Ríos refused to compromise his principles. As people say in Puerto Rico he remained "vertical" when he asked the judge to hold the proceedings in Spanish. It would be a symbolic move "toward the decolonization of our people" and, for Mr. Ojeda Ríos, a man

301

who speaks perfect English, it was one sure way to retain the dignity that years of the harshest jail treatment had not destroyed.

Judge Carmen Consuelo Vargas de Cerezo refused. But she nevertheless made an important concession. "Mr. Ojeda," as she consistently referred to the professional-looking defendant, could speak Spanish. The rest of the trial would be in English. Thus, as Filiberto Ojeda Ríos spoke to his people in their language, a court employee dutifully translated his Spanish for a jury that needed no translation and which refused to be part of any courtroom charade. U.S. law required that a translation occur, but, when the judge offered the jurors headsets to hear the translation, they collectively discarded them.

To many of us in the gallery the English to Spanish to English process seemed bizarre. In Puerto Rico's U.S. District Court it's the norm. The English language requirement means that a Puerto Rican never gets a true jury of his or her peers in a federal court; the roughly 75% of the people who speak only Spanish are disqualified for jury duty; and, as Judge Vargas de Cerezo's soon learned, many of the jurors who serve do not necessarily understand the proceedings. In Ojeda's case, one potential juror asked to be excused for lack of English language ability, even though she had already served on several federal juries. Asked by the judge how she survived the screening process, the juror explained that "other judges" told her that she did not need to speak English, only listen to the testimony she might or might not comprehend.

Because of the English-only requirement, some

302

of the island's best lawyers refuse to plead cases before a federal court. For some it is a question of doubts about their English competency; for others it is a matter of principle. Like Filiberto Ojeda Ríos, they refuse to litigate in somebody else's language, in *their* country.

The judge added a final note of colonial surrealism to the proceedings. She was a supporter of the island's statehood party who had just submitted a Master's in Law thesis to a Northamerican university. On the mainland she won that degree with a thesis that bitterly denounced the colonial condition of her people; at home she presided over a colonial court that decided the fate of the leader of *Los Macheteros*.[1]

Acting as his own attorney, Filiberto Ojeda Ríos never denied that he used an Uzi and a pistol to resist the more than 30 officers who surrounded his home on August 30, 1985. He pled self-defense. After "an invasion of our territory by paramilitary forces of the FBI," agents carrying everything from a bazooka to machine guns stormed his house. Firing his weapons was simply Ojeda's way of protecting a "Puerto Rican home," himself, his wife, and Puerto Rico. In fact, because he refused to concede the rights of a "foreign army" on Puerto Rican soil the trial quickly became a credibility contest between a man who identified himself as dedicated to the struggle for "puertorriqueñidad" (the Puerto Rican identity) "and the federal agency of the United States charged with controlling opposition to colonialism by means fair and foul."[2]

Ojeda (and his four legal advisors) cross-examined Abelardo Alba, one of the alleged victims of an assault by Ojeda. Alba was wounded in the eye during the 2 1/2 hour gun battle that preceded Ojeda's arrest. Trying to create a context for the jurors, defense counsel asked Alba if he was the same agent admonished by Judge Emmet Claire in the Hartford Wells Fargo Trial: The law-man had committed "serious violations of statutory law and FBI regulations" while wiretapping the homes and workplaces of *Machetero* members. Claire asked for sanctions from the FBI, but, as Alba reluctantly admitted to the jury, his only penalty was a "letter of censure" in his bureau file. Apparently the FBI didn't care that its agent had repeatedly broken the law and it also allowed Alba to "invade" Ojeda's home without a valid search warrant. Initially Alba said that he had seen a copy of the warrant before the assault on the defendant's Luquillo home; under cross-examination he admitted he had never seen a valid warrant, only the one a judge would sign after the assault took place.[3]

However, to a Puerto Rican jury, Alba's admissions only confirmed what many already suspected: From Albizu to Ojeda, the FBI did as it pleased when it sought to apprehend the revolutionaries who fought for the independence of *la patria*.

The contradictions mounted. Alba claimed he had been wounded in the eye by the ricochet of a bullet from Ojeda's gun; later he could not recall whether he had told a nurse at the hospital that it was a flying piece of concrete which damaged his eye.

Both Alba and FBI agent Jacques Island told jurors they did not respond to the shots fired by Ojeda; agent Kirk Francis confirmed this story, but he also seemed confounded when Ojeda produced a sworn statement (offered in Hartford) which indicated that, according to Kirk Francis, there had been an "exchange of fire" and "armed battle" in the early stages of the Luquillo operation. Jacques Island told a court in Hartford he had not personally participated in the assault on Ojeda's home; in Puerto Rico he remembered the details of the assault with such precision he assured the jury he was the agent who had picked up Ojeda's weapons after an agent shot them out of the defendant's hands.

Ojeda personally questioned Jacques Island, a veteran of the Navy "seals" intelligence unit. Previous testimony established that the defendant spoke English only once during the entire arrest process. When the agents who broke down the front door to the apartment building arrived at his door, Ojeda said "speak in Spanish; you are in Puerto Rico." No one denied this statement but there was a heated exchange about the nature of Ojeda's next remarks.

Ojeda: "Didn't I then express myself in a clear and strong voice, as I am doing now, that I was exercising the right to defend my home and my country."

Island: "I don't remember anything about that. Your words were 'gibberish.'"

Ojeda: "In other words, the word 'gibberish' you would describe my words as bluster."

Island: "I would have to look it up in a dictionary."

Ojeda: "But what does it mean for you?"

Island: "I would describe it as vomit, as an extremely hollow philosophy."

Ojeda: "Do you mean that talk of patriotism is a senseless expression, that patriotic statements are vomited by people that are supposedly extremists?"

Island: "This does not have anything to do with patriotism."

Ojeda: "What you mean is that it doesn't have any importance for you...what I may say only has importance for you when you say it does."

The prosecutors presented 14 witnesses. The defense called two. One, a next door neighbor who witnessed the assault on Ojeda's home, offered testimony about the alleged (by Ojeda) existence of a bazooka. To the defendant, this was proof positive of his right to, and need for, self-defense. Fourteen Northamerican FBI agents testified that there was no bazooka so prosecutors worked hard when they cross-examined Jacqueline Dosal for eight long and gruelling hours. She lived in the same building as Ojeda and testified "that upon being awakened by loud noises on August 30, 1985, she looked out her bedroom window and saw more than 20 FBI agents, some in face paint and camouflage uniforms and carrying long weapons behind the apartment building. One of them was wielding a bazooka—a weapon she admitted she had never seen except in war movies but which she described so precisely that a juror who once served in the National Guard identified the manufacturer."[4]

Prosecutors flew in a rebuttal witness from Philadelphia. This was Ms. Dosal's former roommate who quickly confirmed that she only saw three or four agents when she first looked out the window. That brought a smile to the prosecutor's face but, when he allowed his rebuttal witness to continue, she first indicated that all the agents wore "blue jackets with FBI emblazoned in yellow"—all, that is, except for the one fellow in face paint and camouflage. He carried a bazooka.

The only other defense witness was a captain in the police of Puerto Rico. He testified that he knew nothing about the raid until it was in progress. Thus, Ojeda established that during the most significant and massive arrest on the island in many years, the Puerto Rican officers found themselves directing traffic. Their job was to keep all Puerto Ricans away from Luquillo while at least 30 FBI agents (not the five originally indicated by the FBI) arrested Filiberto Ojeda Ríos. At the end of his testimony the captain produced a four-year-old report confirming all the details of his testimony.

As they prepared their closing statements to the jury, Ojeda and his advisors felt confident. They believed they had proven their point about the pervasive and corrosive nature of colonialism. And, after so many indisputable contradictions exposed to the jury, the defense easily established reasonable doubt about the truth of the FBI's rendition of the arrest. But, there was also no doubt that a Puerto Rican revolutionary—the leader of a "notorious terrorist" organization—resisted arrest by the FBI and its numerous agents. Not everybody admitted that he burned incriminating documents in his bathtub after the FBI announced its presence; not everybody kept machine guns at home; and even fewer Puerto Ricans fired them at officials who openly identified themselves as the legal representatives of federal authority. The verdict would thus be a test of the "verticalidad" of the Puerto Rican jury.

The night before he offered his closing statement, Filiberto Ojeda Ríos had a meeting with Pedro Albizu Campos. Lying in his makeshift jail cell in the federal courthouse Ojeda dreamed a silent encounter with the Albizu depicted in the photo taken at Columbus Hospital in 1943. Although Albizu said nothing to his revolutionary successor, Ojeda felt blessed and strengthened by the encounter. As in July of 1936, in August of 1989 a *Puerto Rican* jury would once again decide the fate of a home-grown revolutionary.

Ojeda began his closing statement with a reference to the most common of all Puerto Rican weeds. He told the jury that "the truth will rise up again, like the moriviví." To anyone who had not tramped around Puerto Rico this was an esoteric reference. The moriviví is a plant that grows wild in Rio Piedras and Vieques, in Utuado and Ponce. Touch its leaves and the plant appears to shrivel; seconds later the moriviví resurrects. Its tiny green leaves and fuzzy flowers are everywhere, promising that what appears to be dead (*Mori*, I died) will live (*vivir*).

The leader of *Los Macheteros* told the jury that "in the midst of their [the FBI's] many lies, the truth began to flower. And, like the moriviví, the more it was trampled, the greater its capacity to find a new path and a new life."

What was the truth? The FBI meant to assassinate Filiberto Ojeda Ríos. They "fired the first shot and it was this shot that destroyed the windows. What better confirmation could I have of their intention to assassinate me?... you heard several members of the Bravo Team of the Hostage Rescue Squad tell you how much they feared for their lives when they heard shots. They, who came attacking, shooting, breaking down doors, shattering windows...and I, alone with my wife, listening to their screams and deafening blows, their shots, their battering and destruction of glass doors, in their war uniforms with their weapons and painted faces—I was not supposed to fear for my life. I was not supposed to do anything to defend my wife's life or my own.

"This is typical of oppressors. The oppressed are never supposed to think and act according to our own human nature, because for them we are not human! And much less should we, according to their mentality as superior beings with the force of power, have the audacity to prevent their abuses, attacks, and assassin's intentions."

Reading this, I am still startled by Ojeda's words. Oppressor. Assassins. Audacity. *The defendant was talking about the FBI.* Indeed, despite his proud stance as a revolutionary, and despite his organization's boast that it did in fact rob Wells Fargo, Filiberto Ojeda Ríos was nevertheless arguing he had a right to violently resist arrest. In Puerto Rico the "good guys" were the "bad guys." They lied and, even more importantly, they effectively spit on the Puerto Rican people.

Remember "that I was disposed to surrender to the Police of Puerto Rico, whom I know, objectively, are not my enemies because in large measure they too are discriminated against and treated as inferiors. And what did Agent Island have to say about this? That I was talking nonsense. His word in English was 'gibberish.'

"And the lies continued. They wove their little

story which culminated in a subliminal message designed for you, for our people...Supposedly, according to Agent Brown, I made a threatening gesture with a pistol that I had in my left hand and he, with the precision of a cowboy from the West, and with an intention of not killing me—-according to them—knocked the pistol out of my hand with a round from his machine gun."

Nonsense. That never happened. Ojeda argued that he eventually laid down his arms because the FBI wanted to kill him. However, "I won't insult your intelligence by denying that I burned papers. But I ask you to think about this carefully. What was my obligation, at the time, with this *foreign army* below claiming a supposed right to search and enter my house? Wouldn't I have the duty, given what *we* know about the history of repression in our country ...to protect the privacy, if not the lives of all those Puerto Ricans—*independentistas* and non-*independentistas* alike—whose names could have been in my possession?...Indeed, wouldn't any patriot, knowledgeable about the sad history of our country, feel an obligation, a duty to protect these people...." (emphasis added)

"I want you to think about the motive of the government of the United States and the FBI to weave their fabrication in relation to their assault on my home. Decide for yourselves...if it does not have some relation to an intention to discredit and criminalize us, *independentistas* determined to claim the most legitimate rights of this people. Decide for yourselves if this does not demonstrate that intimidation—an effort to prevent our people from making demands which are totally founded in truth, in our desires to feel truly free and fulfilled as human beings, and an effort to show that they are masters and the power—was not part of their motive." (emphasis in original)

"Women and men, members of the jury. You are Puerto Ricans, as I am. I trust you absolutely because of the general knowledge of the context in which these accusations are made by the prosecutor in the name of the government of the United States...I trust your honesty, and, above all, I trust in your moral valor and sense of justice. Your decision is of the highest importance. Not because it has to do with Filiberto Ojeda Ríos. It might well have been about any son of our people. It has to do, in the end, with what it means for the more than century-old struggle of us Puerto Ricans seeking our Puerto Rican identity.

"What matters, above all, is that you do justice for this Puerto Rican homeland. You can judge me. History will judge us all."

Right after the jury announced that it had reached a decision, the sound of music filtered into the federal building. In old San Juan the courthouse sits near the dock. Cruise ships park in the harbor and, as their passengers walk down the gangplank to begin duty-free shopping, a native band generally plays native music. It's like leis in Hawaii but on August 26 the band played *Verde Luz* (Green Light). This is the second "national anthem" of any Puerto Rican independence activist; it meant nothing to the tourists, but it was welcome support for Ojeda Ríos and an obvious source of consternation to Judge Consuelo Vargas.

After less than four hours of deliberation

(including dinner) the jury announced its verdict. "At the first 'not guilty' the silence became absolute. After seven more 'not guilties' the courtroom kept the silence of awed respect for the jury. It was not until it had filed out of the courtroom that cries of jubilation began to fill the night, while a cacophony of car horns began in the streets below."[5]

Ojeda's attorneys demanded his immediate release. But, Judge Vargas washed her hands of the defendant. She "rushed" out of the courtroom with a simple statement: "I have lost jurisdiction over him; he has to go back to Hartford where he came from."

Judge Vargas lacked the courage displayed by the jury. Those Puerto Ricans freed a revolutionary. This one returned him to the administrative detention demanded by the colonial powers that be.

Two days later a beaming Filiberto Ojeda Ríos finally walked out of the federal courthouse. As he talked to the swarm of reporters stationed outside, Ojeda stood beside his two granddaughters and a delighted Oscar Collazo. The man who attacked Blair House in 1950 embraced the man who resisted arrest in 1985 and, together, the two revolutionaries offered their assessment of the verdict: Fifty years after a Puerto Rican jury refused to criminalize the assassination ordered by Pedro Albizu Campos, it also refused to criminalize the revolutionary resistance offered by *Los Macheteros*. One generation after another Puerto Ricans supported, not only the anticolonial struggle, but its intimate links to the *puertorriqueñidad* that caused, demanded and nourished it. Ojeda's grandchildren symbolized his reverence for family which was linked to his defense of the Spanish language which was linked to a band that proudly played *Verde Luz* on the narrow streets of one of the oldest cities in the Western Hemisphere.

Puerto Rico had culture—Latin American culture. The former was a subdivision of the latter because, as Alfredo Palacios told President Roosevelt in 1942, "to call the Puerto Rican patriot who is fighting for his country's freedom an assassin (or a criminal) appears absurd to us who venerate *in our America* the memory of the heroes who through their abnegation and sacrifice gave us independence." (emphasis added)

Ojeda became a very reluctant celebrity. On television talk shows, callers (who were not put on the air) asked how they could join *Los Macheteros* or where they could purchase a machine gun. On the streets, "average" citizens crossed thoroughfares to shake the hand of a "terrorist." Filiberto Ojeda Ríos, a son of the people, was home; and the only label that mattered to pedestrians was the one they all cherished: Puerto Rican.

In Washington, officials lost a wonderful opportunity to learn from history. George Bush or Attorney General Richard Thornburgh could have used the not guilty decision as a face saving way to begin the process of decolonization. They could have freed all the Puerto Rican political prisoners as a sign that Washington finally respected the anticolonial will of the Puerto Rican people. But, instead of correcting history, the Justice Department chose to repeat it. In San Juan, marshals put an electronic bracelet on Ojeda's leg because federal prosecutors wanted to make sure he arrived for a *criminal* trial on Wells Fargo in Hartford.

Meanwhile, in Vieques, another *Machetero*—Attorney Roberto José Maldonado—tried to provide legal assistance to displaced residents. In one of the sharpest and ugliest confrontations in memory, the Navy and Justice Departments used the summer of 1989 to mock the *puertorriqueñad* so proudly defended by Filiberto Ojeda Ríos and a jury of his peers.

Mount Carmelo

As we flew in on Roberto's tiny plane, we could see scores of soldiers working near the rock vestiges of the wall that was, in 1940, to turn Vieques into the Pearl Harbor of the Caribbean. For fifty long years this tiny island symbolized the brutal nature of U.S. colonialism. But, when the Navy attacked Mount Carmelo in the summer of 1989, its actions graphically underlined the *continuing* legitimacy of the prisoners anticolonial position. Mount Carmelo showed that nothing has changed. U.S. colonialism is as indifferent to the will of the Puerto Rican people in the 1990's as it was in the 1930's.

Naval officers said it was an imaginary line. That naturally made it hard to see but for close to fifty years Naval commanders nevertheless argued that the line not only existed, it cut around, across and through Vieques.

The line also moved through time. A woman who lived in the same spot for 64 years was told in 1988 that her home lay right on the imaginary line. She and a number of her neighbors had to move—"for their own good"—because Navy officials feared the families could be injured as a result of the military exercises that were still an everyday fact of

314

Vieques life.

Wire fences, erected to avoid Naval liability for stray cows, cut across the island. Nobody got hurt if they stayed off the Navy's lands, but one price the people paid for safety was a devastated economy. Families survived on what they got from a variety of public and private sources, and, when someone wanted to build a new home, he followed a custom that had deep roots in Puerto Rican history. A man and a woman squatted on land that nobody seemed to own and, especially in *la isla nena*, "the baby island," Viequenses felt comfortable that the authorities in San Juan would look the other way.

In 1988 the imaginary line suddenly reappeared. A number of squatters, including the woman who had lived on the same spot for 64 years, were told that the Navy went to court. The Viequenses now had to explain to a judge why they should not be evicted from lands the Navy said belonged to the United States of America.

The Viequenses managed to obtain attorneys— many worked pro bono—but even then many of the homeowners had a hard time understanding the proceedings. In the federal courts, English is the only medium of legal dialogue, so, in a language they did not understand, Viequenses tried to locate a line they could not see.

Carmelo Felix Matta wanted to know why his house was inside the line but other properties, located directly between Carmelo's home and the Naval base, were not inside the line? He had lived on "his" land since 1976. Some of the other homes were newer. Why weren't they on Navy land?

The Navy's answer was simple: The imaginary

line was not a straight line. It zigged and zagged but only the Navy knew where.[6] This was hard for the Viequenses to grasp because in Carmelo's neighborhood, called Villa Borinquen, islanders had built, over a number of years, some 200 homes. As one local wag noted, for the Navy's argument to make sense, "the line would not only have to be imaginary and zig-zagging, but also moving."[7]

Carmelo fought the Navy for more than a year, but the courts finally upheld the Navy's request for an eviction notice. On April 14, 1989, a number of unarmed federal marshals appeared at Carmelo's home, which is not easily accessible. To get to the house one must leave the main road, itself narrow, and drive up a steep dirt path full of rain-made pot holes. Even a brand new jeep can find trouble in four or five places over the half mile stretch that leads to the Matta property.

Arriving at roughly one in the afternoon, the marshals wanted Carmelo to evacuate the house at once. He refused to do so. Where was the Navy's line? You could see the Navy fence from the rear of the Matta house, but, as Carmelo and his wife Maria correctly stressed, "there were no guards, no posts, no signs, not a single thing" that suggested that this land belonged to the Navy.

The marshals listened, but their job was to enforce the law, not interpret it. The Matta's had to move. Carmelo resisted; the children began to cry; his aged mom began to shout; and both sides finally agreed that the Mattas would move, but, like Filiberto Ojeda Ríos on August 30, 1985, the Mattas requested only that the Puerto Rican police would carry out the eviction order.

316

The Will of The People

As word of the Mattas' plight passed from one end of the island to the other, swarms of angry residents made the trek to what instantly became "Mount Carmelo." Since resentment against the Navy and its activities is often just below the surface on Vieques, the marshals now had the unenviable job of catching the Navy's flak. With not a sailor in sight, the growing crowd complained of everything from noise to poverty, from colonialism to imperialism.

When the local police finally arrived, they refused to help the federal marshals. In part, their reluctance stemmed from the angry glances of neighbors. Walking toward the Matta house was like walking a gauntlet of verbal abuse. The stated basis of the police refusal—"if this is Navy land, we have no jurisdiction"—turned a local issue into a battle that emphasized a century old reality of island life: Almost any legal, political, or economic problem always comes back to the issue of political status. What is Puerto Rico? Who is in charge? What will the United States do this time?

As the crowd of onlookers continued to grow, the marshals tried to maintain order while a squad of sailors, in shorts and tank tops, began to load the Matta furniture on a Navy vehicle. Bedding, books, and musical instruments were quickly and peacefully placed on the trucks. The sailors suddenly started running for their lives. Carmelo, a beekeeper, had failed to mention that there were a number of beehives among the family's final possessions. Like Carmelo, the bees didn't want to move, so they made short work of the sailors who, dressed for a basketball game, hastily regrouped about one hundred yards down the hill.

While Carmelo waited to be evacuated from the scene, bystanders complained about the flames. A fire had mysteriously broken out in one of the Navy vehicles and it threatened to spread to the truck which contained the Mattas' few belongings. One marshal grabbed a small fire extinguisher but his efforts were fruitless. The Vieques fire department arrived at once, but, like the ambulance, they were blocked by federal vehicles. Onlookers pleaded for permission to simply move the truck; if people were allowed to push the vehicle back, it and the Mattas' belongings could be saved.

The marshals refused. The trucks were Navy property which could only be moved by Navy personnel. Unfortunately, the sailors had wisely decided to retreat from Mount Carmelo, so, with everyone watching, the fire spread from one truck to another. It took two hours, but eventually the Mattas' lost everything.

Meanwhile, another squad of marshals arrived on the scene. These fellows wore bulletproof vests and carried automatic rifles, sawed-off shotguns and Uzi, submachine guns.

The new marshals immediately had their own turf battles to fight. A few members of the crowd grabbed shovels to fill in a trench the Navy had dug to keep the crowd contained, but the appearance of shovels upset the Marshals with the Uzis, who were also fighting with Don Carmelo's mother. She screamed that a marshall wearing sunglasses had set the fire, and, adding insult to injury, it was the marshals who had refused to move the truck which contained the family furnishings. The matriarch of the Matta family was hot and, so too, Carmelo's wife Maria. An intelligent, strong and spirited woman, Maria had previously had no strong beliefs about political status; even though her own family had been forcibly evacuated from Vieques in the 1940's, Maria generally steered away from political controversies. But, by day's end, she saw Northamericans in a new light: "Anyone that talks of statehood should be killed in the public plaza."[8]

The marshals, now sitting ducks, decided to follow the Navy's lead. They retreated for the day, but the crowd of neighbors remained on Mount Carmelo. Before darkness fell, friends arrived with cots, blankets, mattresses, and food; the area was quickly cleaned up; and Maria suddenly had one hundred houseguests. Without prior consultation, and with no set strategy in mind, the community had decided to sit-in at the Matta property, daring the Navy and marshals to attempt another eviction.

Force, however, was out the question because officials in Washington immediately understood that the confrontation on Mount Carmelo was political dynamite. Thus, throughout the summer of 1989, Filiberto Ojeda Ríos stood trial while the Navy stood behind its imaginary line. Indeed, sailors remained so patient that they even turned a blind eye to open violations of the law.

On May 27, 1989 two hundred families invaded lands that were clearly labeled "U.S. Government Property—No Entre—Keep Out." In what the locals described as "a rescue of lands monopolized by the Navy" (*un rescate de los terrenos acaparados por la Marina de Guerra*) Viequenses took one-acre plots and began to build shelters from any materials they could find. Plastic roofs on plywood walls became one-room homes to people who declared that, "for forty-eight years the Navy has not used these lands and now we have tremendous needs, so we have decided to rescue these lands."[9]

Through the summer and early fall of 1989, the Navy did nothing to Carmelo and Maria, nor to the islanders who continued to develop their recently "rescued" homeland. The standoff became a way of life until Hurricane Hugo violently solved many of the Navy's problems. Hugo utterly devastated Vieques. It blew away every one of the wood and plastic structures, destroying in hours seeds of hope that had taken 48 years to bloom.

The Navy's response was quick and certain. It first furnished humanitarian aid and it then constructed fences. The *morning after* the storm finally dissipated citizens awoke to walls that were anything but imaginary. Sailors had completely fenced in the rescued lands as they fenced out the Puerto Ricans devastated, first by Hugo and now by the United States Navy.

Meanwhile, the entrances to the beaches, formerly manned by a civilian security guard, now contained a well-armed soldier as well; and the Navy's new fence, instead of moving toward the imaginary line, stood fifty feet deeper into the United States of America's original property claim.

On Mount Carmelo, the Mattas survived. Hugo hurt but never destroyed their cinderblock home. So, as Maria and Carmelo waited for the marshals to reappear, many Puerto Ricans angrily argued that the summer of 1989 yet again substantiated the charges made by organizations like the FALN and *Los Macheteros*.

In August, a jury of his peers told Filiberto Ojeda Ríos that *they* understood the colonial context in which he struggled for freedom. In September, the United States Navy reaffirmed U.S. colonialism by brutally squashing the hopes of islanders whose parents heard sailors promise to leave Vieques at the end of World War II.

In the United States, the political prisoners remained in jail; Filiberto Ojeda Ríos was scheduled for a criminal trial in Hartford; and, in Congress, U.S. Senators once again solemnly promised to respect the will of the Puerto Rican people. However, as Senator Dale Bumpers of Alabama told a government witness in July of 1989, "I do not think you need to bother yourself with independence. That is not going to happen. I do not think there is a person in this room or in Puerto Rico that thinks that."[10]

Prison, Profits and The Plebescite

Senator Bumpers was honest. Like Senator Millard Tydings in 1945, or Congressman William Jones in 1914, Bumpers at least indicated that talk of self-determination was rhetoric rather than reality, a hollow promise not a human right.

Men like Bumpers cleared the air; you knew where you stood, and what had to be done. But, as Congress debated a proposed plebiscite bill from 1989 to 1991, Senator Bumpers colleagues also repeated history. They again acted like the "Great Sphinx of the North" so, in February of 1991 Congress witnessed a rare phenomenon: Unanimity among Puerto Rico's political parties.

Ruben Berríos Martínez (head of the island's

Independence Party) offered the Senate a history lesson. "The fact is that the U.S. government has an obligation because nobody invited them to come to Puerto Rico to start with. So there is an obligation that the United States should discharge before its own image as a freedom loving people and before the world...Now we are telling the central government go ahead and say something because we have already said, and during 93 years you have paid no attention to us. So, if you let this slide, what will happen in Puerto Rico? Well, anything can happen but it is your obligation to speak and to speak clearly because we are tired of waiting. The three of us are tired of waiting. The people of Puerto Rico are tired of waiting. Now is no time to say, go back and you arrange things between yourselves and come out. We have done that hundreds of times. We do not want to do that anymore. We want you to fulfill your obligation now."[11]

This was a surprising outburst from the normally diplomatic Berríos. But, for the last two years the House of Representatives had not only refused to provide specifics, they had refused to be specific about the lack of specifics. As Morris Udall put it on May 9, 1990: "It must be made very clear that the exact details of status implementing legislation cannot be determined in advance, and that while we can assure through this legislation that a winning status will be *considered* by both Houses of Congress, we cannot assure enactment or that the bill will be precisely what the winning political party will prefer."[12]

It was paternalism from the mouth of a liberal Democrat. So, Berríos and his colleagues wanted the Senate to provide the non-revocable specifics never offered by the House of Representatives.

Senators did as they were asked. But, after 94 years of colonialism, the answers given to the Puerto Rico people underlined two important points: the predicament of those who work within the system and the moral and international legitimacy of revolutionary groups like the FALN and Los Macheteros.

Since nobody needed "to bother with independence," the Senate focused on statehood. In Puerto Rico, statehooders claim that statehood is for the poor. To men like Resident Commissioner Carlos Romero Barceló it's a question of pluses and minuses. "Puerto Rico's per capita contribution to the federal treasury, were we a state, would come to less than that of any other state in the Union. At the same time the per capita benefits we'd reap from federal aid programs would be greater than those of any other state in the Union."[13]

Finally, Puerto Rico would also have seven or eight islanders "working up in Washington at all times to help draft and pass new and improved social welfare legislation."[14]

The Senate was worried about the promises of men like Romero Barceló. "It did not want to enact statehood if it costs a huge amount of money. As a practical, political consideration, it would be very difficult to enact statehood and have it cost billions of dollars to the Treasury."[15] So, the Puerto Ricans got their specifics but ones that were quite different from those anticipated. As Senator Bill Bradley (New Jersey) noted, "what you are saying is that the poverty level in the United States, those who are in poverty would receive more than those who are in poverty in Puerto Rico, is that correct."[16]

It was. What the Senate proposed was "permanent" second-class statehood. Programs like Medicaid, Aid to Families With Dependent Children, and Food Stamps would all have budgetary caps. But, there was "another cap" on top of the separate caps. If the total for *all* the poverty programs was, for example, $10 billion then if food stamps went up, Medicaid or some other program would go down. The cap on the cap sent definite limits because the Senate said islanders could have statehood only if it was "revenue neutral"[17] That was a euphemism for "Puerto Ricans are too poor to be equal" and Senator J. Bennett Johnston (Louisiana) wondered if that was constitutional. Could you really treat 50 states in one fashion and Puerto Rico in another?

Assistant Attorney General Gerson assured the Senators that it could be "permanently done." And critics should stop using the word discrimination. "The issue that you [the Senate] face in terms of constitutional analysis is whether there is a rational basis for the distinctions. As I say, discrimination is an unfortunate term. It carries an opprobrium with it. There is a rational basis for the distinctions that the Congress would make."[18]

The rational basis was money. It was rational to permanently cap the state of Puerto Rico and thus offer it another peculiar distinction. It was the nation's first colony, its first unincorporated territory, and now its first second-class state.

In this projected move from permanent possession to permanent poverty, no Senator questioned the negative impact of the 936 laws. None offered the economic strategy which is a prerequisite for self sustaining growth. None mentioned almost a century of Puerto Rican requests for real economic power. And none discussed U.S. colonialism's most incredible achievement: A statehood movement that proudly sought indefinite dependence on the federal government.

The House saved the Senate. It refused to commit to any specifics, and that left Puerto Ricans with a familiar refrain: We are tired of waiting. The Senate was tired of the Puerto Ricans. Staffers indicated that Congress would do nothing more until islanders once again clamored for action; meanwhile, the Puerto Rican economy produced more poverty, the 936 corporations more profits, and Congress rested on a series of discriminatory proposals.

As Senator Pete Domenici (New Mexico) summed up the hearings, "It is fun for this committee to have this kind of issue. We do not get this kind of issue very often. And I think it is always somewhere else that such matters of individual freedom, rights, choices by people, those are never discussed by us. I think we go in, not necessarily without strong feet, but we go at it a little slower perhaps because we do not do this very often."[19]

Domenici did indicate that the novelty of the issue might move the committee to do a better job, but he prefaced that comment by saying: "I also want to conclude by saying I am remiss by not going there thus far. I always find something else and say I am too busy...I do not know where I am going to find the time to be an adequate participant in this...but I think we ought to make at least a public commitment to your people, Puerto Ricans, that we will try to come there and get to know you better. I urge that more of us do."[20]

The Senator would squeeze Puerto Rico in when and if he ever had the time. Or, as Senator Malcolm Wallop (Wyoming) noted, "I would caution patience for all parties, and that is not to say that I regard 92 years of waiting as impatience. But we are in a moment in time in which real decisions can be framed...and I think we ought not to back off from that simply because timetables get jiggered off track."[21]

What track? Just like President Truman's veto of a plebiscite in 1946, Congress disregarded the expressed will of Puerto Rico's elected representatives. Meanwhile, Senator David Pryor of Arkansas published a study which proved that the economic exploitation stressed by the FALN was, in 1992, far greater than ever.

Senator Pryor said the 936 laws allowed pharmaceutical companies to earn tax benefits that were astonishingly high, fully 300% as a percentage of employee compensation. In more human terms the pharmaceutical did *not* boast that they earned over $70,000 in tax benefits for each and every employee. The rationale for the system—jobs—was so out of line that firms like Pfizer made over $156,000 for each employee, while the figure for Merck was $110,000 and for American Home Products it was $80,000. These firms employed, respectively 500, 953, and 1000 Puerto Ricans in the entire country. Meanwhile, for the decade of the eighties, these companies averaged (again respectively) $69 million, $68 million and $75 million in tax free profits each and every year.[22]

This was a farce when President Carter first discovered it in 1978; and it was a farce when President Reagan tried to change the 936 tax laws in 1986. As President Reagan then told Congress, "despite the fact that the inflation adjusted tax-exempt income of corporations which have elected the benefits of section 936 has more than doubled since 1972, *employment levels (both overall and in the manufacturing sector) have remained flat.*"[23]

President Clinton got the point. In 1993, he tried to eliminate the 936 tax laws. Like his predecessors, he failed; the pharmaceutical lobbyists are more powerful than the sharpest facts and Puerto Rico now has so few jobs that islanders also lobby Congress for a perpetuation of the status quo.

However, the most important thing about the president's proposal was its motivation: *He wanted the tax monies for the mainland.* He wanted the pharmaceutical profits because he sought to help close the federal budget deficit with the bonanza earned by the drug companies. A president who is celebrated for his grasp of the most complex facts openly admitted that he knew nothing about Puerto Rico. Thus, he ordered full speed ahead even though—as his friend from Arkansas stressed—the system was so out of balance that "the combined federal and local tax incentives produced a manufacturing sector that provided 63% of Puerto Rico's total net income in 1990, although it accounted for only 17% of total jobs."[24]

Just like President Taft in 1909, President Coolidge in 1925, President Carter in 1978, and President Bush in 1989,[25] President Clinton in 1993 claimed plenary power over the Puerto Rican people.

America ruled the island, but, like his predecessors, this president never argued that primary power equalled primary responsibility.

In Washington, Puerto Rico and its people are invisible. That is a hundred year old fact which is arguably the most damning consequence of U.S. colonialism. From Mc Kinley to Clinton, from Senator Foraker in 1900 to Senator Domenici in 1991, U.S. officials promise to learn something yet they rarely take the time to do so. Thus, while arrogance and indifference rule the colony, those who struggle for revolutionary change are labeled criminals instead of patriots, wrong instead of right.

Pedro Albizu Campos argued that only a crisis would catch America's attention. My hope is that Albizu was wrong. My hope is that we look at the facts and demand that the prisoners be given immediate and unconditional amnesty. A revolution against colonialism is an all-American enterprise, a fight which links heroes as disparate as George Washington and Simòn Bolívar, Sam Adams and Augusto Sandino, Patrick Henry and José Marti.

Free the prisoners because colonialism is the crime; free the prisoners because their liberation could be a first—PEACEFUL—step on the road to decolonization.

What better way to change the system than to courageously face an ugly fact: We the people own a colony. And we the people should finally accept responsibility for the consequences of a century of political and economic imperialism.

The choices is ours. But, along with our revolutionary ancestors, the world is watching, the prisoners are waiting, and the next generation of revolutionaries is....

Epilogue

The hearings occurred on October 5, 1993. About 100 people squeezed into a luxuriously paneled room to hear and give testimony before the Subcommittee on Western Affairs of the House Committee on Foreign Affairs.

The first speaker was Congressman José Sérrano (D. New York). He gave an eloquent presentation which stressed what he said was an indisputable fact: Puerto Rico was a colony of the United States.

No one batted an eyelash! A U.S. congressman repeatedly stressed that, two hundred years after Valley Forge, the United States was an imperial power. Instead of outrage or denials, the congressional panel matter of factly accepted Puerto Rico's status as a colony.

After Congressman Serrano's presentation, three island politicians (one for statehood, one for independence, and one for commonwealth) took the floor. They also said Puerto Rico was a colony and they too met with no challenge from the congressional panel or from Puerto Rico's Resident Commissioner, Carlos Romero Barceló. Romero emphasized Puerto Rico's colonial status as well.

What, then, are the prisoners doing in jail? Since so many government officials openly admit that Puerto Rico is a colony, the prisoners' struggle is not only legitimate, but incorporates ideals of U.S. democracy. As Supreme Court Justice Harlan noted in 1901, "the idea that this country may acquire territories anywhere on earth, by conquest or treaty, and hold them as mere colonies or provinces...is wholly inconsistent with the spirit and genius as well as the words of the Constitution."

The contradiction is ours. The United States owns the colony. The prisoners did their duty. And the president should immediately free them, not only for the sake of justice, but for the sake of the principles embodied in the Declaration of Independence.

Anyone who wishes to help free the prisoners has a number of options available. The umbrella organization to free the prisoners is:

Ofensiva '92
Apartado 20190
Rio Piedras, Puerto Rico 00928
tel: 809-763-0034

In Chicago the National committee to Free Puerto Rican Political Prisoners and Prisoners of War can be reached at

P.O. Box 476698
Chicago, IL 60647
tel: 312-278-6706 or 312-278-0885

Addresses for each of the prisoners are listed at the end of this book. Please write to express your support.

Finally, please write the president. And circulate petitions in support of immediate amnesty for the incarcerated prisoners and those living clandestinely. The president has the authority to offer amnesty; hopefully those who support the prisoners will convince the president to immediately free Puerto Rico's political prisoners and prisoners of war.

Notes

Introduction

1. Congressional Record, April 2, 1900, page 3636.
2. This is based on a document written by Luis Rosa.
3. See the sworn, formal complaint of six attorneys who were a part of these proceedings. I am quoting from page 3 of the May 8, 1980 complaint.
4. President Carter Library, Atlanta, GA, NSC, Box 43, this is an undated memo to the president from Brezenski and Robert Lipschutz.
5. See *People of the State of Illinois vs. Mara Siegal*, Appellate Court of Illinois, First District, Third Division, 430, North Eastern Reporter, 2nd series, page 143.
6. See, *op.cit.*, the attorneys report to the Judicial Inquiry Board, page 4.
7. North Eastern Reporter, op.cit., page 144; for the judge's comment see the formal complaint to the judiciary board, page 4; I have also interviewed attorneys Deutsch and Siegal.
8. Puerto Rico, Hearings Before the Committee On Territories and Insular Affairs, Senate, 78th Congress, first session, May 1943, page 50.

Chapter 1

1. See, for example, Ricardo Alegría, *Temas de la Historia de Puerto Rico* (San Juan : Centro de Estudios Avanzados de Puerto Rico and El Caribe, 1988), page 187 for the details of the agreement.
2. Puerto Rico, Hearings before the Senate Committee on Territories and Insular Affairs, 78th Congress, first session, May 1943, page 50; Papers of Richard

331

Nixon, Nixon Project, Alexandria, Virginia, this is from a White Memo of April 30, 1974. See White House Central Files, ST 51-2.

3. Congressional Record, Senate, February 26, 1900, page 2231.

4. Congressional Record, Senate, 56th Congress, first session, 1900, page 2473.

5. Congressional Record, April 2, 1900, pages 3638-3639.

6. W.F. Willoughby, *The Government of Modern States* (New York: D. Appleton Century,1932) p. 106; see, too, Willoughby's *Territories and Dependencies of the United States* (New York: The Century Company, 1905), especially Chapter 4, pages 79-105. The quote appears on page 86.

7. Congressional Record, House, 1909, page 2923.

8. Mary White Ovington, The United States in Porto Rico, *The New Republic*, July 15, 1916, p. 271.

9. Congressional Record, Senate, June 19, 1922, page 8955.

10. The Civil Government of Puerto Rico, Hearings Before the Committee on Territories and Insular Possessions, Senate, February, 1924, page 6.

11. See the Papers of E. Montgomery Reilly at the New York Public Library. This is from page 6 of a copy of his inaugural address.

12. Marisa Rosado, *Las Llamas de la Aurora* (San Juan, 1991), page 168.

13. Gordon S. Wood, *The Radicalism of the American Revolution* (New York: Vintage, 1991), pages 222-225.

14. Rosado, *op. cit.*, page 31; for the high minded and idealistic comment see Franklin Roosevelt Library, President's Personal Files, this is from a memo to the president dated August 29, 1936. See page 1 of the letter written for Roosevelt by Ernest Gruening.

15. Rosado, *op. cit.*, page 33.

16. Pedro Albizu Campos, *Obras Escogidas,* Tomo II, Manifesto Ante la Visita del Presidente de Estados Unidos, (San Juan: Editorial Jelofe, 1981), page 38.

17. Franklin Roosevelt Library, Hyde Park, New York, President's Personal Files, Puerto Rico, the letter is dated August 29, 1936 and it is addressed to Henry Epstein, then the Solicitor General of the State of New York and, in 1917, a Harvard classmate of Albizu's.

18. Theodore Roosevelt, *Colonial Policies of the United States* (Garden City: Doubleday, Doran, 1937), page 83; see ,too, Earl Parker Hanson, *Transformation* (New York: Simon and Schuster, 1955), pages 41-42.

19. See Sugar, Hearings Before the Committee on Finance, United States Senate, 75th Congress, first session, August, 1937, pages 132-133.

20. See, for example, Pauline Maier, *From Resistance to Revolution* (New York: Vintage, 1972); and Lawrence Henry Gipson, *The Coming of the Revolution* (New York: Harper, 1954).

21. New York Public Library, *op. cit.,* this is from a letter dated August 31, 1921.

22. Civil Government of Porto Rico, Hearings Before the House Committee on Insular Affairs, 68th Congress, first session, page 25.

23. Albizu, *op. cit.,* Tomo I, pages 29-31.

24. *Ibid.,* page 50.

25. Rexford Tugwell, *Puerto Rican Public Papers* (San Juan, 1945), page 95.

26. Albizu, *Orbras Escogidas,* Tomo 2, pp. 120-121.

27. Franklin Roosevelt Library, Official File, 400, Box 24, this report to the president is dated December 8, 1937. See page 2 of the summary for the remarks cited.

28. National Archives, Washington, D.C. Record Group 126, this letter to Governor Blanton Winship is dated

March 9, 1936.

29. Truman Clark, *Puerto Rico and the United States, 1917-1933* (Pittsburgh: University of Pittsburgh Press, 1975), page 146.

30. National Archives, Record Group 126, 9-8-68; this letter to Winship is dated July 31, 1936.

31. See Sugar Hearings, 1937, *op. cit.*, page 133.

32. Estado Libre Associado de Puerto Rico, Comision de Derechos Civiles, Informe, San Juan, February 1989; the lists appear in the appendix to this very extensive and significant study.

33. National Archives, Record Group 126, 9-8-68 status, this letter to the president is stamped April 23, 1937.

34. See Snyder's report to Roosevelt, *op. cit.*, page 3.

35. Ricardo Alegría, editor, *Temas de la Historia de Puerto Rico* (San Juan: Center of Advanced Studies of Puerto Rico and the Caribbean, 1988), page 235.

36. See Federal prisons and the Nation's Rebels, *Research Review*, U.S. Department of Justice, Federal Bureau of Prisons, Washington D.C., September 1988, page 1.

37. This letter is dated October 17, 1938. See The American Civil Liberties Union Archives, Princeton University Library, Volume 2053.

38. Puerto Rico, Hearings Before the Committee on Territories and Insular Affairs, Senate, 78th Congress, first session, Washington, 1943, pages 136 and 55 respectively.

39. See Frank Otto Gatell, "Independence Rejected: Puerto Rico and the Tydings Bill of 1936," *Hispanic American Historical Review*, 38 (February, 1958), pp.26-44, esp. 31-33.

40. See Ernest Gruening, *Many Battles* (New York: Liveright, 1974), page 198.

41. James Deitz, *Economic History of Puerto Rico* (Princeton: Princeton University Press, 1986), page

120.

42. National Archives, Record Group 126, 9-8-68, this letter is dated April 6, 1937.

43. This is from an autobiographical statement written by Mr. Ojeda Ríos while he was being tried in the late 1980's.

44. This is from page 6 of a 1986 video transcript titled, "Have you seen *la nueva mujer.*"

45. *Fortune Magazine*, 1941, page 132.

46. Roosevelt, *op. cit.*, April 6, 1937.

47. See Arturo Morales Carrión, *Puerto Rico: A Political and Cultural History* (New York: Norton, 1985), pages 244-245.

48. Roosevelt Library, Tugwell Papers, Box 47, This first letter is dated May 4, 1942; see page two of the English translation provided for the president.

49. *Ibid.*, page 2 of the letter.

50. *Ibid.*, Palacios response is dated May 16, 1942.

51. William Roger Louis, *Imperialism At Bay* (New York: Oxford University Press, 1978), p.164.

52. Puerto Rico, Hearings Before the Committee on Territories and Insular Affairs, Senate, 78th Congress, first session, May,1943, page 50.

53. *Ibid.*, pages 236-237.

54. Roosevelt Library, Tugwell Papers, this is from a long enclosure from the president to Sumner Welles, it is dated, June 30, 1943.

55. *Ibid.*,page 5 of the memo.

56. *Ibid.*, this letter from Abe Fortas to Rexford Tugwell is dated September 12, 1944.

57. *Ibid.*, page 1 of the letter.

58. Tugwell Diary, Box 34, this is from a letter to Abe Fortas dated September 14, 1944.

59. *Ibid.*, page 67.

60. *Ibid.*, page 67.

61. Roberta Johnson, *Puerto Rico: Commonwealth or Colony?* (New York: Praeger, 1978), page 29.

Chapter 2

1. Hearings Before a Committee on Territories and Insular Affairs, Senate, 78th Congress, first session, May 1943, page 53; for the Muñoz comment Hearings Before the Subcommittee on Insular Affairs, House, 78th Congress, first session, June 1943, page 279.

2. Independence For Puerto Rico, Committee on Territories and Insular Affairs, U.S. Senate, May 8, 1945, pages 423 and 428.

3. *Ibid.*, page 428.

4. See the doctoral dissertation of Carlos Ramon Zapata-Oliveras, *United States-Puerto Rico Relations in the Early Cold War Years (1945-1953)*, University of Pennsylvania, 1986, pages 131-132.

5. National Archives, Record Group 126, Puerto Rico, Legal Status; this is from a document titled *The Problem of the Ultimate Status of Puerto Rico*, Research project 83, September 1948, Division of Historical Policy Research, Office of Public Affairs, Department of State, page 110.

6. Hearings, 1945, *op. cit.*, page 377 and 387.

7. President Truman Library, Independence, Missouri, Papers of Samuel I. Rosenman, this is from a memo dated October 3, 1945.

8. Zapata-Oliveras, *op. cit.*, pages 166-167.

9. Truman Library, Papers of Samuel Rosenman, which includes a transcript of the Tugwell interview and the president's statement.

10. Charles Callan Tansill, editor, *The Making of the American Republic* (New Rochelle: Arlington House, n.d.), page 22.

11. See, e.g., Ronald Fernandez, *The Disenchanted*

Notes

Island: Puerto Rico and the United States in the Twentieth Century (New York: Praeger, 1992).

12. Major General Frank Mc Intyre, American Territorial Administration, *Foreign Affairs*, X, January 1932, page 300.

13. The Virgin Islands, Hearing Before a Subcommittee On Insular Affairs, House, 69th Congress, first session, 1926, page 69.

14. Nomination of Rexford Tugwell, Committee on Territories and Insular Affairs, Senate, 77th Congress, first session, 1941, page 37.

15. See, Fernandez, *op. cit.*, Chapter One.

16. Enoch Crowder, *The Spirit of Selective Service* (New York: The Century Company, 1920), page 84; see, too, Fred Albert Shannon, *The Organization and Administration of the Union Army, 1861-1865* (Glouster: Peter Smith, 1965).

17. Ivonne Acosta, *La Palabra Como Delito* (Rio Piedras: Editorial Cultural, 1993), page 75.

18. Ivonne Acosta, *La Mordaza* (Rio Piedras: Edil, 1987), page 40.

19. Harry S. Truman Library, Independence, Missouri, President's secretary's Files, Report on the Nationalist Party submitted On November 4, 1950; see page one of the introductory letter.

20. Acosta, *op. cit.*, page 233.

21. Gruening, *Many Battles, op. cit.*, page 197.

22. These stories were derived from interviews with Laura Albizu Campos Meneses de Meneses and Manuel Caballer.

23. This report is dated April 18, 1948. See Truman Library, President's secretary's Files.

24. Truman Library, Hoover Report, *op. cit.*, page 1 of the 2 page cover letter.

25. Acosta, *op. cit. La Palabra Como Delito*, page 109.

26. Acosta, *La Mordaza, op. cit.*, page 48.

27. Congressional Record, May 5, 1949, page 5709.

28. Congressional record, House, June 30, 1950, page 9593.

29. Congressional record, House, June 30, 1950, page 9585; for the Senate report see Senate Report 1779, 81st Congress, 2nd session, page 3.

30. Puerto Rico Constitution, Hearing Before the Committee on Public Lands, House, 81st Congress, 1950, page 23

31. Congressional Record, House of Representatives, March 14, 1950.

32. See Johnson. *op. cit.*, page 29.

33. Gordon Wood, *The Radicalism of the American Revolution* (New York: Vintage, 1992), page 176.

34. John Fitzpatrick, editor, *The Writings of George Washington* (Washington, GPO, 1931), Volume 4, page 55. Allen Bowman, *The Morale of the American Revolutionary Army* (New York: Kennikat Press, 1943), page 70; also Richard Ketchum, *The Winter Soldiers* (Anchor: Garden City, 1973); finally, for the quote from Hamilton, see Garrison Keillor, "In Praise of Sunshine Patriots," *The New York Times,* July 4, 1993, page 11.

35. Miñi Seijo Bruno, *La Insurreccion Nacionalista En Puerto Rico- 1950* (Rio Piedras: Edil, 1989), page 211. I also interviewed Mr. Collazo.

36. Congressional Record, House, June 30, 1950, page 9593.

37. Hearings Before the Subcommittee on Interstate and Foreign Commerce, Senate, 80th Congress, 2nd session, 1948, page 781.

38. See The Nationalist Party, a Report prepared at the request of the Hon. Fred Crawford, Member of the Committee on Interior and Insular Affairs, House, Washington, 1951.

39. Hearings, Senate, May 1943, *op. cit.*, page 137; see

Notes

endnote 1 for the full citation.

40. Miñi Seijo Bruno, *La Insurreccion Nacionalista En Puerto Rico - 1950* (Rio Piedras: Edil,1989), page 171.

41. Kal Wagenheim, *Puerto Rico: A Profile* (New York: Praeger, 1972), page 79; also Johnson, *op. cit.*, page 38.

42. House of Representatives, 82nd Congress, 2nd session, Report 1832, April, 30, 1952, page 3.

43. Congressional Record, May 13, 1952, page 5119.

44. *Ibid.*, May 28, 1952, page 6179.

45. President Eisenhower Library, Abeline, Kansas, Office of Special Assistant For National Security Affairs, FBI Series, 4,this particular letter is dated November 16, 1954, see page 5.

46. *Ibid.*, page 5.

47. Marisa Rosado, *Pedro Albizu Campos* (San Juan, 1992), pp. 212- 213. This is my translation.

48. See Betances Entre Nosostros, Instituto De Estudios del Caribe and El Museo de La Universidad de Puerto Rico, San Juan, 1989, page 43.

49. José E. López, editor, *Puerto Rican Nationalism: A Reader* (Chicago: Editorial Coqui, 1977), page 89. This volume contains the entire 1937 report.

50. National Archives, Office of Territories, Record Group 126, the letter to Muñoz is stamped September 25, 1952.

51. For example, Ronald Fernandez, *The Disenchanted Island: Puerto Rico and the United States in the Twentieth Century* (Westport: Praeger, 1992), especially Chapter Seven.

52. Congressional record,83rd Congress, 2nd session, March 1, 1954,pages 2432-2433.

53. *Ibid.*, page 2434.

54. Fererico Ribes Tovar, *Lolita Lebrón, La Prisionera* (New York: Plus Ultra,1974), page 155; see, too, Antonio Gil de La Madrid Navarro, *Los Indomitos* (Rio

Piedras: Edil, 1981), this contains a fine analysis of the motives and activities of the revolutionaries.

55. *New York Times*, March 2, 1954, page 17.

56. President Eisenhower Library, Abilene, Kansas, Dulles Telephone Series, Box 2, the memo is dated November 20, 1953.

57. Eisenhower Library, Dulles- Chronological Series, Box 5, this telegram is dated November 24, 1953.

58. Eisenhower Library, Ann Whitman Files, Administrative Series, Box 23, the letter is dated November 28, 1953.

59. Eisenhower, Ann Whitman Files, International, the letter is dated January 8, 1954.

60. *Ibid.*, page 1 of the Sears letter.

61. *Ibid.*, page 2 of the letter.

62. *Ibid.*, page 2 of the letter.

63. Eisenhower Library, Ann Whitman, Office Files, the letter is dated March 27, 1956 and there are a series of attachments stapled to the letter.

64. *Ibid.*, page 1 of the letter.

65. *Ibid.*, this is one of the attachments to the letter. It is dated April 27, 1956.

Chapter 3

1. Naval Training Activities on the Island of Vieques, Puerto Rico, Hearings Before the Committee on Armed Services, House, 96th Congress, second session, Washington, 1980, page 100.

2. Paolo E. Coletta, editor, *United States Navy and Marine Corps Bases, Overseas* (Westport: Greenwood, 1987), page 272.

3. Facilities, 1992, U.S. Department of Justice, Federal Bureau of Prisons, Washington, 1992, page 34.

4. See Guidelines For the Development of a Security Program, U.S Department of Justice, Washington,

1987, page 77.

5. *Ibid.*, page 77.

6. *Ibid.*, page 77.

7. President Carter Library, Atlanta, Georgia, ST-51-2, Box 80, this memo is dated May 9, 1978, see page 1 of the memo.

8. See the sworn statement of Luis Colón Osorio, U.S.A. v. Luis Colón Osorio, Cr. 93-40 (HL), page 4.

9. *Ibid.*, page 5.

10. *Ibid.*, page 6.

11. Report on Progress of Puerto Rico, Message From the president of the United States, House, 78th Congress, first session, Document 304, page 2.

12. *Papers of Woodrow Wilson, Volume 45*, pages 249-250. (Princeton: PUP, 1979).

13. See, for example, Ronald Fernandez, *Cruising the Caribbean: U.S. Foreign Policy in the Twentieth Century* (Monroe, ME: Common Courage, 1994).

14. See *Building the Navy's Bases in WWII, Volume 2*,(Washington: GPO,1947), page 5.; also Report on Need of Additional Air Bases to Defend the Coast of the Unites States, Its Territories, and Possessions, House, 76th Congress, first session, Document 65. Thus is familiarly known as the Hepburn Report.

15. Fernandez, *op. cit.*, especially Chapters Three, Four and Seven.

16. See the letter from Fortas dated November 13, 1944. It was in response.

17. For example, Elizabeth Langhorne, *Vieques: History of a Small Island* (Vieques: The Vieques Conservation and Historical Trust, 1987), Chapter Six; also Arturo Melendez López, *La Batalla de Vieques* (Rio Piedras: Edil, 1989).

18. Washington Navy Yard, Naval Operational Archives Division, The Greenslade Report, pages 15 and 20.

19. Puerto Rico, Hearings before the Committee on

341

Territories and Insular Affairs, Senate, 78th Congress, first session, Washington, 1943, page 15.

20. Fortas, *op. cit.*, page 2474.

21. National Archives, Record Group 126, 9-8-89, the letter from Forrestal is stamped May 28, 1947; the Culebra comment appears on Admiral William Leahy's August 20, 1948 Memorandum to the president, page 15.

22. *Ibid.*, the letter from the president is dated July 7, 1948 and my quote is from page 2 of the three-page letter.

23. Naval Training Activities on the Island of Vieques, Committee on Armed Services, House, 96th Congress, second session, Committee print #31, page 3.

24. This is from an autobiographical statement which accompanies U.S.A. v. Luis Colón Osorio, Cr. #2: 92CR00063 (TFGD), January 25, 1993, page 1. I confirmed this story in my June 1993 interviews with Mr. Colón Osorio.

25. *Ibid.*, page 1.

26. Carmelo Delgado Cintrón, *Culebra y La Marina De estados Unidos* (Rio Piedras: Edil, 1989), pages 199-234.

27. For example, Maxwell Taylor, *The Uncertain Trumpet* (New York: McGraw Hill, 1959); Bernard Brodie, *Strategy In the Missile Age* (Princeton: PUP, 1959).

28. President Lyndon Johnson Library, Austin, Texas, National Security Files, Puerto Rico; this is a December 14, 1961 memo to the president from Kenneth E. Be Lieu. See page 1 of the memo.

29. *Ibid.*, page 1.

30. Johnson Library, the letter is two pages long.

31. Puerto Rico Federal Relations Act, Hearings Before the Committee on Interior and Insular Affairs, Senate, 86th Congress, first session, Washington,

1959, especially pages 40-55.

32. John F. Kennedy Library, Boston, Massachusetts, page 3 of the December 28, 1961 letter.

33. *Ibid.*, pages 2-3.

34. Johnson Library, NSF, Vance letter, March 10, 1964.

35. *Ibid.*, page 1 of the fact sheet included with the secretary's letter to the White House.

36. *Ibid.*, pages 2-3 of the 1964 memo.

37. John F. Kennedy Library, Boston, Massachusetts, Oral History Interview with Luis Muñoz Marín, June 11, 1965, page 5.

38. *Ibid.*, page 5.

39. Delgado Cintron, *op. cit.*, page 208.

Chapter 4

1. Leonardo Rodríguez, *They Have To Be Puerto Ricans* (Chicago: Adams Press, 1988), page 3.

2. Virgin Islands, 1956, Hearings Before Subcommittee on Territorial and Insular Affairs, House, 84th Congress, second session, 1956, page 149 and page 150 for the first quote.

3. Hearings Interstate and Foreign Commerce, Senate, 80th Congress, second session, 1948, page 784.

4. Robert M. Baker,Puerto Rico's Program of Industrial Tax Exemption, *The George Washington Law Review*, V 18, no. 4, June, 1950, page 470.

5. Hearings, Tax Treatment of U.S. Concerns With Puerto Rican Affiliates, Special Committee of the Select Committee on Small Business, Senate, 88th Congress, second session,1964.

6. *Ibid.*, page 69.

7. Milton C. Taylor, *Industrial Tax-Exemption in Puerto Rico* (Madison: University of Wisconsin Press, 1957), page 13; H.C. Barton Jr., *Puerto Rico's Industrial Development Program* (Cambridge: HUP, 1959), page

17;also David F. Ross, *The Long Uphill Battle* (Rio Piedras: Edil, 1969).

8. For example, Amendment to Increase the Minimum Wage, Hearings before the Committee on Education and Labor, House, 84th Congress, first session, Washington, 1955, Muñoz testimony appears on pages 705-728.

9. Luis M. Falcon, Puerto Rico: Migration and development, *Unauthorized Migration: Addressing the Root Causes* (Washington: Commission For the Study of International Migration and Cooperative Economic Development, 1990), pages 207-247, pages 224-225 for the figures cited.

10. Michael Conniff, *Black Labor on a White Canal* (Pittsburgh: University of Pittsburgh Press, 1985).

11. Barry Commoner, *Making Peace With the Planet* (New York: Pantheon, 1989), page 160; for the birth and death rate figure see James Deitz, *Economic History of Puerto Rico* (Princeton: PUP, 1986), page 284.

12. Hearings Before the Subcommittee on Insular Affairs, House, 78th Congress, 2nd session, 1943, page 1642.

13. *Ibid.*, page 1942.

14. President Truman Library, Independence, Missouri, Papers of Philleo Nash, the ten-page report from O'Connor is dated August 14, 1948.

15. Interstate and Foreign Commerce Hearings, *op. cit.*, page 781.

16. Falcon, *op. cit.*, page 235.

17. Roberta Johnson, *Puerto Rico: Commonwealth or Colony* (New York: Praeger, 1979), page 118.

18. Puertorriqueños en los Estados Unidos Continentales: Un Futuro Incierto, Comision de Derechos Civiles de los Estados Unidos, Washington, 1976, page 27.

19. Francisco Quiñones Vizcarrondo, *El Cerebro*

Puertorriqueño (Caguas: Imprinta Cartagena, 1989); also Antonio S. Pedreira, Insularismo (Rio Piedras: Edil,1985).

20. José Luis Gonzalez, *Nueva Visita Al Cuarto Piso* (San Juan: Libros de Flamboyan, 1986), page 189.

21. John Higham, *Strangers in the Land* (New York: Atheneum, 1971).

22. Most of the quotes about Oscar López Rivera come from correspondence; however, see too, his article "Who is the Terrorist? The Making of a Puerto Rican Freedom Fighter," *Social Justice*, Volume 16, number 4, pages 162-174.

23. Nicholas Lehman, *The Promised Land* (New York: Alfred Knopf, 1991), pages 98-100.

24. President Kennedy Library, Boston, Massachusetts, Central Files, Executive ST 51-2, this memo is dated January 15, 1963. It is to the president, from Lee White.

25. Puerto Rico—1963, Hearings Before the Subcommittee on Territorial and Insular Affairs, House, 88th Congress, first session, May, 1963, page 50.

26. *Ibid.*, page 50.

27. *Ibid.*, page 194.

28. Juan M. García Passalacqua, *La Crisis Política en Puerto Rico* (Rio Piedras: Edil, 1983), page 39.

29. Congressional record, House, October 23, 1963, page 19118 and page 19120.

30. *Ibid.*, page 19120.

31. President Johnson Library, Austin, Texas, Official Files, ST51-2, this is a memo to the president from Lee White. It is dated June 8, 1964.

32. *Ibid.*, page 2 of the memo.

33. *Ibid.*, page 2 of the memo.

34. *Ibid.*, page 2 of the memo.

35. *Ibid.*, see page 1 of a memo to the president dated

July 28, 1966.

36. *Ibid.*, page 2 of the 1966 memo.

37. A fine summary of this documentation appears in *Discrimen y Persecucion Por Razones Politicas* (Commission on Civil Rights, Estado Libre Asociado, 1989), pages 256-286.

38. *Ibid.*, pp. 259-260.

39. President Carter Library, Atlanta, Georgia, Presidential Files, Box 80, this is a three-page memo dated 5/9/78. My final quote is from page 3 of the memo.

40. See *Petition to the U.N. on POW Status*, Submitted by the National Committee to Free Puerto Rican Prisoners of War, 1985, page B-1.

41. The Nixon Project, Alexandria, Virginia, ST51-2, The memos are dated July 30, 1969 and August 28, 1969

42. *Ibid.*, see the memo dated May 20, 1971.

43. *Ibid.*, see the memo dated November 24, 1971.

44. *Ibid.*, see the 2 page memo from Bush dated March 5, 1973.

45. *Ibid.*, this NSC memo is dated March 16, 1973.

46. Nixon Project, see a White House memo of April 30, 1974.

Chapter 5

1. Menachim Begin, *The Revolt* (New York: Dell, 1977), page 90.

2. President Carter Library, Atlanta, Georgia, Counsel's Office, Box 43,the memo is dated July 14, 1977.

3. *Ibid.*, See memo dated October 5, 1977.

4. *Ibid.*, page two of Jordan's October 5 memo; the comments of the attorney general appear in a three-page memo from the Justice Department, also dated October 5. See page 3 of the memo.

5. Carter Library, Domestic Policy Staff, Gutierrez, Box

31, see, too, memos dated May 31, 1978 and June 5, 1978. My quote is from the June 5, 1978 memo.

6. *Ibid.*, pages 1-2 of the June 5, 1978 memo.

7. Carter Library, *op. cit.*, Box 43, see two memos from Zbigniew Brezinski and Bob Lipshutz, dated September 4, 1979 and August 31, 1979. See especially, for the quotes used, the memo of September 4, 1979, pages 2-3.

8. *Ibid.*, Box 43, the Gilman letter is dated May 4, 1979, see page 2.

9. See Begin, *op. cit.*, page 141.

10. *Ibid.*, page 295; see, too, Amos Perlmutter, *The Life and Times of Menachim Begin* (Garden City: Doubleday, 1987).

11. *Ibid.*, page 226.

12. *The Economist*, July 26, 1986, pages 9-10.

13. *Ibid.*, page 11.

14. For example, Herman Kahn, *On Thermonuclear War* (New York: Free Press, 1969), especially page 145.

15. See, for example, General Curtis Le May, *Mission With Le May* (New York, 1965).

16. U.S.A. vs. Haydée Beltrán Torres, 77 Cr, 680, April 16, 1980, page f-3.

17. United States of America vs. Alejandrina, et. al., No. 83, CR 494, August 1, 1985, pages 2363-2364.

18. FBI Oversight Hearings, Senate, Subcommittee on Security and Terrorism, February, 1983, page 18.

19. *Toward People's War For Independence and Socialism in Puerto Rico: In Defense of Armed Struggle*, MLN, 1979, page 58.

20. *Ibid.*, page 59.

21. William Sater, Puerto Rican Terrorists: A Possible Threat to U.S. Energy Installations, Rand Corporation, October 1981, page 2.

22. *Ibid.*, page 4; for the same conclusion see *The Economist*, March 26, 1977.

23. *Ibid.*, page 5.

24. U.S. vs. Oscar López, page 37.

25. Ralph Turner and Lewis Killian, *Collective Behavior,* 2nd edition (Englewood Cliffs: Prentice Hall, 1972), pages 258-259.

26. *Toward Peoples War...*, *op. cit.*, page 60.

27. Christopher Simpson, *The Splendid Blond Beast* (New York: Grove Press, 1993), page 23.

28. Amos Perlmutter, *The Life and Times of Menachim Begin* (Garden City: Doubleday, 1987), page 182-183.

29. *Toward People's War, op. cit.* page 64.

30. President Lyndon Johnson Library, Austin, Texas, Official Files- Puerto Rico, the memo is dated November 30, 1964 and it is signed by Robert M, Sayre.

31. *Ibid.*, see the memo to W.W. Rostow dated January 10, 1968.

32. President Gerald Ford Library, Ann Arbor, Michigan, papers of James Cannon, see the memo dated 6/22/76

33. *Ibid.*, Papers of James Cannon, Box 27, the letter is dated December 30, 1975.

34. *Toward People's War, op. cit.*, page 70.

35. Hearings, House Ways and Means Committee, 94th Congress, first session, July, 1975, page 1039.

36. *Ibid.*, page 1040.

37. Arguably the most powerful critique of the tax laws was by a statehooder, Luis P. Costas Elena. See his series of articles in *Revista Del Colegio de Abogados de Puerto Rico,* Nov 1979, February 1980, May 1980, and November 1981.

38. President Carter Library, Atlanta, Georgia, Domestic Policy Staff, Stern, see Mr. Stern's June 23, 1978 memo, page 1.

39. *Ibid.*, pages 5-6 of the memo.

40. Dr. Manuel Escobar, *The 936 Market: An*

Introduction, San Juan Citibank, 1980, pages 52-53.

41. U.S. v Carlos Alberto Torres, etc., No. 80 CR 736, U.S. District Court, Northern District of Illinois, Eastern Division, February 3, 1981, pages 5-6.

42. *Ibid.,* pages 19-25.

43. *Ibid.,* pages 171-172.

44. A Civil Government For Porto Rico, Hearings Before the Committee on Insular Affairs, House, 63rd Congress, second session, February, 1914, page 31.

45. *Ibid.,* page 13.

46. U.S. v. Torres, *op. cit.,* pages 36 and 48.

47. *Ibid.,* page 47.

48. Jan Susler, *The Situation of the Puerto Rican Political Prisoners and Prisoners of War and the Campaign For Their Freedom,* People's Law Office, Chicago, page 21.

49. U.S. v Carlos Torres, sentencing on February 18, 1981, page 55.

Chapter 6

1. *El Nueva Dia,* October 3, 1978.

2. *San Juan Star,* March 15, 1980, page 8.

3. Bail statement of Filiberto Ojeda Ríos, dated January 26, 1988, see pages 7-9.

4. *Hartford Courant,* editorial page, June 5, 1987, page B8.

5. See *El Reportero,* September 4, 1985, page 2; and *El Mundo,* September 9, 1985, for an article by Antonio Gonzalez, page 19.

6. *Nuevo Dia,* September 3, 1985, page 41.

7. Ronald Fernandez, *Los Macheteros* (New York: Prentice Hall Press, 1987), page 227.

8. *Ibid.,* pages 229-230.

9. For example, Luis Angel Ferrao, *Pedro Albizu Campos y el Nacionalismo Puertorriqueño* (Rio Piedras: Editorial Cultural, 1990).

10. United States District Court, District of Connecticut, U.S. vs. Víctor Gerena, Criminal # H-85-50, change of venue motion submitted on June 17, 1986, especially pages 24-26.

11. *Ibid.*, see the defendants' motion to dismiss dated December 22, 1986, page 8.

Chapter 7

1. Scott Styles, Conditions of Confinement Suits: What Has the Bureau Learned, *Federal Prison Journal*, 1991, page 42.

2. Affidavit of Warden Dennis Luther, U.S. District Court, Northern District of Illinois, Eastern Division, No. 84, C 1695, see pages 1-2 of the March 20, 1984 affidavit.

3. *Ibid.*, for the case number, see the Emergency Petition of the Prisoners, page 3.

4. Guidelines For the Development of a Security program, National Institute of Corrections, U.S. Department of Justice, 1987, page 77.

5. Memorandum Decision of Judge Plunkett, No.83 C4616, page 3, July 11, 1983.

6. *Ibid.*, page 9 of the judge 's decision.

7. Sworn affidavit of Edwin Cortés, dated March 5, 1984., see endnote 2 for the full citation.

8. *Ibid.*, page 2 of Edwin Cortés sworn statement.

9. See Guidelines, *op. cit.*, page 127.

10. Videotaped television interview in 1986. See page 17 of the manuscript "Have you seen la nueva mujer?"

11. Testimony offered by Luz Rodríguez in 1990, see page 5. This is in private communications with friends and relatives.

12. This is from private correspondence written by Alicia Rodriguez

13. Bureau of Justice Statistics, State and federal

Notes

Prisoners, 1925-85; also Prisoners in 1991, Washington,. D.C. 1986 and 1992 respectively

14. Malcolm Feeley and Johnathan Simon, The New Penology, *Criminology*, Volume 30, no. 4, November, 1992, pages 449-474, especially 451-453.

15. Robert Buchanan and Karen Whitlow,Guidelines For developing, Implementing, and Revising an Objective Prison Classification System, National Institute of Justice, Washington D.C., June 1987, page A-6 has a copy of the chart and an explanation of the classification process accompanies the "custody classification."

16. Feeley and Simon, *op. cit.*, page 459.

17. See the sworn affidavit of Luz Berríos-Berríos, U.S. District Court, District of Connecticut, U.S. vs. Víctor Gerena, H-85- 56,C.D. August 26, 1987.

18. See Amnesty International, United States of America, The High Security Unit, Federal Prison, Kentucky, London, August of 1988; See too *Social Justice*, Volume 15, No. 1, Spring of 1988; this issue of the journal contains three detailed articles about Lexington. For a facility even more secure see Connie Gardner, State of the Art Segregation, *Federal Prison Journal*, Department of Justice, Washington, D.C., 1991.

19. See, for example, Federal Bureau of Prisons, Oversight Hearing, Committee On the Judiciary, 98th Congress, 2nd session, March, 1984, page 18 for a comment by then Director Norman Carlson.

20. See Baraldini vs. Meese, Federal Supplement, 432 (D.D.C., 1988), page 435.

21. *Ibid.*, page 438.

22. *Ibid.*, page 447.

23. Amnesty International, *op. cit.*, second page of their unpaginated summary from August of 1988.

24. Styles, *op. cit.*, page 40.

25. For example, Estelle v Gamble, 429 U.S. 97, page 258.

26. Raymond Holt and Richard Phillips, Marion: Separating Fact From Fiction, *Federal Prison Journal*, Spring, 1991, page 30.

27. Allegations of Ill-Treatment in Marion Prison, Illinois, Amnesty International U.S.A., New York, May 1987, page 14.

28. This number represents 365 days x 7 years.

29. Federal Bureau of Prisons, Oversight Hearings, Committee on the Judiciary, House, 98th Congress, second session, 1984, page 16.

30. *Ibid.*, page 16.

31. Marion Penitentiary -1985, Oversight Hearing, Committee on the Judiciary, House, 99th Congress, first session, 1985, page 35.

32. Holt and Phillips, *op. cit.*, page 29.

33. Oversight Hearings on Corrections, Committee on the Judiciary, House, 101st Congress, first session, 1989, page 33.

34. *Ibid.*, page 34.

35. Holt and Phillips, *op. cit.*, page 34.

36. Holt and Phillips, *op. cit.*, page 34.

37. Hearing, Committee on the Judiciary, House, 102nd Congress, first session, 1991, the justice's opinion is from Wilson vs. Seiter, see page 75.

38. See, for example, *The San Juan Star*, September 1, 1988.

39. See the statement of Filiberto Ojeda Ríos made on September 10, 1988, page 2.

Chapter 8

1. Juan Manuel García Passalacqua, El Juicio de la historia, *Nueveo Dia*, 12 de Septiembre, 1988.

2. This is from a statement by Attorney Linda Backiel.

Notes

It was made available to the press after the trial and is called "Historic Verdict in Puerto Rico."

3. For example, *The San Juan Star*, July 20, 1989.

4. Backiel, *op. cit.*, page 6.

5. See page 4 of a summary by Attorney Linda Backiel. It is called "Historic Verdict in Puerto Rico."

6. The best analysis of what happened on Vieques appears in *The Vieques Times*, written and edited by Charlie Connelly. I have used Volumes 29, dated April of 1989 and Volume 30, dated May of 1989. Mr. Connelly was also good enough to sit through an interview in November of 1990.

7. See *Vieques Times*, April of 1989, p.2.

8. See *El Mundo*, April 15, 1989, p.6; also *The San Juan Star* for April 15,1989.

9. *El Mundo*, May 27, 1989.

10. Political Status of Puerto Rico, Hearings Before the Committee on Energy and Natural Resources, Senate, 101st Congress, first session, Washington, 1989, page 225.

11. Political Status of Puerto Rico, Hearings Before the Committee on Energy and Natural Resources, Senate, 102nd Congress, first session, Washington, 1991, page 173.

12. Congressional Record, House, 101st Congress, 2nd session, May 9, 1990, page E1439.

13. Romero Barceló, *op. cit.*, page 87.

14. *Ibid*, page 87.

15. Political Status of Puerto Rico, *op. cit.*, pages 217-218.

16. *Ibid.*, page 227.

17. *Ibid.*, pages 223-225.

18. *Ibid.*, page 217.

19. *Ibid.*, page 108.

20. *Ibid.*, pages 107-108

21. *Ibid.*, page 103.
22. Pharmaceutical Industry, Tax Benefits of Operating in Puerto Rico, Washington, GPO, May, 1992, pages 18-24.
23. Puerto Rico's Economy, Hearing, Committee on Interior and Insular Affairs, House, 99th Congress, 2nd session, Washington, 1986, page 131.
24. Pharmaceutical Industry, *op. cit.*, page 3.
25. For a discussion of the events which involved each of these presidents see Ronald Fernandez, *The Disenchanted Island: Puerto Rico and the United States in the Twentieth Century* (New York: Praeger, 1992); also *Cruising the Caribbean* (Monroe, ME: Common Courage, 1994).
26. *New York Times,* The Week in Review, September 26, 1993, Page 1.

Prisoners' Addresses

Antonio Camacho -Negron
No. 03587-069
FCI Mc Ken-Unit 2
P.O. Box 8000
Bradford, PA 16701

Luis Colón Osorio
Under House Arrest in
Puerto Rico

Edwin Cortés
No. 92153-024
P.O. Box 1000 (A-3 #503)
Leavenworth, KS 66048-
1000

Elizam Escobar
No. 88969-024
P.O. Bx 1500, Colorado 2
El Reno, OK 73036

Ricardo Jimenez
No. 88967-024
P.O. Box 1000
Lewisburg, PA 17837

Oscar López Rivera
No. 87651-024
P.O. Box 1000
Marion, IL 62959

Adolfo Matos Antongiorgi
No. 88968-024 Unit J
3901 Klein Blvd
Lompoc, CA 93436

Dylcia Pagán
No. 88971-024
5701 8th Street
Camp Parks
Dublin, CA 94558

Alberto Rodríguez
No. 92150-024
P.O. Box 1000
Lewisburg, PA 17837

Alicia Rodríguez
No. NO7157
P.O. Box 5007
Dwight, IL 60420

Ida Luz Rodríguez
No. 88973-024
5701 8th Street
Camp Parks
Dublin, CA 94568

Luis Rosa
No. NO2743
Box 711
Menard, IL 62259

Juan E. Segarra-Palmer
No. 15357-077
USP Atlanta
Atlanta, GA 30315

Alejandrina Torres
No. 92152-024
5701 8th Street
Camp Parks
Dublin, CA 94568

Carlos Alberto Torres
No. 88976-024
P.O. Box 1000
Oxford, WI 53952

Carmen Valentín
No. 88974-024
5701 8th Street
Camp Parks
Dublin, CA 94568

PRISONERS OF COLONIALISM

Norman Ramírez Talavera
  No. 03171-069
  Reybrooke
  Lake Placid, NY   12977

Roberto José Maldonado
  No. 03588-069
  Federal Medical Facility
  3150 Horton Road
  Fort Worth, TX 76119

Index

Index

Index

H

I

Index

Independence
independence and the
Cold War, 71, 98
Independence bill, 47, 48
independence concerns,
7, 97
independence offer, 96,
98
Independence Party,
186, 187
independentistas, 56, 57,
184, 187, 191, 206,
243
international tribunal,
10
Irgun, 199-200
Island, Jacques, 304,
305, 309

J

Jackson, Henry, 20, 130,
183, 188, 194, 203,
206, 263
Jauco, 240
Javits, Jacob, 77, 90
Jayuya, 39, 44, 156
jíbaro, 51, 115
Jiménez, Ricardo, 15,
141 *(photograph)*, 223
Johnson, Lyndon, 182,
184

Johnston, J. Bennett,
324
Jones, Walter, 218
Jones, William, 222, 321
Jones Act, 223
Jordan, Hamilton, 195
Juarbe Juarbe, Juan,
249
jury duty, 45, 302, 307,
308, 311-312

K

Kastenmeier, Charles,
291
Kennedy, John F., 126,
127, 129, 130, 177,
179
Kent, Rockwell, 45
King, Martin Luther, 162
King David Hotel, 200
King Monty. *see* Reilly,
E. Montgomery
Kings Day. *see* Three
Kings Day
Kinoy, Arthur, 254
Knoizen, Arthur, 101

365

Index

370

Q

Index

Index

V

W

Y